Becoming a Family

Parents' Stories
and Their Implications
for Practice, Policy, and Research

Becoming a Family

Parents' Stories
and Their Implications
for Practice, Policy, and Research

Rena D. Harold

With

Lisa G. Colarossi
Lucy R. Mercier
Patricia Stow Bolea
Carol R. Freedman-Doan
Susan A. Lynch
Margaret L. Palmiter
Jacquelynne S. Eccles

2000

LAWRENCE ERLBAUM ASSOCIATES, PUBLISHERS
Mahwah, New Jersey   London

Lawrence Erlbaum Associates, Inc., Publishers
10 Industrial Avenue
Mahwah, NJ 07430

Cover design by Kathryn Houghtaling Lacey

Library of Congress Cataloging-in-Publication Data

Harold, Rena D.
Becoming a family : parents' stories and their implications for practice,
policy, and research / Rena D. Harold, with Lisa G. Collarosi... [et al.].
        p. cm.
Includes bibliographical references and indexes.
ISBN 0-8058-1961-4 (cloth : alk. paper)
ISBN 0-8058-1962-2 (pbk. : alk. paper)
    1. Family—United States. 2. Family life surveys—United States.
3. Parents—United States—Interviews.   I. Collarosi, Lisa G.
II. Title.
    HQ536 .H319   2000
    306.85'0973 —dc21   00-027035
                                                          CIP

Books published by Lawrence Erlbaum Associates are printed on acid-free
paper, and their bindings are chosen for strength and durability.

Printed in the United States of America
10   9   8   7   6   5   4   3   2   1

For my family

Linda, Lonny, and Noah

Peg -
thanks for being a part of
"my family of choice" —
love.
Rene

Contents

Preface

The movement from young adulthood, through coupling, and the transition to parenthood may be among the most universal adult developmental transitions. These passages hold interest for all of us, but especially for those who study the psychological, familial, and sociocultural components of development, all of which interact and influence one another. The primary purpose of this book is to enhance understanding of family life development by shedding light on the meanings that family members ascribe to the developmental process of becoming a family. This is achieved by qualitative analysis of narratives through which individuals and families explain themselves, their thinking, and their behavior. These family narratives are indicators of individual and family identity, as well as descriptions of connections to others.

Our interest in the ways in which the families develop stems from the notion that family dynamics and relationships affect the ideas and beliefs of children, the choices they make, and how they learn to define themselves within a family system. We began our research quantitatively with a set of ideas about how family environments affect children's self-perceptions and their achievement motivation. As we collected data from the families, however, we became intrigued by the themes the families themselves identified as important. We have used an adaptation of narrative and storytelling techniques in our family development study to provide parents with an opportunity to talk about experiences and beliefs they found meaningful. Giving "voice" to parents, as we have done in this book, allows them to define themselves, their family members, the way they interact with their world, that, in turn, impact the thinking, affect, and behavior of family members. It also gives the parents the opportunity to examine how their views and self-definitions may have changed over time, and the events they think led to these changes. We need this kind of research that examines the family as a naturally occurring unit, gathers data from multiple family members, and documents the nature of their interactions over time in order to have a complete and meaningful picture of family life. Thus, the challenge in fully investigating families and their relationships both within and outside the family structure is to observe not only the behavior of the participants but also to understand the experience or meaning the interactions have for them in order to consider the implications for practice, policy, and research.

The large number of interviews conducted as well as the use of constant comparison between these meanings and the theoretical frame of the researchers provided a thick data set that allows for the investigation of many aspects of family life and development. The specific issues discussed in the chapters that follow include creating a family identity; child characteristics, for example, the causes for the similarities or differences parents see in their children; social support, for example, changes in their relationship with each other, with their extended families, and with their friends after they become parents; and work, for example, for mothers, making the decision about when, or if, to return to work. Each chapter includes a review of seminal literature, parents' comments and ideas about the topic, and a discussion of practice, policy, and research implications that are relevant to the issue.

The book begins with a brief description of three perspectives that framed our study of family development and informed our interpretations of the data: developmental life span, family-in-environment (ecological systems theory), and family roles. It also includes a thorough discussion of the methodology that was used in this study. Although much has been written that uses qualitative methods, fewer writings detail the specific process that is used to collect, organize, and analyze such data. Sharing this information can be helpful for both researchers and practitioners. Gender differences and a feminist perspective on the family, as well as a model for viewing diverse family types, are discussed at the end of the book. Illuminating these differences can further an understanding of the social structure of the family and its implications for maintaining the broader social order through parents' expectations of themselves and of their children. Additionally, despite the fact that the study participants were primarily members of two-parent heterosexual families, it is very important to acknowledge that the process of "becoming a family" is not tied to only one type of family.

Each of us has a story to tell, and are glad when someone is interested in listening. The stories of the parents in this study are compelling, sometimes because of their notability, and sometimes because of their ordinariness and similarity to family life as it is stereotypically known. These stories illustrate social and psychological issues, and because of that, we hope this book will be of interest to those who are teaching about family theory and practice, human behavior in the social environment, social policy, qualitative research methods, and women's studies, as well as to those who share our fascination with the development of families and the creation of the family story.

Many of the ideas that led to the undertaking of this study and resulted in the writing of this book, were nourished on the patio of Zingerman's Deli in Ann Arbor, Michigan! Research funding was provided by grants from the National Institute of Child Health and Human Development to Jacquelynne S. Eccles, Phyllis C. Blumenfeld, Rena D. Harold, and Allan L. Wigfield, and by a grant from the Directors's Discretionary Fund at the Institute for Social Research at The University of Michigan to Jacquelynne S. Eccles and Rena D. Harold.

The authors acknowledge the many parents who willingly gave of their time and energy to share their experiences. Needless to say, they made this book possible, as did the help of several graduate students and staff who helped interview parents and transcribe their stories. Particular thanks go to Cle Milojevic and Dana Johnston, and to Judi Amsel, Executive Editor at Lawrence Erlbaum Associates, who saw us through the process of writing this book.

Although each story is unique, there is also a sense of universality in telling the story of *Becoming a Family*, one to which each of us can relate. In analyzing the stories, we spent much time reflecting on our own life experiences as the children we were, as partners, and, for many of us, as parents. We would like to acknowledge our families of origin and the families we have created—through relation and choice.

1

Telling the Family Story: The Backdrop

Rena D. Harold
Michigan State University

Patricia Stow Bolea
Grand Valley State University

> People tell stories about everything, particularly about important life transitions such as birth and death, arrivings and leavings, and of the important rituals that mark these and other passages.
> —Laird, (1989, p. 435)

Through stories and myths, people define and punctuate their lives in particular ways, revealing interpretive systems for explaining themselves in relation to the world as they move through the life span (Laird, 1989).

The movement from young adulthood, through partnering, and the transition to parenthood may be among the most universal adult developmental transitions. These passages hold interest for all of us, but especially for those who are studying the psychological, sociocultural, and biological components of development, all of which interact and influence one another. These transitions are also important because of the unique position they hold at the interface of individual and family systems models of understanding behavior (Goldberg, 1988). A thorough examination of such transitions requires that each person be viewed both from an individual psychological perspective and within his or her own family system, with all its powers to mold and influence attitudes, values, and behavior.

Although there has been considerable study of life events and transitions over the last 2 decades, the primary emphasis of these investigations has been based on biological or sociopsychological models of stress and family interaction. Traditionally, these studies have been conducted by outsider observations, surveys, and questionnaires. These studies often fail to inquire about the inner subjective perceptions of self from the perspective of that individual (Borden, 1992).

Progress in the use of a narrative method as a tool for exploring the subjective nature of individual and family life transitions has occurred within the context of the "new epistemology" and of the constructivist movement in family research. This signifies a movement away from the traditional positivistic approach and from standard notions of family structure and functioning, from the search for "truth" to a search for meaning, and toward new ways of comprehending how families construct their worlds (Laird, 1989). One of the richest sources of meaning lies in the narratives through which individuals and families explain themselves, their thinking, and their behavior. Within family narratives are indicators of individual and family identity, as well as descriptions of connections to others.

The primary purpose of this book is to enhance understanding of family-life development by shedding some light on the meanings that family members ascribe to the process of becoming a family. Sixty families, each with at least two children, who were part of a much larger longitudinal research project, were asked if they would be interested in participating in this study. It is their "stories" that are used to highlight issues that families deal with in the course of family-life development.

The specific issues discussed in the book emerged through the process of qualitatively analyzing these stories. The first two chapters of the book place the stories in context. The first chapter describes the theoretical foundation of the study. The second describes the methodology used in collecting and analyzing the data, with examples of how the method worked for this study and how it could be adapted for use with other populations. Chapters 3 to 6 present particular issues raised by the parents, including a review of seminal literature and parents' comments and ideas about the topic. In each area, mothers' and fathers' comments are compared and contrasted when appropriate. In addition, each of these chapters includes some interpretations of the stories in a discussion of practice, policy, and research implications that may be relevant to the issue. The final chapter highlights themes that run through all the chapters, discusses the implications of this methodology and the data for other family types, and looks to the future to consider what questions come next in the story of family development.

FAMILY

The first issue that must be addressed in any discussion of family development is what is meant by *family*. Despite the fact that in recent years the definition of family has entered the arena of political debate, it has always been a concept that is somewhat difficult to pin down. White and Epston (1990) suggested this is due to the many levels of analysis on which one can view the family. Thus, we can talk in terms of *a family*—a single group or organization; we can talk in terms of *families*—a population of such groups; or we can talk in terms of *the family*—a social institution.

A further complication is the many forms a family can take. There are "traditional" (i.e., heterosexual) two-parent nuclear families, multigenerational families, single-parent families, blended families, gay and lesbian families, extended families, families of choice, etcetera. However, there is some consensus among family researchers that a necessary characteristic of a family is that it be *intergenerational* (White & Epston, 1990). According to this definition, the affinal relationship between two adults does not constitute a family. It is only when a child is brought into the adult dyad for long-term nurturing and socialization that a family is formed. For most families, this occurs with the birth of the first child, although the child's entry obviously can occur through a variety of means. Despite the fact that many families are formed through blending one or two divorced, widowed, or single families, White and Epston (1990) argue that the formation of such a family is really a middle-stage development in an ongoing family career. Thus, the birth or the adoption of the first child into one or both of the families who eventually blend is the event that initiates the formation of the respective families. In this book, we take one step back to life before the birth of the first child. It is at this pivotal point, on the road to "becoming a family," where our families' stories begin.

THEORETICAL MODELS

This work has its underpinnings in three theories that can be used to interpret the stories. The first draws on social and developmental psychological literature, including a model that looks at family development over the life span, milestones or transitions in the life of the family, and the family's internal processes (Carter & McGoldrick, 1988). The second theory utilizes a largely social work perspective, in that it examines the family as it interacts with its environ-ment. This ecosystem approach (Bronfenbrenner, 1979; Harold, Mercier, & Colarossi, 1997 Hartman, 1978) is very helpful in understanding the interac-tion between family developmental processes and the institutions and other systems external to the family unit. The third theory, then, borrows from socio-logical theory as it looks at roles and social structures in the family and suggests that these are socially constructed (Feld & Radin, 1982). That is, notions of family and parenting are important because of the meanings they have for the individual. Furthermore, these meanings are created through a social process that reflects expectations about what an adult should do (e.g., marry and have children), that is, the roles and behaviors in which adults should engage, and when these should take place (Wapner & Craig-Bray, 1992).

These three frameworks, then, are the backdrop for examining such issues as how couples maintain individual identities while creating a family identity; families' explanations of intrafamily similarities and differences; social support needs of families at different developmental stages; the interface of work and family life; and the dynamics that surround decision-making processes and choices about what has been termed the family career (White & Epston, 1990).

Developmental Life Span

In their seminal work, Carter and McGoldrick (1988) present a contemporary approach to the intersection of family systems theory and family development models to examine the evolution of family life. This includes a conceptualiza-tion of the nuclear family as a three-generational system that reacts to pressure from generational tensions as well as developmental transitions, depicting this interactive process with a vertical and horizontal axis in their model (Fig. 1.1). In assessing families, Carter and McGoldrick incorporate activities of the en-tire three-generational system as it moves through time. Relationships with parents, siblings, and other family members go through stages as one moves along the life cycle, just as do parent–child and spousal relationships. These au-thors note the difficulty of examination of the family as a whole, due to the complexity involved. Their model provides an overview of the family cycle, and when used as a guide for family therapy offers clinical suggestions for work-ing with families at each developmental stage.

An important characteristic of their model is that it begins with young adults rather than married couples. Carter and McGoldrick posit that young adults' resolution of family of origin issues profoundly influences who, when, how, and whether they will marry/couple and how they will carry out all other succeeding phases of the life cycle. This life phase is viewed as a cornerstone, a

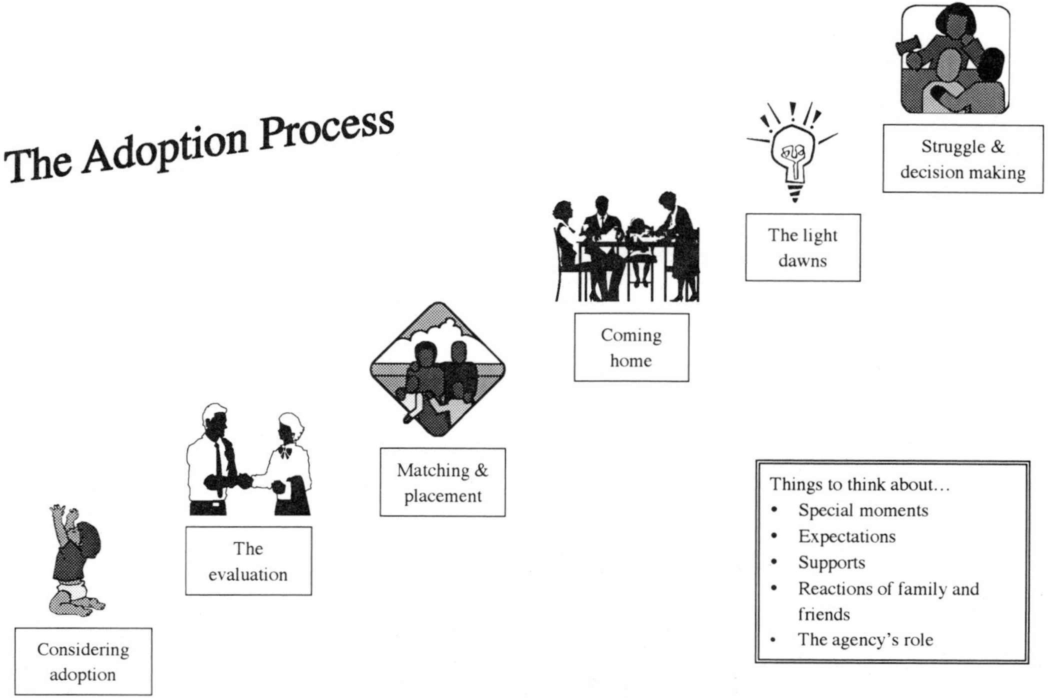

The Adoption Process

Struggle &
decision making

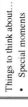

The light
dawns

Coming
home

Matching &
placement

The
evaluation

Considering
adoption

Things to think about...
- Special moments
- Expectations
- Supports
- Reactions of family and friends
- The agency's role

FIG. 1.1.   Depiction of Carter and McGoldrick's model of the family as a three-dimensional system moving through time.

5

time to formulate identity and goals before partnering or forming another new family subsystem. In the authors' view, the more adequately young adults are able to differentiate themselves from the emotional configurations of their family of origin experiences, the fewer vertical stressors they will encounter in the future. In addition, the authors' address the issue of career preparation for young adults. Our subjects were asked to tell their stories beginning as individual young adults. They talk about their first encounters with one another, their individual and joint decisions about work, school, geographic location, and marriage. They continue on to describe the process of becoming a family, thus allowing for the use of Carter and McGoldrick's work as a theoretical backdrop to the exploration of family development.

Carter and McGoldrick (1988) did not consider the influence of the family to be restricted to the members of a particular household or to a given nuclear family branch of the system. Although they acknowledge the stereotypical American pattern of separately domiciled nuclear families, there are subsystems within the larger family system, including the extended and intergenerational family, which react to past, present, and anticipated future relationships. In addition, they recognize the interplay between the family system and the larger environment, as discussed in the next section.

Family-in-Environment

Although the family is the principal arena in which individual development occurs, individuals and families are located within and interact with several levels of systems (Bronfenbrenner, 1986). Further, according to ecological systems theory, change in relationships with one part of the interacting systems may impact on or result in a shift in all other relationships (Bronfenbrenner, 1979). This concept is central to diverse philosophies of change, including most family therapy work. In this book, many issues are examined that impact not only on a specific family member, but the family as a whole. For example, a child's temperament may affect the way a child is treated within the family, which may in turn affect the child's ability to form relationships in the school setting. A parent's home life can certainly influence his/her behavior at work just as events at work can impact on family life. Similarly, parents' access to social support can have a positive effect on their children, for example, providing the parents with respite care, financial aid, adult outlets for expression of feelings, education about appropriate child development, and so on. Thus, using an ecosystems approach to understanding families acknowledges the interactive influences and connections between individual members as well as between individuals, families, and their environments (McMahon, 1990). It assumes a dynamic picture and takes into account that people are influenced by their personal characteristics as well as by their external contextual environments as depicted in Fig. 1.2.

Each variation within and between systems interacts to affect the individual's and the family's development. The focus of ecological systems theory, then, is on the interface where the person or family and the environment come together (McMahon, 1990). This person-in-environment perspective and the "fit" between the person or family and their surroundings is a characteristic of our stories. Families define who they are, relate to their children, feel supported or not, and occupy multiple roles including worker and parent, in the context of their extended family, peer group, community, etcetera.

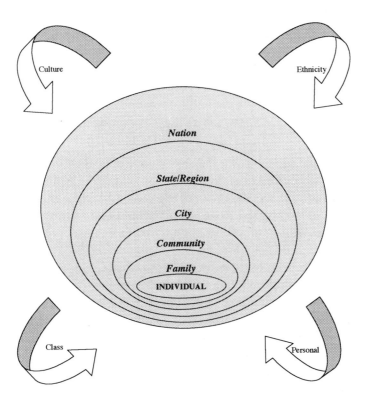

FIG. 1.2. An ecological systems perspective offers a model for understanding individual and family development as they are influenced by their contextual environments and a variety of variables, including culture, race/ethnicity, class, and personal values and attributes.

Within this framework, the family is viewed as a *system*, a set or arrangement of people related or connected in such a way that they form a unity. Within that system, there are *subsystems*, parts or components of a larger system, which may include parents, siblings, one parent and one child, etcetera. Equally important is the *suprasystem* to which the family belongs, the larger, more encompassing whole like a nation or culture. Each family has *boundaries* that keep the system enclosed (e.g., allow people to identify themselves as part of that family); but these boundaries are also permeable and some families may choose to let in nonfamily members. Families may, however, also have *barriers* that tend to prevent movement in and out of the system (Minuchin, 1988).

Using this model to understand family development, the following assumptions are made:

- Change in one part/person in the system affects all other parts/persons
- To survive, a system must have goals and strive to achieve them
- Systems must have input—some form of energy from the external environment
- Systems must have a way of processing input
- Systems must produce output, which then becomes input for other systems and reinforces the cyclical or interactive nature of systems
- There must be feedback from the environment
- Systems are self-regulating and can adjust and readjust as needed

"Elements [people] in a system are necessarily interdependent, contributing to the formation of patterns and organized in their behavior by their participation in those patterns" (Minuchin, 1988, p. 9).

Family Roles

Role theory and role analysis consider the individual and the social system in which the individual exists to explain his or her experiences and behaviors (Wapner & Craig-Bray, 1992). People's behaviors are influenced, in part, by the expectations, rewards, and sanctions that are associated with a given role or position. Further, these expectations come from a variety of sources, for example, society, family, community, class structure, and may change depending on the particular context. Thus, being a wife may have a different set of behavioral expectations depending on whether that woman is in her workplace or at home, whether she is part of a dual-earner family, and whether she has children. In addition, the expectations will vary as a result of her own conception of the role, her partner's ideas, the environment in which she lives, the couple's friends' and coworkers' attitudes and patterns of behavior, her own and her partner's family of origin messages about the role, etcetera (Feld & Radin, 1982; Wapner & Craig-Bray, 1992) (see Fig. 1.3).

Examining families in this way allows us to look at the role demands that parents in our study articulated. Some women described the role conflict that they felt when there were contradictory expectations about how they should behave—for example, as wife, mother, or professional worker. In trying to hold

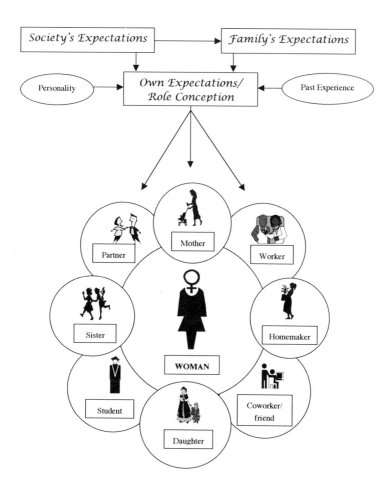

FIG. 1.3. A woman may occupy many overlapping roles, with potentially competing expectations from multiple sources, which may result in role strain and role conflict.

two or more roles simultaneously, the men and women in our study had to deal with their own definitions, and those of their extended families, as well as societal definitions of what constituted appropriate role behavior for those positions, that is, which need or role takes priority in which situations, as well as what to do about conflicting expectations. The role strain that accompanied these issues was particularly apparent at times of transition, for example, partner to parent, from worker to parent and back to worker, etcetera. This perspective is particularly important because it suggests a way of analyzing problems that does not focus on a personal inadequacy, but rather considers roles and structures in the family as being socially constructed, and therefore in need of examination and perhaps re-creation.

THE CHAPTERS

The authors in this book were all involved in some aspect of developing, collecting, and/or analyzing the family stories. They represent three different but related social science foci: social work, clinical psychology, and developmental psychology, and are associated with six different institutions/organizations. They work in both academic and practice settings, and have taught family development theory and research as well as working clinically with families. Each author has examined the data against the backdrop of the theories that have been briefly described, and has looked at parents' stories for the implications they may have for social work/clinical practice, research, and social policy. In presenting the stories themselves, names of parents, their children, and employers have been substituted with a description of the relationship (e.g., my husband, my wife, Child A, etc.) to maintain and preserve the confidentiality of the participants.

Chapter 2, "Telling the Family Story: The Process," by Rena Harold, Margaret Palmiter, Susan Lynch, Carol Freedman-Doan, and Jacquelynne Eccles, documents a detailed description of the development of the storyboard and the data collection and analysis processes unique to the qualitative research approach that was utilized. In particular, it describes a process for investigating the development of families as described by parents themselves in an open-ended parental narrative relating the development of the family in story form.

Parents were asked to tell the story of how they became a family, beginning with couplehood, through the birth of the first child across time to living with the first and second children. The storyboard technique that was utilized gave "voice" to parents, allowing the meanings that parents impart about family development to emerge from the data. This chapter also describes two additional applications of this methodology for readers to consider.

In chapter 3, "Talking About Identity: Individual, Family, and Intergenerational Issues," Patricia Stow Bolea uses the stories to address a set of questions related to ways in which families describe their own sense of who they are, as they define a family heritage together. In addition, parents' stories are reviewed for evidence of the influence or contribution of family of origin issues as they construct their family identity.

Past work in this area has focused on marital quality, effects of the family of origin on parents' child rearing, and the psychological role of the extended family in supporting family identity development. This information provides a backdrop for dividing the family stories into three categories: individual identity, family identity, and connections to others, which subsumes intergenerational issues and cultural ties and traditions. Within each grouping, various themes are described that detail the assorted ways in which families talk about their beliefs, hopes, and plans for their children as well as their description of who they are as a family unit. Research has shown, and our stories corroborate, that parents' goals, expectations, rituals, and traditions, as well as their connection to their families of origin and to their cultures, all impact on how families define themselves.

Lastly, family identity and intergenerational issues are discussed in terms of their implications for practice with diverse families. Included in this discussion are an emphasis on the important role of culture in defining family identity, and a look at additional implications for research and policy.

Chapter 4, "Narratives of Temperament: Same or Different?" is written by Carol Freedman-Doan. The often-voiced question, "How can children in the same family be so different?" was one of those that led to the qualitative study and collection of family stories, and is examined in this chapter along with the notion of whether childhood temperaments are perceived as stable across time. Children's characteristics preoccupy many parents' thoughts. They struggle with how to describe their children, and often do this by comparing them with one another, using dichotomous characteristics (e.g., "He was the fussy baby, she was the easy one"). This chapter explores the factors, such as parents' own childhood experiences, expectations of parenthood, and experiences with taking care of children, that shape parents' perceptions of their child even before the child is born.

Furthermore, this chapter identifies the characteristics parents find most notable in describing their young children, such as: preference for a particular gender; concern about the size and health of the baby (e.g., big baby/small baby, healthy/sick); whether the child is early or late in his/her cognitive and physical development, or has an easy or fussy temperament; whether the parent has a positive or negative affective reaction to the baby; whether the child is a loner or tends to be sociable, the dependence or independence of the child in his or her need for adult attention; and how much change the infant brings to the parents' lives. This chapter also investigates the potential impact that parents' perceptions of their child as an infant has on their perceptions of the child later into childhood. The implications of these findings for child and family practitioners, as well as general health providers, are explored.

Lisa Colarossi and Susan Lynch are the authors of chapter 5, "Tales of Social Support Throughout Family Development." This chapter highlights how the process of becoming a family can create changes in the amount and kind of social support that people give and receive. The chapter discusses social support across three time frames: before the birth of the first child, after the birth of the first child, and after the birth of additional children. Different themes emerged in each time frame that involved the nature of support in the spousal relationship, support from extended family members, support provided to children, and support received from friends and professionals.

The participants' stories revealed that changes in their social contexts and social roles effected changes in social support. For example, social roles include spouse, coworker, friend, and family member, in which all of the parents in our study participated. All of these roles influenced the amount and kind of social support they described. As our participants became parents, they had to provide more support to each other and to the baby than they were used to providing as a couple before their first child. Extended family members also provided different kinds of support to participants across the different time frames of becoming a family.

The chapter also discusses how the influence of gender roles on social support created differences in the stories that mothers and fathers told. For example, a change in social context due to geographic relocation is described by females as causing decreases in social support, often resulting in feelings of isolation. In addition, whether a women's social context includes work makes a difference in the amount of support she receives from peers. Alternatively, men do not describe the same sense of loss of support after a relocation, possibly because they continue to work and, therefore, maintain consistent access to friends and coworkers. Mothers and fathers also provide different kinds of support to children. The chapter concludes with suggestions for clinical practice with couples and families for the healthy development of all family members, and implications for social policy and further research.

In chapter 6, "Job Talk: The Role of Work in Family Life," Lucy Mercier and Rena Harold explore "worker" as one of the roles that define an individual as an adult in society. The definition of *work* is value laden and has been further complicated by changes in traditional family roles, that is, men as breadwinners, women as caretakers of family and home. This chapter explores the ways in which the women and men in this study discussed how work impacted on family-life decisions and vice versa.

The themes of the family stories about work revolved around several axes: the meaning of work for personal and family identity, the intersection of work and gender roles; work as a source of support (as well as of stress and worry); and the importance of work in family decision making. Much of the data about work in family life came from women's stories, and the majority of the themes discussed were closely linked to the birth of children and the amplification of gender roles after the beginning of parenting. In fact, the themes in this chapter are most logically divided into "Work and Family Before Babies" and "Work and Family Life with Children," since the first child's birth seems to have created lasting change for interactions within and outside of the family. This chapter examines parents' reactions to changes in the work–family interface and reveals the resilience and creativity with which many families can respond to work and family pressures. Implications for practice, policy, and research complete this chapter.

The book concludes with chapter 7, "Telling the Family Story: Subplots and Next Chapters." In it, Lisa Colarossi, Rena Harold, and Lucy Mercier summarize the themes that are raised in the chapters and consider them in the context of the three theoretical perspectives discussed earlier. Gender issues and gender roles are also discussed, as is the notion of choices that parents made or, in some cases, felt they were forced to make, as their family life developed. In addition, this chapter discusses the applicability of the storyboard methodology to diverse family types and considers the impact of race/ethnicity, class, and gender on family development, before concluding by summarizing the overall implications for future practice, policy, and research.

REFERENCES

Borden, W. (1992). Narrative perspectives in psychosocial intervention following adverse life events. *Social Work, 37*(2), 135–141.

Bronfenbrenner, U. (1979). *The ecology of human development: Experiments by nature and design.* Cambridge, MA: Harvard University Press.

Bronfenbrenner, U. (1986). Ecology of the family as a context for human development: Research perspectives. *Developmental Psychology, 22,* 723–742.

Carter, B., & McGoldrick, M. (1988). Overview: The changing family life cycle: A framework for family therapy. In B. Carter & M. McGoldrick (Eds.), *The changing family life cycle* (2nd ed., pp. 3–28). New York: Gardner.

Feld, S., & Radin, N. (1982). *Social psychology for social work and the mental health professions*. New York: Columbia University Press.

Goldberg, W. A. (1988). Introduction: Perspectives on the transition to parenthood. In G. Y. Michaels & W. A. Goldberg (Eds.), *The transition to parenthood: Current theory and research* (pp. 1–20) Cambridge, England: Cambridge University Press.

Harold, R. D., Mercier, L. R., & Colarossi, L. G. (1997). Using the eco-map to bridge the practice research gap. *Journal of Sociology and Social Welfare, 24,* 29–44.

Hartman, A. (1978). Diagrammatic assessment of family relationships. *Social Casework, 59,* 465–476.

Laird, J. (1989). Women and stories: Restorying women's self-constructions. In M. McGoldrick, C. Anderson & F. Walsh (Eds.), *Women in families:* A framework for family therapy (pp. 427–450) New York: Norton.

McMahon, M. O. (1990). *The general method of social work practice: A problem-solving approach* (2nd ed.). Englewood Cliffs, NJ: Prentice-Hall.

Minuchin, P. (1988). Relationships within the family: A systems perspective on development. In R. A. Hinde & J. Stevenson-Hinde (Eds.), *Relationships within families* (pp. 7–26). Oxford, England: Clarendon.

Wapner, S., & Craig-Bray, L. (1992). Person-in-environment transitions. *Environment and Behavior, 24,* 161–188.

White, M., & Epston, D. (1990). *Narrative means to therapeutic ends*. New York: Norton.

2

Telling the Family Story: The Process

Rena D. Harold
Michigan State University

Margaret L. Palmiter
Child Trends, Inc.

Susan A. Lynch
University of Arkansas at Little Rock

Carol R. Freedman-Doan
Eastern Michigan University

Jacquelynne S. Eccles
The University of Michigan

As chapter 1 indicated, when viewed from a systems perspective, the family is a complex, integrated whole whose patterns of interaction are circular rather than linear in form (Minuchin, 1988). What, then, are the appropriate strategies for studying the family's developmental process? Traditional research has focused on effects rather than process, constructing the family statistically, and has often been limited to exploring dyadic relationships, that is, subsystems of family units, rather than examining the whole. Thus, research is needed that

15

will take the family as a naturally occurring unit, gather data from multiple family members, and document the nature of their interactions over time (Minuchin, 1988). Giving "voice" to parents, as we have done in this book, allows them to tell their own story, that is, to define themselves, their family members, and the way they interact with their world, that impacts the thinking, affect, and behavior of family members (Watzlawick, 1996). The challenge in investigating families and their relationships both within and outside the family structure is "to try to assess not only the behavior of the participants but also the experience or meaning the interactions have for them" (Ratke-Yarrow, Richters, & Wilson, 1988, p. 61).

Our interest in the ways in which families develop stems from the notion that family dynamics and relationships affect the ideas and beliefs of children, the choices they make, and how they learn to define themselves within a family system (e.g., Eccles [Parsons], 1983). We began our research quantitatively with a set of ideas about how family environments affect children's self-perceptions and their achievement motivation. As we collected data from the families, however, we became intrigued by the themes the families themselves identified as important. We decided to add a qualitative component to our study in order to explore these themes in greater depth, allowing parents' own voices to be heard. This chapter describes how we gathered information from families, how this information was used to identify significant issues in family development, and how a similar "storytelling" process could be used in other settings to understand the meanings people assign to important events in their lives (Harold, Palmiter, Freedman-Doan, Lynch, & Eccles, 1993; Harold, Palmiter, Lynch, & Freedman-Doan, 1995).

Storytelling as a form of narrative is one type of data collection method that encourages individuals to give information about their lives in their own words. This qualitative method has become an increasingly popular tool for understanding human behavior and experience (e.g., Gergen & Gergen, 1984; McAdams, 1985) because individuals can relate the information about their experiences that is most relevant to them and organize this information in a way that is representative of how they see themselves (Veroff, Chadiha, Leber, & Sutherland, 1993a; Veroff, Sutherland, Chadiha, & Ortega, 1993b). We used an adaptation of narrative and storytelling techniques in our family development study to provide parents with an opportunity to talk about experiences and beliefs they found meaningful. With the storytelling technique, we gained information about how the parents viewed themselves as parents, how this view may have changed over time, and the events they thought led to these changes.

THE FAMILIES

The families who told us their stories were selected from a large-scale longitudinal study conducted in 12 schools, in four primarily White, lower-middle to middle-class school districts in a midwestern urban community (Eccles & Blumenfeld, 1984; Eccles, Blumenfeld, Harold, & Wigfield, 1990). The study began with groups of children in kindergarten and the first and third grades, and followed them for 4 years, at which time the children were in the third, fourth, and sixth grades, thus spanning the elementary school years.

Approximately 900 students, two thirds of their parents, and their teachers participated by completing questionnaires and interviews. A unique opportunity existed within the larger study to examine sibling pairs. Because of the grades originally targeted (i.e., kindergarten, first, and third), there were several naturally occurring sibling pairs in the sample. We became interested in the differences that often characterize members of the same family, and that were already apparent in our findings.

How many times have you heard someone say, "I can't believe how different my children are—you'd think they had different parents and were raised in different homes!"? In fact, siblings can be quite different from each other in terms of their personalities and learning styles (Plomin & Foch, 1981; Scarr & Grajek, 1982). Some studies have found that siblings are no more similar to each other than randomly paired individuals (Plomin & Daniels, 1987). This influenced our decision to supplement our sample in the third year of the original study by adding the elementary-aged siblings of students already participating. The decision to limit the age span of the children was made to facilitate the comparison of the siblings within the family, that is, the likelihood of siblings experiencing a similar family environment. We also contacted the parents of these sibships to see if they would agree to be interviewed more extensively on the development of their families. In all, 88 families agreed to tell us their "story."

This chapter will include information from 60 participating families whose children were first and second in birth order. Of these families, there were stories from 38 sets of parents, 18 additional mothers, and 4 additional fathers. Thirty-seven pairs of parents were married and one set of parents was divorced at the time of the interview. Of the 18 additional mothers, 14 were married but their spouses declined to participate, 3 were divorced and were custodial parents, and one was widowed. All four of the additional fathers were married, but their spouses chose not to participate. The average age of the mothers was 34 years; for fathers it was 40 years.

Of the children who were represented in their parents' stories, 65 were girls and 55 were boys. Nineteen of the sibling pairs were both girls, 14 were both boys, 11 consisted of an older sister with a younger brother, and 16 consisted of an older brother with a younger sister. The average age of firstborn children at the time of the interviews was 10 years old and the average age of second-born children was 8 years old.

Approximately 47% of the families were Catholic, approximately 34% identified themselves as some denomination of Protestant, and another 19% listed no preference for their religion. The average education level for mothers was some college education, whereas the average education level for fathers was college graduate. About 60% of the mothers worked for pay, averaging between 21 and 30 hours of work per week, whereas 94% of the fathers worked for pay, averaging between 41 and 50 hours of work per week.

GATHERING FAMILY STORIES

The family interview of the parents consisted of two parts: an open-ended narrative relating the development of the family in story form; and a structured interview containing both open- and close-ended questions asking the parents about each child's specific interests, abilities, and behaviors and then asking them to compare the siblings to each other on these dimensions.

Our process for having families tell us their stories grew out of a method developed by Veroff and his colleagues (1993a; 1993b). We first practiced using this method on several families who were not in the study. These practice interviews reinforced our belief that the family-story technique would give us information about how parents view their parenting, how their expectations about parenting have been influenced by having children, and how they have adapted their parenting to the needs and temperaments of their two children.

For the study, each parent was interviewed separately in a private room of their home where there were few interruptions or distractions. All interviews were tape recorded, after receiving participant consent, and later transcribed verbatim. The following instructions were given to the parents:

> When we began this project we had several pairs of brothers and/or sisters (siblings) in the study because of the grades that we targeted. We noticed that some of these sib pairs were quite alike in their interests and abilities, but others were not. This year, we have asked many other families who have more than one child in elementary school if they would be interested in participating and, as you know, the purpose of this interview is to take a more in depth look at how children within the same family are both similar to and different from one another. The interview is divided into two sections: The first is more informal; the second asks you to respond to specific questions.

> To begin, I'd like to take about 20 minutes and ask you to tell me in your own words the story of your family. I have no set questions to ask you. I'd just like you to tell me about your family as if it were a story with a beginning, a middle, and how things will look in the future. Most parents enjoy talking about their family, and there is no right or wrong way to tell the story. Just tell me in any way that is most comfortable.

Parents were then shown the storyboard depicted in Fig. 2.1 (Harold et al., 1995) and told:

> To help you think of your story, we've put together this storyboard that seems to describe most people's story line. You see that a story line for the formation of a family includes each of these parts [interviewer points to parts of the storyboard]: Your family relationships Prior to the Birth of Child A; Becoming the Parent of Child A [birth experiences and complications]; Living with Child A; Becoming the Parent of Child B [birth experiences and complications]; and Living with Children A and B [then and now].

Interviewers also told parents that they were especially interested in changes parents had experienced in their family relationships, in their expectations of themselves as parents, and in their expectations for their children's development. Interviewers also asked parents how critical life events had affected everyone in the family. Finally, parents were told:

> As you see, this is a very different way of getting a picture of the formation of a family [i.e., different from the close-ended questionnaires used previously in this study]. Everyone seems to come up with a different and interesting story. Please use the story line as a guide, a way to think of what to include in your story. Would you begin by talking about your family relationships prior to the birth of [first child's name]?

Interviewers were chosen purposely for their ability to collect information of this nature without allowing their own biases to influence what they heard. Interviewers were told to keep this part of the interview as open ended as possible. They were also told that what parents say spontaneously often provides an accurate reflection of their thoughts and feelings about their family's development. Interviewers were given suggestions on how to keep the story moving along and how to ask questions effectively without implying a specific response (e.g., "Can you tell me more about that?" "And then what happened?").

We trained each interviewer extensively. During this training, each interviewer practiced the storytelling technique on nonparticipating families in preparation for beginning with the actual study participants. After the actual interviews began, regular group meetings were held with the interviewers to

Your Family Story

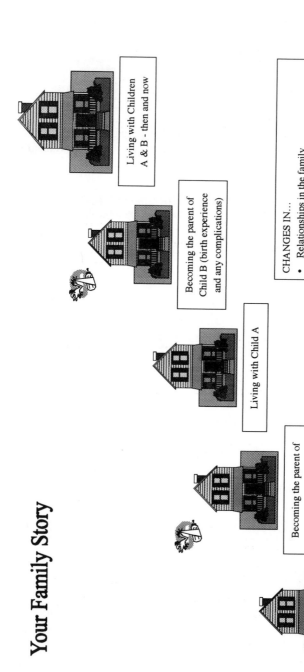

Living with Children
A & B - then and now

Becoming the parent of
Child B (birth experience
and any complications)

CHANGES IN...

- Relationships in the family
- Expectations you have for your role as parent
- Expectations you have for how the children
  will develop
- The differential impact of critical events on
  everyone in the family

Living with Child A

Becoming the parent of
Child A (birth experience
and any complications)

Your family relationships
prior to the birth of Child A

FIG. 2.1   Storyboard.

give them an opportunity to discuss questions or problems, and also to allow them to get feedback on the interviews they had completed. In keeping with the principles of qualitative data collection, these meetings encouraged an interactive relationship between data collection and data analysis (Altheide, 1987; Berg, 1989).

ORGANIZING AND CODING THE STORIES

In the next few sections of this chapter we discuss how we coded the family stories and how we then began to analyze some of the information we had gained. Although the technical aspects of this process will not be of interest to everyone, our intention is to provide a road map of the qualitative methods we used so that they will be useful to others in exploring the richness of these types of data.

We decided that the initial approach to organizing the stories should be influenced by the design of the collection process and our beginning assumptions. Thus, the stories were first divided into the initial theoretical classes outlined on the storyboard (e.g., Prior to the Birth of A). However, it became clear that the families had attached their own meanings to these classes. These meanings emerged by examining the story classes, and a set of *categories* were developed for each class (e.g., *Birth Decisions*). The *characteristics* of the particular categories (e.g., *planned or unplanned births*) and their *connecting themes* have been the result of an interactive process between our initial assumptions and the meanings of the various classes and categories to the families (Fig. 2.2).

Level I Coding—Classes

The storyboard placed a developmental framework on the process of the families telling their story. An important first step in coding the stories was to organize the information presented by the families into each class: Prior to the Birth of Child A, the Birth of Child A, Living with Child A, the Birth of Child B, and Living with Children A and B.

Two of the classes were coded on a copy of the family story by two of the coders. Each coder worked independently, using the definitions of the particular class outlined in the previous discussions. The other two coders coded three classes on a second copy of the family story, again working independently. Mothers' and fathers' stories were coded separately. Coders responsible for coding the mothers' stories for classes Prior to the Birth of A and Birth of B, for instance, coded the corresponding fathers' stories for Birth of A, Living with A, and Living with A and B. This helped to keep coders open to the content of the stories themselves, rather than the influences of other coders or other family members.

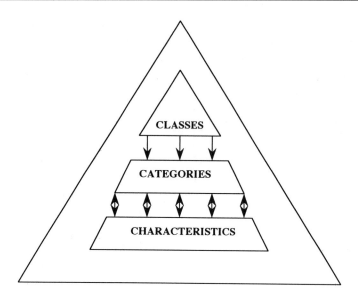

FIG. 2.2.   Coding frame: Classes are divided into categories that are described by
characteristics.

Each coder included in a class those statements that reflected that stage of
family development. For example, comments about dating, the influence of extended families on marriage decisions, and descriptions of how the couple met
were coded in Prior to the Birth of A. This approach is referred to by Altheide
(1987) as conceptual coding, and requires that coders identify a series of comments that reflect information about a particular concept.

The amount of information within each class varied from family to family.
For example, a couple whose first child was born 10 months after their marriage
may have spent relatively little time commenting on the period Prior to the
Birth of A. In addition, comments were sometimes made that seemed out of se-
quence, in that they referred to a time period different from the one currently
being examined. However, these comments were often made in the context of
the parents' current living situation. For example, a divorced mother describing Living with A and B, made the statement: "I am their sole disciplinarian."
She followed this with a recollection from her childhood that was coded in the
class Prior to the Birth of A: "And I remember when I was growing up, my
mother's word never meant as much as my father's word. Dad held more power
behind his words than Mom did." Although this might seem to be out of se-
quence, in that it came at the end of her story, it appeared that she said this as a

comment on her role as a single parent to her two children. Conversely, some parents told about the time period Prior to the Birth of A and interjected comments about how something that occurred in their past related to their current parenting practices: "And I guess I was most disappointed in the experiences that were offered to me.... Because of that I've always wanted to kind of overdo for my own children." This comment was coded in Living with A and B.

Once each coder had assigned comments to a class, the coders compared their decisions. To accomplish this, the group read through each story, and each coder indicated which comments they had assigned to which classes. When the two primary coders were in agreement, the comment was placed in the class they had chosen. In cases of disagreement between the two primary coders, the other group members gave their opinions. This process increased the likelihood that there would be a shared understanding about which story data should be included in the coding of each class.

This coding process resulted in several important phenomena that would influence the analysis. First, classes were not mutually exclusive. It became clear that, as Altheide suggests, one item is frequently relevant for several purposes, in this case, for several classes (Altheide, 1987). This phenomenon was incorporated into the coding process during all of the stages. For example, statements regarding the birth and infancy of the second child may have been coded in the class Birth of B and in the class Living with A and B where data that compared the two children were coded:

> And I did have another baby, and things were totally different with the second child. I think it was much more exhausting, it was more than twice the work. But the new baby slept better immediately, nursed real well, was a better baby, a much more pleasant baby.

The second phenomenon was that the information presented by the participants in their description of the various theoretical classes, or developmental stages, elicited content that had not been of primary interest to the researchers, but was significant to the parents who told their family stories. For example, while the researchers anticipated parents talking about planned or unplanned pregnancies, they had not identified some of the specific factors that parents felt precipitated the decision to have children, such as the purchase of a new home or the celebration of holidays. Quantitative, close ended questions about decisions to have children might not have tapped this rich and interesting data about birth decisions. This began an interplay between the deductive framework of the researchers and the topics, issues, and meanings that had been inductively derived from the participants themselves.

Level II Coding—Categories and Characteristics

This first level of coding organized the data to make it more manageable and produced a framework that laid a path for the next level of analysis. In keeping with the commitment to utilize an interactive approach between deductive (the original research framework) and inductive (meanings that were identified by parents) analyses, and because the foundation for the Level I classes was the theoretical frame of the researchers, Level II coding began with a return to the stories. Coders reviewed the stories and recorded all topical areas discussed. Some of these were present in the initial description of the class developed by the researchers, and others came from the participants' discussion of issues that were important for them in that particular class. This list of topics became the *categories* for Level II coding.

The Level II coding process outlined here is modeled, in part, after Glaser and Strauss's (1967) description of constant comparison. Qualitative analysis takes a grounded approach to the data, expecting ideas, concepts, and even theories to develop from the data. But perhaps even more importantly, the approach of this project reflects the interaction of induction, deduction, and verification (Strauss, 1987). It demonstrates how concepts, issues, and hypotheses can be derived either from theory or from the data. Level II coding used a process of joint coding and analysis. Discussion and comparison were used to ground the theoretical classes to the data, thereby creating data-driven categories (Berg, 1989; Lofland & Lofland, 1984).

After organizing the stories into the five classes, the coders independently read the material in each of the five classes for mothers and fathers to get an overall sense of that particular class. The coders then met as a group and reviewed the first class, Prior to the Birth of A—mothers' stories. As this material was read aloud, each coder identified concepts, events, ideas, and/or feelings that emerged from within that class. This group review process allowed the coders to discuss and compare these issues, and develop a list. The interaction between the coders resulted in further clarification of several issues, and the addition of some that no individual coder had identified alone. Some examples of these issues were the motivation for having children, definitions of "good/bad" babies; characteristics of the birth/delivery; relationships with spouse, friends, and extended families; and work issues around pregnancy or birth.

Once the issues were identified, the coders examined the list looking for ways in which the various ideas fit together or reflected similar categories. Using the issues that had been lifted from the stories, the coders organized the second level of the coding frame around the following four *categories* that were identified across all classes: *Birth Issues, Family Life, Description or Expectations of the Children*, and *Work Life*.

The next step was to continue coding the data to this further level of specificity, organizing the issues within each class by *category*. The coders met as a group to read each class of material, line by line, and describe the nature of the issues in the class. Decisions to place issues within certain categories were discussed among the coders until consensus was reached regarding the appropriate placement. These issues within each *category* became the *characteristics* that defined that category.

The categories and their various characteristics allowed for a logical coding of the data for the first four classes. When beginning the coding process on the class Living with A and B, however, it became clear to the coders that this particular class contained a large amount of varying information. The decision was made to divide the Living with A and B class into more than the four categories. It was the category *Family Life* that seemed to hold the largest amount of varying information. For example, one mother told us:

> I find that as they get older, more independent, there's more time for us. Uh, it's like today, he had the day off, I had the day off, so we spent the day together.

> You know, [Child A] is in soccer, so we spend quite a bit of time at practice, at games and so forth. [Child B] is in Girl Scouts, I'm like assistant teacher to that. So, we do spend enough time with the kids. I don't want to miss the field trips and the involvement with the kids, you know.

> So, I think some of my expectations as a parent, I feel I'm hard on myself, I feel the pressure of being a responsible parent, you know, because it's my job to raise them to be good adults. You know, I think that's the hardest part of parenting for me that, you know, I don't come on too strong so that I turn them off to the values that we have, that I don't, you know, that I do come on strong enough when I need to be the disciplinarian and that kind of thing.

This story typifies the varied topics parents included in describing their family life: the relationship between the spouses as well as with extended family members, the activities the children and family get involved in, and the parent's beliefs and values. Consequently, the coders divided the category *Family Life* into three separate categories: *Family Relationships, Family Activities*, and *Family Goals and Beliefs*. These categories were defined and described using the same process that was outlined previously. The coders then returned to the *Family Life* category in the other four classes and recoded the data into these three categories.

The only other difference for coding the class Living with A and B was the addition of comparative data regarding the two children. This particular category is only appropriate for that class. There are now six categories for each class, with the exception of the class Living with A and B, which has seven. The final coding frame is shown in Table 2.1 (Harold et al., 1995).

Level III Coding—Linkages and Connecting Themes

The data were then divided, utilizing the entire coding frame, into the 31 categories depicted in Table 2.1. The next step in the process was to examine meanings and connections between various sets of categories. The 31 categories were analyzed using a number of approaches. Relationships between the various categories were explored, looking both vertically and horizontally. For example, looking at how the families describe birth decisions across the developmental cycle of the family may tell us something about how decisions to have children change as the needs and demands of the families change. Looking at the relationships between categories during the developmental stage of the Birth of Child A, on the other hand, could give us insight into the preparation families do before they begin to have their children.

Additionally, data were examined in depth within a particular category prior to exploring linkages and connecting themes. For example, the decision to have children has provided an interesting example of data analysis within a particular class around a specific process identified by the parents. Information about the decision to have Child A was contained in the class Prior to the Birth of A. This class was read for mothers and fathers and coded for such comments, and the data were analyzed. Out of the 56 mothers, 26 indicated that their first pregnancy was planned, and 15 said it was unplanned. Four were unclear and 11 did not mention the decision. In contrast, 18 fathers said the pregnancy was planned, 7 said it was unplanned, and 17 did not mention a birth decision. Before hypothesizing about any possible meaning of the differences in numbers between mothers and fathers regarding the mention of birth decisions, it was important to examine the stories to see if anyone who did not mention a decision explicitly, did so implicitly. Of the 17 fathers, only 2 implied a decision making process, although they did not state how or when they enacted that process. For example, one of the fathers said: "We had more or less decided that we were going to have children early … because I felt it would be easier to understand what the kids were thinking and why if we were younger than if we were older." Only one of the mothers who did not explicitly discuss their birth decision referred to motivation for having children: "Basically I grew up in a big family. I had like two sisters and four brothers. So I've always been around kids and I've always wanted a big family myself."

Thus, even considering implied decisions, mothers were still more likely to discuss the decision-making process than fathers. This may be because as child bearers, mothers are more cognizant of the birth decision process or may find it a more salient memory. However, the nature of qualitative stories where individuals may make conscious or unconscious choices about what to discuss makes it difficult to accurately interpret the absence of data on a particular topic.

Among those families who said they planned their first birth, the precipitating factors fell into seven different areas:

1. They had enough resources
2. Biological or physical reasons were compelling (e.g., the "biological clock was ticking")
3. They liked children
4. There had been a recent death in their family prompting the decision to honor or celebrate life with a new pregnancy
5. They experienced pressure from their family(ies) of origin
6. They felt they had attained a psychological readiness to have children
7. It was the correct timing in their work/career

Both mothers and fathers frequently endorsed the first two factors. However, more fathers mentioned being "psychologically ready" to take on family responsibilities, while more mothers discussed the pressure they felt from their family or their spouse's family of origin to produce children.

A careful analysis of the small number of stories where parents indicated that the birth of Child A was unplanned versus those who said it was planned revealed no systematic differences in how the child or their relationship with the child were described. The planfulness of the birth decision may also be diagnostic of the parents' relationship. For example, do parents who plan when to have children communicate more effectively than parents who do not plan? Although these data cannot answer this question conclusively, there were some indications that parents who describe the process as planned, continue to work at their relationship as an entity separate from their roles as parents and family members:

> We had waited 5 years before we had any kids and they used to refer to us as the married single people.... But we started thinking about if we wanted to have kids ... and we talked about what it was going to be like. Your lifestyle changes as soon as you have a kid ... You know we traveled an awful lot still. We would still take the kid with us, and we made time to make sure we always went on vacation by ourselves. So we tried not to let the baby dominate our life.

TABLE 2.1
Final Coding Frame

Level I: Theoretical Classes	Prior to the Birth of A	Birth of Child A	Living With Child A	Birth of Child B	Living With Child A & B
LEVEL II: CATEGORIES • Characteristics	BIRTH DECISION—CHILD A • Information on birth decision: choice or accident planned/unplanned • Precipitating factors	BIRTH PROCESS • Additional decision information • Birth itself • Pregnancy • Expectations of birth	BIRTH DECISION—CHILD B • Information on birth decision: choice or accident planned/unplanned • Precipitating factors	BIRTH PROCESS • Additional decision information • Birth itself • Pregnancy • Expectations of birth	BIRTH DECISIONS • Additional children? • Overview information on having children
	FAMILY RELATIONSHIPS • Extended family descriptive • Marital relationship • Living situation	*FAMILY RELATIONSHIPS* • Extended family descriptive • Marital relationship • Living situation	*FAMILY RELATIONSHIPS* • Extended family descriptive • Marital relationship • Living situation	*FAMILY RELATIONSHIPS* • Extended family descriptive • Marital relationship • Living situation	*FAMILY RELATIONSHIPS* • Extended family descriptive • Marital relationship • Living situation
	FAMILY ACTIVITIES • Events and activities • Trips • School involvement	*FAMILY ACTIVITIES* • Events and activities • Trips • School involvement	*FAMILY ACTIVITIES* • Events and activities • Trips • School involvement	*FAMILY ACTIVITIES* • Events and activities • Trips • School involvement	*FAMILY ACTIVITIES* • Events and activities • Trips • School involvement

	EXPECTATIONS/CHARACTERISTICS	FAMILY GOALS & BELIEFS	WORK LIFE
Level II: CATEGORIES • Characteristics	• Expectations or characteristics of : pregnancy parental role child	• School involvement: goals/beliefs • Future goals • Parenting beliefs	• Mother's work life • Father's work life • Before children work life • Changes expected?
	• Physical problems • Personality of child • Looks of child • Initial impressions • Gender preferences	• School involvement: goals/beliefs • Future goals • Parenting beliefs	• Mother's work life • Father's work life • Effect of birth on parents' work • Financial issues
	• Personality • Skill • Physical issues or problems • Achievement issues	• School involvement: goals/beliefs • Future goals • Parenting beliefs	• Mother's work life • Father's work life • Work and child rearing
	• Physical problems • Personality of child • Looks of child • Initial impressions • Gender preferences • Expectations of two	• School involvement: goals/beliefs • Future goals • Parenting beliefs	• Mother's work life • Father's work life • Effect of birth on parents' work • Financial issues
	Child B Child A & B • Personality • Comparison child A & B • Skill • Life with two • Physical • Achievement issues	• School involvement: goals/beliefs • Future goals • Parenting beliefs	• Mother's work life • Father's work life • Work and raising a family • Work life with two children

The similarities and differences in the stories that couples tell about their birth decision process can also be examined. The following process discussed by one couple demonstrates their different views or memories of what that time was like for them:

> *Mother.* Well, my husband and I were married for 6 years before we had [Child A]. And that time was spent working. We both had jobs and we worked until we got enough money to buy the house, and we got the house and worked on it for a while and then we were ready to start a family so we had [Child A] and she was born a month before she was expected so we've been catching up ever since it seems like.

> *Father.* I didn't really care to have kids until my sister-in-law got divorced. She had a 3-year-old and a 3-month-old, and he just left. Then she moved in the house, so I started helping out and taking care of the kids and found out I liked it. I finally decided to myself, hey, I want to have kids. And then we decided to try, took us a while. And we had [Child A], and that was a big event.

Two questions raised by the this example are whether the differences in their recollections reflect individual differences between couples (e.g., communication patterns or differences in interpretation of events), or whether the differences reflect how gender plays a role in viewing life events. It is interesting to note that in discussing resources, this mother's story is representative of the reasons that 31% of mothers (as compared to 17% of the fathers) gave for planning to have their first child. This father's story discusses his psychological readiness to have children and is indicative of the reasons that 22% of the fathers (as compared to 8% of the mothers) gave for planning their first child. This suggests that men and women may find different issues salient in their view of family development.

The above examples demonstrate how a thick, richer picture of family development begins to emerge from the stories. These findings can be compared to existing research and theory. Furthermore, quantitative analyses linking these data with data collected from parents and their children for the larger study may reveal how birth decisions impact on other family development issues.

It is also possible to analyze the data by examining an issue important to how the family relates to external people and/or institutions, such as will be found in chapter 6, "Job Talk: The Role of Work in Family Life." As the parents talk about the development of their family, they frequently refer to the interaction between that development and the rest of the social structure within which they live. For example, what have been the influences of various stages of family development on the work lives of men and women, and vice versa. Is the impact different for men than for women? How do the experiences of this group of families compare to those of families in other studies?

CONCLUSIONS AND IMPLICATIONS

This chapter describes a process for investigating the development of families as described by the parents themselves. The methods of both data collection and analysis have allowed the meanings that parents attach to family development to emerge from the data. The large number of interviews conducted as well as the use of constant comparison between these meanings and the theoretical frame of the researchers provide a thick data set that allows for the investigation of many aspects of family life and development. In the following chapters, we relate the information we gained from parents as they discussed such issues as deciding to become parents and creating a family identity; the causes for the similarities or differences they see in their children; changes in their relationship with each other, with their extended families, and with their friends after they became parents; and, for mothers, making the decision about when, or if, to return to work.

Documenting the methodological process that was followed is, in and of itself, an important goal of this chapter. Although much has been written that uses qualitative methods, fewer writings detail the specific process that is used to collect, organize, and analyze such data. Sharing this information could be helpful for both researchers and practitioners. For example, the process described herein is particularly well suited to the collection, organization, and analysis of client data secured through clinical practice. What follows is a brief description of two client populations with which this method could be incorporated effectively, not only to increase immediate knowledge about the clients, but also to allow the practitioners to play a more integral role in on-going research, which might eventually impact on policy (see Harold et al., 1995 for a more complete discussion of this topic).

Application for Use With Adoptive Families

Research evaluating the impact of adoptive family characteristics on adoption disruption has been contradictory. Some studies suggest that the presence of other biological children in the home increases the likelihood of disruption, whereas other studies suggest just the opposite. The income level of families has also been found to be a predictor of both the disruption and preservation of the adoption (Westhues & Cohen, 1990). Clear preferences about the characteristics of the child on the part of the adoptive family seem to support a sustained adoption, if the list of preferences does not get too long or too specific (Partridge, Hornby, & McDonald, 1986). The involvement of the adoptive father also seems to be a strong predictor for a positive outcome in two-parent adoptive families (Partridge et al., 1986; Westhues & Cohen, 1990).

Adoption workers and supervisors continue to struggle with how these findings can inform practice. The contradictory results found in aggregate research also appear in case-by-case supervision, leaving adoption workers feeling uncertain about which characteristics of children, families, or their own practice can lead to a greater likelihood that an adoption will have a successful outcome. There is little research regarding the process of adoption placement (Meezan & Shireman, 1985; Westhues & Cohen, 1990). Because the impact of demographic variables are contradictory, it suggests that the process itself may be as significant as the characteristics of those who engage in it. An adaptation of the family storyboard, as seen in Fig. 2.3 (Harold et al., 1995) could be helpful both to individual practitioners and families in understanding the process dynamics in adoptive placements of special needs children. Information from this process could also lead to the development of themes and issues that families found significant in the process of their individual adoption situation.

Several questions begin to emerge. What are the dynamics of the placement process and integration of the child into the family that affect the success of that placement? How do the qualities of the adoptive family members interact with the qualities of the child and the services of the agency to result in successful adoptive placements? When participants are encouraged to "tell their family story," what themes or key issues emerge from that open recounting of the process? Is there a set of dynamics or components in the adoption process that can be identified and quantified, and then used by adoption practitioners to evaluate a placement that is being considered?

Given the inconsistent findings regarding the impact of family dynamics on the success of an adoptive placement, and the level of information about the process of the adoption itself, this method offers an excellent technique to inform adoption practice. The information would shed light on individual, clinical practice with adoptive families, and on the field of adoption practice as a whole.

Application to the Field of Chemical Dependency

As with adoption agencies, the process outlined in this chapter can provide an innovative structure for gathering extensive client life–history information within chemical dependency treatment settings. Such an extensive history is important, especially in light of recent research suggesting that, to be effective, treatment must begin with an examination of historical and current biological,

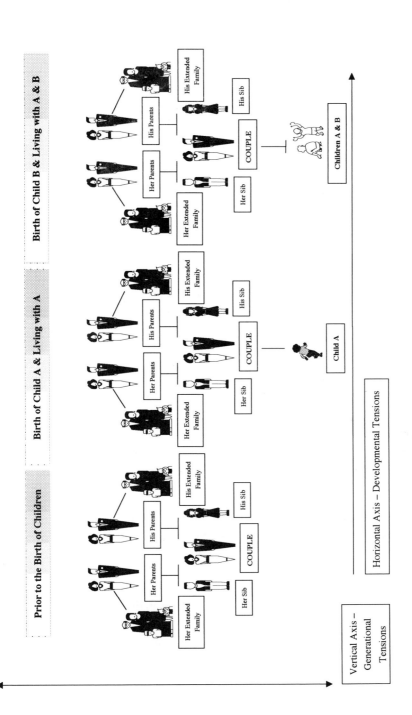

Prior to the Birth of Children   Birth of Child A & Living with A   Birth of Child B & Living with A & B

Vertical Axis – Generational Tensions

Horizontal Axis – Developmental Tensions

FIG. 2.3. The adoption story board

33

psychological, and social functioning. This bio/psycho/social history helps not only to determine the effects of the chemical use on each area of functioning, but also to identify those areas that may either facilitate or hamper recovery (Henderson & Anderson, 1989; Isaacson, 1991; Nirenberg & Maisto, 1990; Polcin, 1992; Smith, Frawley, & Howard, 1991; Smith & Margolis, 1991; Tarter, 1990; Weiner, Wallen, Wilson, & Deal, 1991).

Through the use of "storytelling," clients can provide a bio/psycho/social history of the development of their addiction in a way that is most congruent and meaningful to them. The practitioner would gain immediate knowledge about the events and influences the client believes to be most significant in shaping their addiction while also identifying current strengths and limitations in client functioning.

Once again, the storyboard could be adapted to establish parameters for the information to be provided by the client, utilizing stages/classes such as: Before the Use of Substances; Experimentation with Substances; Increased Use; Problems Due to Use; Acknowledged addiction; Living with addiction, etc. This would insure that certain topical areas are addressed, such as the history and pattern of drug use, the client's level of denial regarding the addiction and the motivation for treatment, at the same time also providing enough flexibility for the client to focus on the content most relevant to her or him.

The practitioner gains individualized information about how the client frames both the antecedents to and the present context of the addiction, as well as the client's current beliefs regarding her/his level of functioning. This information is important to the practitioner in formulating the diagnosis, the prognosis, and the treatment plan. Using more traditional means of data collection may result in information that is less personalized and thus lacks "depth." Consequently, clients who initially look very similar on paper may, in reality, have significant differences that would greatly influence treatment.

For example, when filling out an initial clinical questionnaire, two clients may both indicate that they began drinking at age 16, that they have recently lost a job, and that they currently drink every day. Although these clients may initially look very similar, the meaning each client attaches to this information will have a significant impact on treatment. Thus, Client A may perceive sixteen as an early age at which to start drinking, may attribute her/his recent job loss to her/his drinking, and may believe daily drinking is excessive. Client B, on the other hand, may believe sixteen is a normal age at which to begin drinking, may blame his/her job loss on his/her boss, and may believe daily drinking is not excessive at all. Obviously, these clients would have very different treatment plans.

Due to its capacity to function as both a practice and a research method, the process of information gathering outlined in this paper provides a rich source of data useful to both the researcher and the practitioner. In turn, the process strengthens the link between researcher and practitioner, and could lead to the development of policy based on the findings, i.e., the stories of the subjects, and their interpretations.

The process of encoding themes across parents' stories, as previously discussed, was used by each author in the following chapters to highlight areas of interest and concern for families. Although the chapters discuss different topics, they are all organized around the developmental time line of the storyboard. Each chapter also identifies themes, gives examples of the parents' statements reflecting these themes; and, based on these statements and the literature, discusses possible implications of these issues for practice, policy, and research developments.

REFERENCES

Altheide, D. (1987). Reflections: Ethnographic content analysis. *Qualitative Sociology, 10,* 65–77.

Babbie, E. (1983). *The practice of social research* (2nd ed.). Belmont, CA: Wadsworth.

Berg, B. (1989). *Qualitative research methods for the social sciences*. Boston: Allyn and Bacon.

Eccles (Parsons), J. (1983). Expectancies, values, and academic behaviors. In J. T. Spence (Ed.), *Achievement and achievement motives* (pp. 75–146). San Francisco: Freeman.

Eccles, J. S., & Blumenfeld, P. C. (1984). *Psychological predictors of competence development.* (Grant No. 2 R01 HD17553–01). Bethesda, Maryland: National Institute of Child Health and Human Development.

Eccles, J. S., Blumenfeld, P. C., Harold, R. D., & Wigfield, A. L. (1990). *Ontogeny of self and task concepts and activity choice.* (Grant No. 2 R01 HD17553–06). Bethesda, Maryland: National Institute of Child Health and Human Development.

Emerson, R. M. (1983). Introduction: Theory and evidence in field research. In R. M. Emerson (Ed.), *Contemporary field research.* New York: Little, Brown.

Emerson, R. M. (1985). Introduction: Ethnography and understanding members' worlds. In R. M. Emerson (Ed.), *Contemporary field research.* New York: Little, Brown.

Fielding, N., & Fielding, J. (1986). *Linking data.* Beverly Hills, CA: Sage.

Geertz, C. (1983). Thick description: Toward an interpretive theory of culture. In Emerson, R. M. (Ed.), *Contemporary field research.* New York: Little, Brown.

Gergen, M., & Gergen, K. (1984). The social construction of narrative accounts. In K. Gergen & M. Gergen (Eds.), *Historical social psychology* (pp. 173–189). Hillsdale, NJ: Lawrence Erlbaum Associates.

Glaser, B., & Strauss, A. (1967). *The discovery of grounded theory: Strategies for qualitative research.* Chicago: Aldine.

Gummeson, E. (1991). *Qualitative methods in management research.* Beverly Hills, CA: Sage.

Harold, R. D., Palmiter, M. L., Freedman-Doan, C. R., Lynch, S. A., & Eccles, J. S. (1993, March). *An ethnographic content analysis of family stories: An examination of the process.* Paper presented at the Biennial Meeting of the Society for Research in Child Development, New Orleans, LA.

Harold, R. D., Palmiter, M. L., Lynch, S. A., & Freedman-Doan, C. R. (1995). Life stories: A practice-based research technique. *Journal of Sociology and Social Welfare, 22*, 23–44.

Henderson, D. C., & Anderson, S. C. (1989). Adolescents and chemical dependency. *Social Work in Health Care, 14*, 87–105.

Isaacson, E. B. (1991). Chemical addiction: Individuals and family systems. Special Issue: Chemical dependency: Theoretical approaches and strategies working with individuals and families. *Journal of Chemical Dependency Treatment, 4*, 7–27.

Kelly, G. A. (1955). *The psychology of personal constructs.* New York: Norton.

Lincoln, Y. S., & Guba, E. G. (1985). *Naturalistic inquiry.* Beverly Hills, CA: Sage.

Lofland, J., & Lofland, L. (1984). *A guide to qualitative observation and analysis.* Belmont, CA: Wadsworth.

Marshall, C., & Rossman, G. B. (1989). *Designing qualitative research.* Beverly Hills, CA: Sage.

McAdams, D. P. (1985). *Power, intimacy, and the life story.* Homewood, IL: Dorsey.

Meezan, W., & Shireman, J. F. (1985). *Care and commitment: Foster parent adoption decisions.* Albany: State University of New York Press.

Miles, M. B., & Huberman, A. M. (1984). *Qualitative data analysis: A sourcebook of new methods.* Beverly Hills, CA: Sage.

Minuchin, P. (1988). Relationships within the family: A systems perspective on development. In R. A. Hinde & J. Stevenson-Hinde (Eds.), *Relationships within families* (pp. 7–26). Oxford, England: Clarendon.

Nirenberg, T. D., & Maisto, S. A. (1990). The relationship between assessment and alcohol treatment. *International Journal of the Addictions, 25*, 1275–1285.

Partridge, S., Hornby, H., & McDonald, T. (1986). *Legacies of loss, visions of gain: An inside look at adoption disruption.* Portland: University of Southern Maine.

Patton, M. (1980). *Qualitative evaluation methods.* Beverly Hills, CA: Sage.

Patton, M. (1982). *Practical evaluation.* Beverly Hills, CA: Sage.

Plomin, R., & Daniels, D. (1987). Why are children in the same family so different from each other? *Behavioral and Brain Sciences, 10*, 1–16.

Plomin, R., & Foch, T. (1981). Sex differences and individual differences. *Child Development, 52*, 383–385.

Polcin, D. L. (1992). A comprehensive model for adolescent chemical dependency treatment. *Journal of Counseling and Development, 70*, 376–382.

Ratke-Yarrow, M., Richters, J., & Wilson, W. E. (1988). Child development in a network of relationships. In R. A. Hinde & J. Stevenson-Hinde (Eds.), *Relationships within families* (pp. 48–67). Oxford, England: Clarendon.

Scarr, S., & Grajek, S. (1982). Similarities and differences among siblings. In M. E. Lamb & B. Sutton-Smith (Eds.), *Sibling relationships: Their nature and significance across the life-span.* Hillsdale, NJ: Lawrence Erlbaum Associates.

Schatzman, L., & Strauss, A. (1973). *Field research: Strategies for a natural sociology.* Englewood Cliffs, NJ: Prentice-Hall.

Smith, H. E., Frawley, P., & Howard, M. O. (1991). Environmental risks to be considered in substance user treatment planning, implementation and assessment. *International Journal of the Addictions, 26*, 371–375.

Smith, H. E., & Margolis, R. D. (1991). Adolescent inpatient and outpatient chemical dependence treatment: An overview. *Psychiatric Annals, 21*, 105–108.

Strauss, A. (1987). *Qualitative analysis for social scientists.* New York: Cambridge University Press.

Strauss, A., & Corbin, J. (1990). *Basics of qualitative research: Grounded theory procedures and techniques.* Beverly Hills, CA: Sage.

Tarter, R. E. (1990). Evaluation and treatment of adolescent substance abuse: A decision tree method. *American Journal of Drug & Alcohol Abuse, 16*, 1–46.

Veroff, J., Chadiha, L., Leber, D., & Sutherland, L. (1993a). Affects and interactions in newlyweds' narratives: Black and white couples compared. *Journal of Narrative and Life History*, 3, 361–390.

Veroff, J., Sutherland, L., Chadiha, L., & Ortega, R. (1993b). Newlyweds tell their stories: A narrative method for assessing marital experiences. *Journal of Social and Personal Relationships*, 11, 437–457.

Watzlawick, P. (1996). The construction of clinical "realities." In H. Rosen (Ed.) *Constructing realities: Meaning-making perspectives for psychotherapists* (pp. 55–70). San Francisco: Jossey-Bass.

Weber, M. (1949). *From Max Weber: Essays in sociology.* New York: Oxford University Press.

Weiner, H., Wallen, M., Wilson, R., & Deal, D. (1991). The treatment of cocaine addiction: A case study. *Alcoholism Treatment Quarterly, 8,* 95–105.

Westhues, A., & Cohen, J. S. (1990). Preventing disruption of special-needs adoptions. *Child Welfare, 69,* 141–155.

3

Talking About Identity: Individual, Family, and Intergenerational Issues

Patricia Stow Bolea
Grand Valley State University

In 1973, Troll asked:

> What happens to [parent–child bonds] before, during, and after the various transitions or crises of individual development? To what extent are changes in family relationships quantitative only, and to what extent qualitative? To what extent may there be ebbs and flows in connectedness and separateness, in fusion or individuation? (p. 68)

The desire and need to connect is a universal phenomenon. In this chapter, the family stories are used to explore a set of questions related to the ways families form their own specific identity, different or separate from individual identity. Additionally, their stories provide information related to the connections they develop with others, with a particular emphasis on intergenerational issues. Individual identity, for the purposes of this chapter, is defined as a person's sense of "Who am I?" Family identity is described as the ways in which families define themselves and communicate their shared character or personality. Both individual and family identity, although shaped by a variety of factors, are closely related to connections with others, including preceding generations of family members.

The chapter begins with a brief review of the work that has been done in creating a framework for the investigation of family identity and connections to others. Many of the provisions of the Carter and McGoldrick (1988) model of the family life cycle, as discussed in chapter 1, serve as a backdrop against which researchers may evaluate relevant studies of families in transition. For example, researchers suggest that family stresses, which are likely to occur around life cycle transition points (e.g., getting married, having a baby, etc.), frequently create disruptions of the life cycle and produce symptoms of dysfunction (Hadley, Jacob, Milliones, Caplan, & Spitz, 1974; Walsh, 1978). There is also growing evidence demonstrating the continuing impact of life cycle events on family development over time.

Using this model as a framework, this chapter then provides an analysis of the family stories in a way that explores participants' comments regarding their transition from young adulthood, through couplehood, and the transition to parenthood. In particular, the following questions are explored: What do parents report regarding their own identity? How are families defining a heritage together for themselves, and how is family identity formation communicated in their stories? What, if any, is the influence or contribution of family of origin and kinship groups? What are the experiences and reflections of these parents as they describe their acclimation to these major transitions in their lives and consider the role that prior generations (or the messages passed down) may play?

FAMILY TRANSITIONS TO PARENTHOOD

The transition to parenthood has been defined to include the brief period of time from the beginning of a pregnancy through the first months of having a child. Traditionally, the transition is studied from either the time of conception or from birth. From a psychological and sociocultural perspective, however, there is no requisite that the transition to parenthood be confined to this period. As we will see, much has been noted about the ways in which the contextual family experience, expectations, and events that both precede and follow conception and delivery, also affect the transition experience (Goldberg, 1988).

New parents' capacities to make a successful adjustment at this time may set a future course of effective, competent parenting. Critical difficulties during this adjustment may lead to, or exacerbate, marital discord and thereby create difficulty in providing for the child's needs. Both preventive and clinical interventions may be necessary to modify an unwanted trajectory and ensure the healthy psychological adjustment of the parent and child, the marital couple, and the family system (Goldberg, 1988).

Early studies of the transition to parenthood often perpetuated a "transition as crisis" ideology (LeMasters, 1978). Recent studies using longitudinal methodology have explored this premise and have raised more differentiated questions, examining the process of change for individuals, couples, and families. There are now a variety of models that propose to separate the issues and define the path for individuals and couples immersed in the transition to parenthood (Cowan, P. A. & Cowan, C. P., 1988).

The Transition to Parenthood: What Happens to Couples?

A repeated finding in recent transition to parenthood research is that with the transition from being a couple to becoming parents comes a general decline in marital satisfaction, especially for women (Belsky & Pensky, 1988; Heinicke & Guthrie, 1992). This phenomenon is recognized as quite complex. In addition, it is believed that the strongest predictor of the marital adjustment to parenthood is the prebirth condition of the marital relationship (Belsky & Kelly, 1994; Cowan & Cowan, 1992; Cowan, Cowan, Heming, & Miller, 1991; Heinicke & Guthrie, 1992).

Although a variety of hypotheses have been offered to explain this occurrence, evidence points toward issues of couples' division of labor and expectations. Research consistently indicates that regardless of where couples rate themselves on scales measuring egalitarianism versus traditionalism in their marital relationship, once the baby is born there is a shift toward a more traditional division of labor with regard to household chores (Belsky & Kelly, 1994; Cowan, P. A. & Cowan, C. P., 1988; Cowan, C. P. & Cowan, P. A., 1988; Cowan et al., 1991). The division of labor issue is the most commonly cited reason for disagreement among couples (Cowan et al., 1991). This issue has a profound effect on couples whose expectations of "who would do what" differed from the reality of caring for their child (Belsky & Kelly, 1994; Cowan & Cowan, 1992; Cowan et al., 1991). And these expectations, as we see, have an effect on a family's identity as they adjust to childrearing.

Clearly there is no "ideal" arrangement for new parents. Both individual and family identity incorporate a wide variety of roles and family definitions. When both parents in a heterosexual marriage work outside the home, their feelings about themselves and the marriage tend to be more positive, at the cost of increased overall stress and fatigue (see chap. 6 for more information regarding "The Role of Work in Family Life"). On the other hand, women who reduce outside work in exchange for more time at home have reported feeling underappreciated (Belsky & Kelly, 1994), and fathers feel the pressure of financial burdens. Although both of these alternatives have costs and benefits, research also tells us that when men are more involved in the direct care of their children, they feel better about themselves, as do their wives about themselves, and both report feeling better about their marriage (Belsky & Kelly, 1994). Lastly, what is currently being reported as more important than the actual outcome of division of labor is how that arrangement is negotiated (Belsky & Kelly, 1994; Cowan, C. P. & Cowan, P. A., 1988). This information speaks to the current transition in our culture regarding gender role expectations, the shift toward reducing authoritarianism in organizations and families, as well as the economic conditions requiring two incomes in most families. Consequently, couples face the need for more negotiation on every front. As our culture makes such transitions, one may expect to see these changes reflected in the narratives describing individual and family identity included in this study.

Family identity issues, as evidenced by the ways in which families together define expectations, goals, and plans for their young, are explicit during the transition to parenthood phase of family development. In addition, the decisions that each parent makes about career, philosophy of child rearing, and commitment to the marital partnership are examples of themes that weigh heavily on their own identity formation as adults, and as a family.

As the volume of research seeking to incorporate the above ideas has grown over the past decade, investigators have begun to conceptualize the findings into models. The Cowan et al. (1991) model is one example of a comprehensive approach that allows the prospective adjustment outcome to be determined by the unique characteristics possessed by each family. Cowan et. al. (1991) suggested that to gain an understanding of what happens to relationships and to individuals, it is necessary to examine the interconnections among all five of the following domains:

1. Sense of Self—individual characteristics including: self-concept, self-esteem, symptoms of depression, and emotional distress
2. Parents' Marriage—with special emphasis on their division of labor and patterns of communication
3. Parent–Child Relationship—the quality of relationship between each parent and the child
4. Intergenerational Relationships—among grandparents, parents, and grandchildren
5. Life Stress/Social Support/Employment—the relationship between nuclear family members and individuals or institutions outside the family

The Cowan et al. (1991) model has demonstrated an important point. There is an underlying continuity of adaptation that exists for parents during a time of profound individual and relationship change. Negative and positive outcomes of the transition to parenthood appear to be predictable from parents' prebaby levels of distress and adaptation. It is the additional stress involved in parenting and the way it manifests itself that contributes to their later feelings about themselves, their marriage, and their parenting style.

Parents in our study have described their own transitions by telling their stories. They reflected on the meaning of this transition for their lives. In the process, information was provided that portrays the essence of individual identity, family identity, and intergenerational issues in their lives.

Family of Origin Issues

Recent studies have indicated that family of origin experiences may have a profound effect on subsequent marital adjustment during the transition to parenthood (Lane, Wilcoxon, & Cecil, 1988). An examination of intergenerational influences includes historical family of origin information, as well as information relating to the current evolution of adult children's relationships with their parents, and their new baby. Belsky and Isabella (1985) have noted, however, that the role of these developmental factors has received little attention with respect to the quality of marriage, except in cases of divorce. Indeed, few studies to date have pinpointed the family of origin and developmental antecedents of marital adjustment during the transition to parenthood as a target for study (Wallace & Gotlib, 1990). Research has indicated, however, that the transition to parenthood is a stimulus for increased contact with families of origin, as well as with other social support systems (Belsky & Rovine, 1990; Fischer, 1988). This knowledge, pointing to increased contact with families of origin, highlights the need to gain more information surrounding the nature and meaning of this contact for parents and grandchildren in the development of family identity.

Belsky and Isabella (1985) investigated the relationship between subjects' current marital functioning, and childrearing experiences within their family of origin. Specifically, subjects' perceptions of their own childhood and of their parents' marital functioning were used to predict the quality of their own marital functioning during the transition to parenthood. The findings of this study indicated that subjects who experienced poor childrearing (defined as cold or hostile caregiving by parents) or a poor parental marital relationship are at risk for the likelihood of negative changes in their own marriage. These findings have been replicated by Lane, Wilcoxon, and Cecil (1988), who report a healthier transition to parenthood for husbands and wives with undamaged family of origin experiences. They additionally report that the family of origin issue is a more important consideration than many others in predicting marital change, especially for women.

Belsky, Youngblade, and Pensky (1989) explored the potential for marital quality to act as a protective factor for those who experienced poor childrearing from their parents. They found that mothers who experienced high levels of rejection and low levels of support during their own childhood were more likely to have highly negative interactions with their children, but *only* in cases where negative/poor marital quality was also present. Women with similar childhoods who were in positive marital situations, did not exhibit negative parental behavior. This points to the protective potential for a good marriage to operate as a buffer with respect to the intergenerational transmission of mother's negative affect toward their children. These results provide support for the contention that a person's degree of vulnerability to risk and stress is strongly influenced by the ability to develop and maintain current healthy intimate relationships (Bowlby, 1988).

Thus far, research related to new parents' childhood experiences and the effect of those experiences on their parenting has been described. Given the geographic mobility within American culture, a true exploration of the effect of intergenerational issues on the transition to parenthood must be expanded to include the wider family context.

Effects of Kinship Ties on Family Development

Kinship structure has been defined as the combination of people—both family members and/or friends—who surround, encircle, and participate in the development of one individual or set of siblings. This group for example, surrounding a new baby, is one that changes as that child ages over the life course. Relationships between daughters and mothers (Fischer, 1981, 1991), sons and mothers (Fischer, 1983a), daughters and mothers-in-law (Fischer, 1983b), and grandmothers and daughters (Fischer, 1983c) all shift in response to the birth of a child.

Most studies of kinship in American and British culture point toward a tendency for stronger ties with maternal than with paternal kin. This has been explained by noting gender roles and trends in family behavior. Women tend to act as "gatekeepers," monitoring family business, providing direct childcare, and determining relatives' access to children. Childbirth appears to stimulate increased interaction between grandmother and mother, naturally drawing in the maternal family. It has also been noted that while the birth of a child stimulates increased contact with both sides of a family, paternal grandparents are reportedly less likely to drop in for informal visits in the home in comparison to maternal grandparents (Fischer, 1983a, 1983b, 1988).

Fischer (1988) noted the following distinctions in her discussion of kinship influences on new parents and their child. She asserts that kinship groups affect the developing child in three ways: as audience, through influence, and through the allocation of resources. When discussing kin as audience, she notes reports in which mothers tell of the importance of maintaining face-to-face contact with their family and friends, and grandmothers describe the enjoyment of watching the child grow. The doting audience serves to support the child as "center of the universe" for the parents and family.

Kinship groups influencing family development also occur via direct involvement in childrearing, as well as through role modeling of adult behavior. This transpires as grandparents and others offer advice and coaching to new parents, and direct childcare for grandchildren. Grandmothers specifically are called upon to assist with parenting issues as basic as feeding, toilet-training, and healthcare, and later more complicated and abstract challenges. Lastly, in their provision of resources to families, kinship circles have an impact on the development of children which may go unnoticed. Grandparents and other relatives may help to enrich a child's financial or physical environment, and alternately needy relatives may serve to siphon off resources otherwise intended for the child (Fischer, 1988).

In summary, a brief examination has been provided detailing examples of ways families and kinship groups groom and socialize new parents. Viewed practically, one sees how kinship groups have the potential either to complicate or to soften and absorb some of the major responsibilities new parents face. In this chapter, subjects' stories were examined with regard to families' connections to others, including the marital relationship, extended family, kinship groups, and intergenerational issues.

Family of Origin Issues Replayed in the New Family

Having a baby reawakens issues from one's childhood. Cowan et al. (1991) report that both men's and women's relationships with their own parents undergo marked changes as they themselves enter parenthood. For some, the "becoming a family" period seemed to be an intense period of reconciliation and reconnection with their parents, but others were faced with a reawakening of earlier tensions and family struggles (Fischer, 1983b, 1988, 1991). The parental role is uniquely and emotionally evocative because old feelings and concerns about developmental issues such as control, dependence, autonomy, intimacy, sexuality, and aggression are reawakened in people as they experience pregnancy and early parenthood (Antonucci & Mikus, 1988; Colman & Colman, 1971; Cowan & Cowan, 1992). Reactivation of old issues may be accompanied by a strong regressive pull or by viewing the opportunity as one for change and growth. The opportunity to confront an issue again as an adult, with more psychological resources than one had as a child, may enable a parent to rework and resolve old issues. The reexperience can perhaps facilitate resolution. At the same time, repeated encounters with unresolved developmental and emotional issues can be distressing and unsettling. One's ability to address these family issues varies from individual to individual. The sensitivity and involvement of one's social and family network may be a powerful factor in the occurrence of the reactivation process and its outcome (Antonucci & Mikus, 1988).

Specifically, Fischer (1981) reported in her research with mothers and daughters who are transitioning into parenthood, that the daughters report wanting their mothers to come and "take care" of them. When daughters become mothers they understand simultaneously both what it is to be the subject of mothering (as their new baby is) and the object of the mothering (as the baby's mother). This results in the tendency for a new identification and understanding of their own mothers.

Research documenting specific intergenerational issues in father-son adjustment to parenting is more scarce. The focus of available research was limited to new fathers' tendency either to model their skills after their own fathers' or to compensate for perceived deficiencies in their childhood relationships with their fathers (Parke, 1995). For mothers and sons, Fischer (1983a) indicates that parenthood has the potential to create tension, perhaps reflecting strain between daughters and mothers-in-law.

INDIVIDUAL AND FAMILY IDENTITY: DEFINITIONS AND PROCESSES

Men and women differ qualitatively in their psychological response to childbirth. Their identities are altered in very different ways.

Individual Identity

Cowan (1991) and Cowan and Cowan (1992) as well as Belsky and Kelly (1994) have utilized a tool called the "Pie" to understand better the ways in which the transition to parenthood affects a person's identity and self concept. The instrument requires that each person in their study divide a circle into pieces, using size to indicate salience regarding adult roles both before and after the birth. Not surprisingly, the roles of mother and father become larger pieces for both men and women. What gets reduced for both in this process are the roles of husband/wife/lover. What makes this difficult for women, however, is that women's sense of self as worker/student becomes a smaller piece, whereas men's tends to remain unchanged. A common pattern for couples in their adjustment to child care is for women to reduce work/career energy, whereas their husbands often increase their work to compensate financially. This alteration in roles, along with all the other adjustments to parenthood results in major challenges for parents psychologically, as well as in their couple relationships.

Another perspective for examination of individual identity issues concerns the role implications related to adult development. Parenthood is often valued as a key to adulthood, in that the birth of a child makes the parent not only a mother or a father but simultaneously an adult (Antonucci & Mikus, 1988). Within the tradition of psychological research focusing on the self and identity, investigators discuss people's conceptualizations about their "possible selves." Markus and Nurius (1986, 1987) indicated that this concept is meant to represent what individuals conceive they might become, with both positive and negative implications.

Within the infant mental health literature, researchers are attending to maternal representations of the infant in the prospective parent's mind (Stern, 1991). The roots of the current work were developed by Bowlby (1969), on internal working models; by Fraiberg (Fraiberg, Adelson, & Shapiro, 1975), on parental fantasies; and by Lebovici (1983), on the "imaginary" baby constructed by parents (cited in Stern, 1991).

Recent research explores the variety of ways in which maternal representations of the "self" and the "future baby" change during pregnancy, and the ways in which these changes potentially affect outcomes for the family (Ammaniti, 1991; Ammaniti, Baumgartner, Candelori, Perucchini, Pola, Tambelli, & Zampino, 1992; Fonagy, 1994; Stern, 1991). Stern (1989) asserts that a mother's representation of her infant incorporates the representation of infant as well as the representation of self-as-mother. This research bridges the gap between individual and family identity issues, as the focus moves back and forth between how a mother sees herself, her infant, and the developing relationship that occurs within the family. Additionally, this research also examines the mother–infant relationship within the context of the previous generation of parenting. Chapter 4 discusses some of these issues in looking at the close relationship between mothers' representations of the child's characteristics before and after birth.

Family Identity

Wamboldt and Reiss (1989) suggest that couples who are transitioning into parenthood have before them two tasks: (a) they must define a family heritage together, that is, they must resolve those questions of "From where have we come?" and "What do we think of those experiences?"; and (b) they must address the task of defining a new relationship identity, or deciding who they are. Agreement concerning the ground rules of one's current relationship is interpretable as indicating the degree to which the new couple has articulated their relationship identity. How they define their heritage together has been shown to be more important than the actual experiences.

"A first child reorganizes generational boundaries, making grandparents of parents, uncles and aunts of siblings and parents of children" (Clulow, 1991, p. 263). Like individuals, families and social institutions have self-perceptions. Couples and families have a sense of "we-ness," and a generally agreed on conception or myth about the nature of their family unit, as alluded to in chapter 1. Individuals within the family may not share the same view completely, but decisions and collective actions are often based on common perceptions. As with individual life changes, family transitions open the view of self/we-ness to questions, to redefinition, and/or to reorganization.

The discussion of possible selves relates to the conception of family identity as well. How have we imagined our family to be? Until the research exploring maternal representations, investigators used the concept of family myth to explain this. The family myth is part of "the inner image" of the family, to which all contribute and which all strive to preserve. It expresses shared convictions about the people and their relationship in the family (Ferreira, 1963). Family myths are defined as a set of role images that are accepted by the whole family together, giving each person an allotted pattern of interaction (Byng-Hall, 1988). Viewed in this way, one's family myth not only fulfills one's notion of who one is, but also prescribes the ways in which one behaves within the family group.

The concept of family scripts is similar to the idea of a blueprint. Family scripts prescribe the pattern of family interaction in particular contexts. According to Byng-Hall (1988), children learn how to be parents from their parents. One generation later this can lead to replicative scripts, or to corrective scripts in which an attempt is made to correct earlier mistakes. As described above, the likelihood of recreating a negative family experience appears to hinge somewhat on the ability of the new parents to maintain a positive marital relationship (Belsky, Youngblade, & Pensky, 1989).

Much of the available research on the creation of family identity relies on recollections of family of origin experiences. Again, this highlights the importance of the adult's memory and representation of early experiences (Belsky et al., 1989). What follows here are the stories of the families represented in this book as they talked about themselves as individuals who are creating families with unique life experiences and definitions.

THE STORIES

Following the developmental framework utilized for this research, the emphasis of the analysis of stories for this chapter includes the transitions of adult identity development, the move to couplehood and family formation, and an examination of intergenerational connections. These categories were developed following a review of the literature and an initial review of the stories themselves. Chapter 2 offered considerable detail regarding coding methodology, in general. The coding frame for these particular issues is displayed in Table 3.1. In this chapter, story information is presented using the following format: Individual Identity, Family Identity, and Connections to Others, each of which is described separately. Information within each of these classes is reviewed by presentation of important themes and issues, as well as other interesting results. For each point, parents' own words are provided as evidence of the results.

Individual Identity

Description of self

Generally, data regarding parents' discussion of themselves were integrated with other data throughout their stories. More definitive remarks about themselves as individuals could be grouped into a discussion of life history, ca-

TABLE 3.1
Identity Classes and Themes Across Time Periods

Classes Across Time Periods	*Major Themes Across Parent Stories*
Individual identity	1) Description of self
Family identity	1) Dating and marriage relationship
	2) Family beliefs
	3) Expectations, hopes, and plans
	4) Critical Events
Connections to others	1) Extended family relationships
	2) Kinship groups
	3) Intergenerational themes
	4) Cultural ties and traditions

reer, and their reactions to childrearing. Within the family narratives, three major themes became clear in parents' stories: Chronology; Individual Response to Birth; and, most prominently, Attention to Vocational Issues.

Chronology. Individual identity is found in chronological reports of adult developmental milestones. Parents' stories included information related to their life course before marriage and children. Much of this information described details around their own educational/career paths. An example:

> We were married in April of 1975 when I graduated college. At that time I decided to go to law school. After I graduated we came here because I was in school. And she was working, and I was working part time. I went through school and in between bought a house, and then decided about the time I was ready to finish up school that it was time to start a family.

An important note is that getting married did not end a focus on career preparation for these families. One husband notes:

> I've always worked, and [my wife] quit working after she had the first child, and I went to night school and just finished. And I've always been going to school since we've been married....

Numerous parents, especially fathers, noted the ways their educational training continued after they had children, thus adding to the demands the new family faced. This information supports trends in family development theory that are systems oriented (Bronfenbrenner, 1979), and eliminates the use of distinct/finite categories that preclude the reality of overlapping cycles and patterns of family members.

Individual Response to Birth. Another important theme became clear. Distinct differences appeared when reviewing parents' responses to parenthood. For women, the narratives were found to include excitement and happiness, but were also characterized by tremendous distress adjusting to childrearing. Descriptions included adjectives like "sadness," "boredom," and "isolation." For example, one woman reports:

> Uh, everything was different. I had been working and then I'm home with a baby. I found it a big adjustment, I really did. Mostly because we were new in the neighborhood, I didn't know anybody. So you're isolated with a baby, it's wintertime, you're in a house alone with a baby all day. It was a lonely time, really. I found having a baby takes up so much of your time. I didn't have much time for myself, and with each baby you have less and less.

The response for men in describing their reactions to the birth of their children included excitement, as well. However their narratives were characterized by an absence of the previously noted isolation or boredom, and instead included remarks about their work life, pride, and identity as a father. Additionally, several men noted the value/importance of family time:

> … And I like to see—like us to be a close-knit family, where the kids enjoy being around each other. And I want that to grow in years to come. One of the things we try to do is to take family vacations, trips where everybody can go and do things. That's important for them.

Family stories support the literature findings related to the complex demands parents face during the transition to parenthood (Cowan & Cowan, 1992), and tendencies for couples' reverting to a traditional division of labor when the baby is born (Belsky & Kelly, 1994). Additionally, these stories provide interesting evidence, describing in detail the experience of women who have been a part of the workforce prior to giving birth. This third theme, surrounding vocational issues, is explored in detail in chapter 6.

Family Identity

As indicated previously, family identity is defined in this chapter as the way(s) in which families describe themselves and communicate their shared character or personality. The related questions in this section are: How are these families defining a family heritage together? and How is family identity formation communicated in their stories?

Dating and marriage relationship

Five different issues became clear in discussing parents' dating and marriage relationships: Chronology, Transitional Adjustments, Emotional Tone, Parental Preparation, and Relationship Building.

Chronology. Chronological reports of life events in the development of family identity included dating and marriage as well. Fourteen parents noted the way in which they met their spouses, with work and school cited most frequently. This information was typically presented as part of a summary chronology that included meeting the spouse, getting married, a reference to work, and the number of years until children were born. In fact, 40 parents noted the length of time from marriage to conception/birth, making this information one of the central markers in the family stories in this study. A representative quote is as follows:

> Okay. My husband and I were married in 1971, going on almost 18 years ago. It's hard to believe. We had a very short courtship and we were married within 3

months. And we were married for 7 years before we had children—we both worked.

Transitional Adjustments.   A second theme emerging within the discussions of the Dating and Marriage Relationship included comments regarding transitional adjustments. In particular, parents noted the carefree lifestyle they enjoyed, prior to having children, as part of their family identity development. For example:

> I was married at 29. My wife was 24 at the time. So I was a little bit older than the average married person, I would—I would assume. Uh, the first 2 or 3 years we had a carefree type of existence—going to the plays in New York when we felt like it type of thing, kind of getting to know each other period, and also, like I say, pretty much when we felt like going—anticipating that when the children came, that this would, uh, and rightfully so, this would end abruptly, which it has.

Relatedly, parents were clear about other adjustments corresponding to their marriage and childrearing experience:

> Well, we got married in 1976 in April and we moved out here in November. And I was pregnant with [Child A]. He was not a planned baby. And I had a rough adjustment moving out to [the state], away from the family, being pregnant, and all the feelings that you have when you're pregnant for the first time. But everything went well—we had a good delivery and everything.

Emotional Tone.   Corresponding to these family identity descriptors of chronology, and commentary regarding adjustments, the family stories in this study contained evidence of the emotional tone, or un/happiness these parents experienced in their marriage relationship. An example of a particularly happy report:

> … [My wife] and I have been best friends.… I don't think we ever had a fight until probably about 8 years after we had been married. Things just jelled real well. We enjoyed doing things together. Similar interests. Getting up to [Child A]. We were just excited to beat the band.

Or:

> We were married for 2 years before I got—I was pregnant with [Child A] And, we have had a good marriage. We had it then; we do have a good one now.

While a few of the family stories detailed conflicts that ultimately resulted in divorce, this was not the norm. Rather, stories incorporated all the complexities the parents experienced as they dealt with many transitions simultaneously. An example of a father's story with more typical stress and negative emotions is as follows:

> … Because she was stuck at home sometimes during the day with two kids—I think, in that sense, it made me a lot more aware of some pressures she was under during the day. It made it tough for her at times, I know. And she'd get upset during the day more so than she did when she had one child. And sometimes I'd come home and she'd be on edge and she'd kinda jump on me for something and I'd jump back at her. It made for—when the kids were real small, I'd say, situations were on edge 'cause of the responsibilities and stuff.

A wife discusses the particular challenges in their family:

> Okay, well, [my husband] and I were married in '80 … oh, no we weren't, '79. Prior to that we both lived at home. We were 20 when we got married so I guess that's okay. [Child A] was born almost 2 years after we were married. Yes. Yeah, uh huh. We both were working full time and [my husband] was going—is still going to school at night. So, we were very rarely home alone, I mean, together—so were very rarely home alone, if ever, and it just could be very stressful on the marriage, I guess, as well as everything else.

Parental Preparation. Another related theme became clear as parents talked about their families and included the question of whether or not parents knew what to expect from parenting. Generally, the consensus was that parents described feeling prepared. However, narratives of both men and women also included fear and anxiety, as well as difficulty adjusting. Women more often specifically noted their lack of preparation for infant care, and both mothers and fathers noted the increased feelings of responsibility and loss of freedom/personal time. For example, a father reports:

> Yeah, let's have children, and yeah, it's going to change our life and that's about as far as you go. And then, as soon as the child comes, then all of a sudden all of these other ramifications come into play. Life insurance. Deeds and wills. Schooling, oh gosh—jeans. My gosh. Oh, gosh. Whatever they are. You know. All of these things start hitting you all at once. You have to start thinking about them, and they do change your life.

A mother's thoughts:

> Yeah, I'd always worked, and I really felt tied down—or I—I felt—I don't know if tied down is the word but I wasn't prepared for how much responsibility I had. And I had to adjust to that, and I did. But I—that was the part of it that I didn't really care for too much—was the being at home all the time and being with him, being with the baby. My husband was working afternoons at that time so I didn't see my friends real often.

Relationship Building.   In developing a family identity, stories also told of the importance of time for relationship building, as well as maintenance, in the marriage. For example:

> Well, my husband and I were married for 7 years before the birth of [Child A], and we had a really good time. We were married when we were 21, so we were fairly young in today's standards I guess. But we had decided not to have a family right away because we wanted to build our relationship first. So we did that....

Those couples who did not get time together before the children were born commented on their future plans to reconnect and enjoy activities together. For example:

> ... before the children were born we had just begun to know each other before we had the children, so we're still looking forward to times, a little bit later on in the future, where it's just going to be the two of us—and the time to go hiking and camping and all those great things again so....

or another example:

> Right now, the relationship—I don't know, you're real busy with the kids but, you know, we find time to be alone too. Like we just took off for, you know, Friday night.

In summary, couples discussed the ways they came together, and the initial experience of adjusting to one another in a marriage relationship. Additionally, the narratives of these families clearly demonstrate the pressures on marriage and family and struggles related to limited time, childrearing, and career.

Family beliefs

As a key element in family identity development, family stories were examined for evidence of their convictions or beliefs. Three themes emerged within this area: Structure, which included beliefs or decisions regarding the structure of the current family; Beliefs about Childrearing; and Family Philosophies.

Structure.   The first theme that became apparent within the category of Family Beliefs was a tendency toward description of family structure. Issues present in description of family structure included: the desire to have children early in marriage; the number of children desired; the number of years between children; and the desire to delay childrearing. These remarks summarily describe family formation, with details regarding how parents visualized their family structure and identity. Additionally, family stories describe the negotiation process between couples involved in defining a family, supporting Wamboldt and Reiss (1989) in their discussion regarding the need for couples to define a family heritage together. For example, one husband explains:

> Our philosophy with our children was that we wanted to have—[my wife] wanted four and I wanted two, so, we said we would compromise at three. She ultimately won out. Umm, we wanted to have our children when we were relatively young and, we also wanted to have our children fairly close together.

Childrearing Beliefs.   Once family structure has been established, a second task families confront in developing a family identity together is determining the manner in which they will parent their young. A second issue in understanding family beliefs includes parents' beliefs about child rearing.

Family beliefs regarding child care prescribe vocational decisions (see chap. 6 for a more in-depth discussion of this issue). These decisions were inseparable from childrearing beliefs in some families. For example, many parents were explicit in their belief that mothers need to be at home raising the children. A father remarks:

> [My wife's] relationship and mine hasn't changed at all. We pretty much agree on the upbringing of kids and [our] thoughts were pretty much the same as far as having traditionally—having the woman home and man working, and it worked out financially. We didn't have any problems. Our upbringing, as far as raising the kids and what they should be doing, is pretty much similar.

Although more men than women commented on family structure/roles, statements regarding childrearing beliefs were evenly distributed between mothers and fathers. Other childrearing belief topics were: (a) the importance of discipline; (b) the importance of teaching values/morals; (c) the importance of children learning responsibility; (d) discussion of specific parenting techniques; and (e) teaching children respect for others. For example:

> You know, I wanted, not that I wanted perfect children, I wanted mannerly children, polite children, not perfect. You know, they wrote on the walls, and I'm like, "Knock it off." I never screamed or yelled, but I did want respect. I am from the old school when it comes to, you respect me, you say, "Please," you say, "Thank you," and you don't go to someone's house and take their knickknacks. I'm not from the generation where you go, "They're just experiencing life"—that's bull. You know, you teach your children right and wrong and good and bad, and that was one of the key factors.

Family Philosophies.   Although similar to beliefs about childrearing, the family philosophies were more general and less behavioral in focus. The most prominent philosophy expressed by parents in this group included the *value of education* or the desire to instill in children a thirst for knowledge. An example follows:

> We had the same philosophy with him, we wanted to read to him, and we wanted to instill in him a sense of curiosity and learning, knowing what's about him as early as possible. So we, again, read to him as early as possible. And we tried to get [Child B] involved in the process, too.

A second philosophy discussed by parents, and another key element in family identity development was the importance placed on creating a *sense of family*, which included placing kids first. For example, one mother notes:

> So our family may change a little just because I would be going to work. But both for [my husband] and I it's been a real priority for us to have a strong family.... We love to be with our friends, but if it's been a bad week or [my husband] is gone 3 nights and I'm going to be gone 2, if friends ask us to do something for the weekend, we wouldn't, we'd say, "No, we want to stay home with the kids." So, I—They've been a big priority and I think that—that, I don't think will change.

One father comments:

> One of the things we have tried to do and it's been helpful is to have a close family circle. Umm, dinner times are extremely important, especially when I'm—I travel quite a bit with business and I'm gone sometimes 3, 4 nights a week, a couple weeks in a row. And so when I'm at home with the family, the family time is important.

A third area within the family philosophy theme includes the recognition of the *responsibility of the parent role* and the subsequent importance of role modeling for children. For example, one mother discusses her philosophy of parenting:

> I think that's probably one of the most difficult jobs in the world. It really is, because what we're raising today is tomorrow's decision makers. Whether we're going to blow ourselves up or all make friends.

Or:

> I don't know, the biggest, the biggest, the biggest change, I guess, was the realization that these kids were yours and that you—It's not like babysitting where you could get rid of them at night and take them away. But that you had to become a role model for them. I believe, we've both done a pretty good job of that. I wouldn't trade them for the world. It's the greatest thing that ever happened to us.

The last area emphasized by parents within the Family Philosophy theme included frequent references to the debate of whether or not to allow children to watch television. Although initially somewhat puzzling, a more contextual view resulted in this being understood within the category of worries and *vulnerabilities to outside influences*. Included in discussion of the importance of instilling values in their children, many parents also discussed their concerns as children moved outside the realm of family influence. For example:

> ... and I don't want to have to sit here for the next 10 years and worry about what's going to happen when they're 16. I want to be able to instill certain things, certain morals, certain fibers in them now, so when they're 16 I don't have to worry about them.

Or:

> But it's—it's hard as far as, you know, raising the kids now because they've got so much going on out there—you've got to be so careful. Like when I was a kid I never had to worry about going down the street to play or anything like that and nowadays you can't let the kids out of your sight because there is all this stuff going on.

And:

> And, so we went out and bought a television and a—that was a change in direction, I think, for us, than what we originally wanted to go on. Then about '84, '85, both of us got totally fed up with the thing. The kids became walking TV guides—they knew when all the shows were on and it really was not a good influence for them. And so, we just simply, instead of trying to control the one that we had, we just got rid of it. That's the best way to control it. So, I think that it is a decision that we have made for the better.

In summary, family beliefs as a mechanism for defining family identity incorporated three categories: structure, childrearing beliefs, and philosophies. Narratives of parents' negotiations and views of their family's structure, as well as their values and beliefs, offer clear indicators of family identity. Parents in this study were similar in their collective wishes for their children that they grow to become respectful individuals, with educational aspirations. Parents' stories were clear about the power of their parenting role, and the responsibility they shoulder as they create community within their family group.

Family expectations, hopes, and plans   Within the discussion of family identity, a third category was called Family Expectations, Hopes, and Plans. Just as families envision their family structure, as previously described, and outline guiding beliefs for their children, they also continue the process by imagining the future of their family life.

Goals and Hopes for Children.   The first theme within this category was the way in which parents communicated their hopes and expectations both for and from their children. Similar to family beliefs, these goals/hopes fell generally into three groups including: education, citizenship, and family. Not surprisingly, based on earlier descriptions of espoused beliefs in the value of *education*, parents expressed goals for their children that included a college education. Parents also included comments regarding their belief that children were expected to do their best within their chosen interests. An example:

> I'd like to see them graduate from college.... I believe that nowadays kids have to be in college. You know, it's sort of mandatory now. I just want them to grow up believing they're going to graduate from high school and go straight to college—Get that idea into their heads now. As far as what they want to be, whatever makes them happy. As long as they're happy doing what they're doing.

Closely related to parents' beliefs that children should behave and know right from wrong, they also expressed goals/hopes for their children to become *good citizens*, or caring people in the future. One father expressed this in a very general way:

> My role as a parent—I don't know. I never had any expectations. I just play it daily. You know, I—I never set a goal as a parent. Just have good kids. Honest, honest good people. That's all I can ask of them.

Or:

> I would just like my children to be, like I say, well-rounded individuals. I want them to respect life because they are human beings and I think if—I think if they can respect others and respect themselves and be responsible to themselves that will be—That will make me happy as a parent. It really will. If they can do those things.

Family Relationships.   Stories highlight the element of time in defining a family identity together. Several parents indicated their hopes or expectations that their children would marry and have children. Additionally, several parents expressed the desire for their children to remain close with siblings in the future, resolving existing sibling rivalry. And lastly, with regard to family relationships, parents expressed within their narratives hopes that children would be able to reflect back on their childhood with happy memories, valuing their family experience. For example:

Well, basically what my real intention is [is] that they grow up liking themselves as adults or as people and [that] they feel good about the family as a supporting unit. And I hope they take that with them. I think our strongest—probably our strongest value I think for them as people is to be thoughtful, caring individuals. And sometimes we feel like we've failed miserably. But I mean, you know, that's a continuing process.

Or:

I'm a single parent, so that's kind of different, too. I just talk to other adult friends, and a lot of them have good memories of their families, and I have others who have bad memories of their families. I just hope my kids have good memories, and I hope I can offer them help when they are adults.

In summary, Family Expectations, Hopes, and Plans as a mechanism for defining family identity incorporated two areas: Goals/Hopes for Children and Family Relationships, which outlined parents' images of the future for their children. Within the previous discussion, attention was given to the notion of possible selves, representing what individuals conceive they might become (Markus & Nurius, 1986, 1987). Stories support this notion, both with regard to family beliefs about structure of families and with regard to future images of their families, specifically, what they imagine their children's futures to include.

Critical events   Story information here related to happenings that were outside of the planned/expected series of life course events or disrupted family identity patterns, for example job losses or medical problems, including permanent disabilities. Also included in this coding category were descriptions of events interpreted by parents as particularly difficult. A full range of critical events was present in these stories. The most commonly reported kind of critical events were medical crises of family members. Next were deaths in the family (often a grandparent or great-grandparent), and lastly, accounts of miscarriages during the childbearing years. Other critical events noted in the family stories were divorces, pregnancy and birth complications, or a reference to a period of time with many stressful changes that the family experienced.

An interesting pattern was noted regarding critical events. Regardless of the kind of adversity described by the family, it was usually followed by a comment that suggested some type of resolution. An example of this can be seen in this father's narrative about his son:

... He's good in athletics, but he's not real naturally coordinated and that's due in part to his cerebral palsy. His right side is partially paralyzed so that he has—I think that has an impact on his ability to perform and to achieve things.... But he's very determined and very stubborn, and, if you will, very determined to accomplish things.

According to Borden (1992), "people revise accounts of life experience in the face of unexpected or adverse events so as to maintain a sense of coherence, continuity, and meaning" (p. 135). The resolution in these family stories supports this point, as parents often incorporated the way their family coped with a problem, or discussed pride at the way they handled a trying situation. For example, one mother discusses her divorce:

> But one thing [my ex-husband] and I do is we really try to get along for the sake of the children. And that meant putting our hatred aside which is really hard to do. You know he resents me for pushing him into this, and I resented him for leaving. But we got over that and it was a hard thing to do. But that's one thing we're proud of, I think the most. Not so much that we had children, but what we're doing now with them. We're—that's something that we're just so proud of we can't.... We're like "Look at us! We get along!"

Critical events that did not include some type of positively framed resolution were most often descriptions of miscarriages or stillborn children. This was the only category of critical events in which the number of unresolved accounts was larger than the resolved accounts. For example:

> ... [my wife] had two bad pregnancies prior to [Child A] where she miscarried, so I guess you'd call those complications. The first one was about 2 years before [Child A's birth] and the second one was about a year before so that was pretty hard.

The interviewer then asked how the woman had been able to deal with these difficult situations, to which the husband responded:

> Very badly ... it wasn't one of the easiest things to go through in a relationship.

A common way to follow up on the report of a miscarriage was to report when the next child was born. It is possible that this is the family's way of positively resolving the loss. Among the more unusual and severe critical events noted within this sample were one death of a husband/father and one report of a child dying from sudden infant death syndrome.

Inclusion of critical events in family narratives is important because it is another way in which the family defines itself, as having undergone a particular problem together. The coping and striving necessary for the family to survive become a key part of that family's identity.

Connections to Others

What if any is the influence or contribution of family of origin and kinship groups? These family stories contained details related to cultural family contexts, as well as information about relationships with friends and kinship groups. The families' connections to others were communicated in their stories through coded material in four areas: Extended Family Relationships, Kinship Groups, Intergenerational Themes, and Cultural Ties and Traditions. Results from the last two areas are reviewed in this chapter; the first two areas are focused on in chapter 5, "Tales of Social Support Throughout Family Development."

Intergenerational issues

As discussed in chapter 1, Carter and McGoldrick (Carter, 1978; Carter & McGoldrick, 1988) suggest that the nuclear family is a three-generational system that reacts to pressure from generational tensions as well as from developmental transitions. These family stories were studied for information describing intergenerational influences in family identity development, separate from current relationships with families. Five different themes became clear in their stories.

Structure.   Intergenerational influences on family identity were noted, at a basic level, on individual choices regarding family structure. Parents, in the narratives examined here, reflected on their own childhood experiences in making determinations of whether or not they wished to create a replication of their own family constellation, or produce something different. A common approach was to space the years between children in some pattern that related to their own childhood experience. For example:

> The interesting thing was … I guess that was kinda' a goal, too, to have two kids close in age. Why? So we can raise them at once. Secondly, so these two are able to become best pals, which was something that I really didn't have when I was a kid, because my sister and brother are 4 and ½ and 6 years younger than me, respectively.

Likewise, parents addressed the issue of family size, based on their own family experience, either replicating or making adjustments. One mother noted the following:

> I think the other thing that influenced me was that I was one of five children, and I was extremely aware of how busy my mother's life was for having…. And I didn't want to be the mother of that for a long time because I knew what work it was.

The creation of a new family identity based on intergenerational experiences also included the issue of gender:

> Um, when she came along, it was another interesting story. I never wanted any girls, because my mother and I never were very close and I didn't want to have to submit my daughter to the same relationship that I had with my mother. And the only reason my mother and I don't get along is because we are so much alike. You know, we get along okay now. So, when she was born, I was disappointed, and my husband was ecstatic. He was ecstatic the first one was a boy and he was ecstatic because the second one was a girl.

Direct Messages.   Stories were also examined for explicit information related to the influences of previous generations. Only two parents quoted specific messages they had received from their families of origin. One woman noted her husband's keeping a job that was destructive to him:

> I think what happened, if you want our life story in a nutshell: we got together, we fell in love, we screwed a lot, we got married, the kids came and it was instant adult and time to grow up, and both of us bolted. My being a mother, God must do something to mothers to make them a little more hardened I guess. But he bolted, I mean he stuck with a job that he hated, just to be a good provider, because I'm sure that's all he heard all his life, "You provide for your kids, no matter what.... "

In discussing her family's response to the excessive attention given to her first child, one mother notes a family saying:

> You know, his grandmother had a saying that there should be a rule against first babies. She died the year [our child] was born. That was kinda' sad, because I identified with her, she made me think of my own grandmother, the one I named her after.

Heredity.   Separate from such messages being handed down generation to generation, several parents noted family heredity as a way to explain a variety of phenomena in their family identity, ranging from medical issues to personality styles. For example, one mother notes her daughter's similarity to her own sister:

> It could be heredity. I have a sister that's 13 months older than me and she's exactly the same. My sister has no friends. When we—she's in [state] now and I'm in [another state]—when we go back to [third state where they're from]—if we go out with friends, it's my friends because she doesn't have any. Umm, she just doesn't seem to need them, [Child A is] kind of like that.

Another mother talks about her family history with pregnancies:

They took her too soon. She—because I carried 10 months—and that's history. My mother, my grandmother, my sister, my whole family carries 10 months.

Replication.   Beyond structure, a theme discussed by parents included whether or not to replicate/repeat versus compensate/repair family patterns. Several families noted their intent to replicate a generally positive family experience. For example:

> We had known each other from before, and I think our families are alike, there are a lot of similarities. In fact, both parents had mothers and fathers from the old country. And we are all pretty close knit. We all had some pretty strong values about families and loving each other. I think that was a real connection between [my wife] and I when we first met. I think once we got married, a lot of what we had grown up with influenced the way we raise our kids now. There might be a few things we do differently than my parents did, but probably not a lot. I suspect that a lot of the guidelines I know I had when I was a kid, I still follow now. So far, it seems to have worked pretty good.

Another area in which parents strive to replicate their families of origin related to gender roles. One father explains the perpetuation of the traditional female gender role in their family:

> [My wife] didn't work after she had the.… And she wanted to spend as much time as she could with her children. And I think it's paid off. The kids have commented that it's nice to have Mommy home when they come home from school. My mother never worked and her mother never worked either, so we always felt that it was nice to have Mommy home when you get home from school and we were fortunate that we were able to provide that for our kids.

Or a mother notes her son's modeling of his father's temper:

> You know, I think he's watched—of course being a boy he's going to look up to his dad—so his dad has a temper—when things don't go right his way, you know about it. You know if he's working on a car—you know things start flying and he gets mad and swears. Well [Child A] has picked that up too. So when he was working on his bike and it doesn't go … he's mad at everybody. You know, he'll have his tantrum out there.

One mother notes the way in which she replicated a marital pattern:

> I was raised with a father who was a salesman. So he [husband] was gone, back and forth, in and out, so it didn't seem strange to me. And I'm pretty independent, too, so that didn't bother me …

Compensation and Repair.   Parents noted similarities between themselves and their children, both positive and negative. However, when a negative similarity was noted, parents also discussed the ways they were trying to change this trait in their child. For example, a father describes:

> ... but with him being the oldest I expect more out of him and see a lot of me in him. When I was younger and I had a pet die—[I'd get] really emotional and so he's the same way. He's more emotional though than what I was. And his attitude is the same as mine. "Well I want to go out so I'm going to bug you until you let me out." And that's the way I was. He doesn't get into as much trouble as I did, that's one thing I'm glad about. But I think a lot of it is because I do see me in him, that's why I'm so tough on him though.

Or:

> [Child A] is more like me, she's a loud mouth and a talker, and if you don't slap her or shut her up she just takes over the whole family situation.

Just as families handed down gender roles, families try to undo gender roles as well, as was the case with this mother:

> One tantrum after another, and we never broke them up. And I felt I was raising him the way I had seen my father being treated, you know the male role model—get everything you want and you get it by having a tantrum, having a fit. And I felt that's how I was raising him. I see now that it's wrong. And it isn't working, but, um we're working on that one.

Parents recalled parental difficulties in their own experience as children, and discussed their efforts to compensate in this generation as parents, as suggested by Parke (1995).

> ... but I hope they have good memories and that they always feel like they were loved. That is the most important thing to me, that they know they were wanted and loved, and that they are very special to me, and they're not a burden, and I'm really glad that they were born. I kind of feel like that with my parents—they really didn't make me feel loved enough, and I really want my kids to feel that self-confidence stuff.

In summary, intergenerational issues, as an extension of connections to others in family identity formation, are a powerful influence, with solid representation in these family stories. Viewing families as a three-generational system, which reacts to beliefs and pressures (Carter & McGoldrick, 1988) that precede the current generations under study, is supported by the stories in this study. Families' inclusion of intergenerational material was reflexive and spontaneous, indicating the centrality of its presence during this transitional phase of family development.

Cultural ties and traditions

Family identity must be studied within the unique cultural, religious, and ethnic context (Saleeby, 1994). Story material described here as Cultural Ties and Traditions included references to cultural, religious, or ethnic origin, as well as descriptions of unique family traditions. Although it is known that parents in this study are primarily European Americans, relatively few noted this or any reference to culture or country of origin. However, a few who were first or second generation in this country did include some descriptive information related to their particular family background. For example:

> I grew up with a good set of parents that always took care of me and loved me. My mother is a lot more cheerful and lot more optimistic. My dad grew up in kinda—a strict, not strict, but somewhat strict, Italian home. His parents were born in Italy. So, his family was much more rigid than my mom's was. And our house tended to be, when I grew up at least, a lot more like my mother's, a lot more flexible than my dad's.

Another example in which a mother notes both her cultural heritage as well as related family traditions, is as follows:

> And we're real close with my parents, probably more than my husband's parents. So they spend a lot of time with those grandparents. I was born in Finland so my family is bilingual in that respect. And so that's maybe a little bit different in terms that—when [Child A] was a baby I spoke nothing but Finnish to him. So his first word was "Mother" in Finnish. That, of course, when I went back to work, that became harder when he was with English-speaking people but we've kept that part, we're sort of ethnic. In that, we were in Finland last summer with our whole family. And so some of the traditions like Christmas Eve, we have a big family tradition of going over to my mom and dad's. And we have a very traditional Finnish meal and stuff like that. So they've kind of kept—both kids have had that exposure that's maybe a little bit different than some—a family that's completely American.

References to American culture and religious traditions were not identified as such, although they were also included in the narratives. For example, several families noted Christian Christmas holiday traditions:

> Um, I don't know, we were real active after he was born, as far as not hiding from the rest of the world. We always had chopped down our own Christmas tree and we put him in a little front pack under our winter coats when he was 6 weeks old and went out and cut a tree down.

Additionally, several parents noted family-owned cottages "up north" and holiday visits. This tradition could be considered a geographically based norm that several families in this sample shared. Lastly, at least one family shared a description of a ritual or tradition established within their own family:

> We—nothing—maybe nothing extravagant or anything like that, but like in the winter time we have—Friday night usually is family night where we'll either—I'll make homemade pizza and they'll help me pile the junk on, or a taco or a nacho or something like that, and then we'll get a movie, either rent a movie or have a movie. Or lots of times it ends up being that we'll watch a sporting event because they're really all into sports....

In summary, parents described the effects of their own family of origin experience, heredity, and culture in forming and sustaining their own family identity. By reflectively evaluating their own experience being parented, they also include reparations in their family stories. Additionally, family beliefs and values assessed to have merit are preserved by instilling them in their children. In this way family identity is consolidated and transferred to the next generation of members.

CONCLUSION AND IMPLICATIONS

Several points regarding the literature on transition to parenthood have been included throughout the preceding report. Several other findings must also be included to form a comprehensive exploration. Family development theory, with its focus on the *life cycle* itself (Mattessich & Hill, 1987), is supported by these family stories, as these parents have incorporated and defined for themselves developmental themes related to the challenges of building a career/economic base, marriage, and family.

These stories highlight the need for flexible and interactive systems models of family development, such as the model proposed by Carter and McGoldrick (1988), as their stories are filled with examples of the overlapping complexities involved in raising children in contemporary society. These families are constantly interacting with culture, community, extended family, and kinship groups as they move through time.

Another dimension of this model (Carter & McGoldrick, 1988), the need for attention to the young adult phase of development, with its focus on family individuation issues and career preparation, is supported by stories in this study. Parents constantly referenced career development, as well as their connection to families of origin, by describing their structure and discussing ongoing support, ambivalence, and conflict. More research is needed to specifically address particular patterns resulting from this juncture in development.

Relatedly, repeated themes of replication/repair in the stories support the literature pointing to the psychological reawakening of childhood issues

(Antonucci & Mikus, 1988; Fischer, 1988). A number of parents reported such an experience, " … you kind of sort of relive part of your own childhood in terms of what they are going through.… ," factoring their reflections into decision-making while creating a new family. Intergenerational themes and issues were readily apparent as parents re-created family patterns or re-ordered their new families.

More specific literature findings related to attachment and maternal representations of self were not able to be fully explored with this data set, given the more general nature of parents' comments. However, support was noted for the development of coherent narratives in the face of adverse circumstances, as the mothers had done in studies predicting secure and insecure attachments through narrative exploration (Main, Kaplan, & Cassidy, 1985). Parents developed coherent narratives as evidenced by their comments incorporating resolution in response to accounts of critical events.

While narratives in this study do not provide us with numbers of contacts with community and family members, they provide us with important information regarding the function and meaning of these contacts for parents. One parent noted the meaning of having her children:

> Obviously we were—we didn't have any children for a while and so were free to go out—to go on vacation or whatever. And then when you have kids, it's a different story. You give—a lot of giving, but that's just how it is. But I think a—having kids is more important than worldly things. You know, the experience of having them I would never trade it for.… And, living with a child—right, the same—it's a lot of giving. Definitely. It can be difficult at times, but you look at the good. There's more good than anything.

Another mother comments on her perception of the transition to parenthood:

> And my relationship with my husband was a friendship, you know we were really good friends. And we had a lot of fun together. I remember telling [my husband] that I was pregnant. It was so much fun. He brought flowers home and we were both really excited. Getting ready and preparing was a lot of fun.

Practice Implications

The focus on individual and family identity in this chapter is important, as much research and subsequent practice filters back to interventions with individuals themselves. The value of viewing individual development embedded in family development is critical when considering that each parent's individual adaptation to parenthood will bear heavily on the evolving parent–infant relationship, and subsequent infants' development (Goldberg, 1988). The unique needs of families during the transition to parenthood have stimulated a number of research and intervention strategies designed to assess maladaptive potentials and promote growth in families. Results in this study confirm the need for continued efforts in this vein, as stories detail the myriad pressures existing for parents in a contemporary society where gender roles and prescriptions for behavior are in flux, and economic demands are high. Clinical practitioners must be aware of these contextual issues, stressors, and expectations.

Family myth, defined as a series of well-integrated beliefs that preserve homeostasis, was a concept created by Ferreira (1963). Byng-Hall (1973, 1979, 1988) expanded the use and discussion of the construct with his focus on family legends as central to family history. Today, structural or transgenerational theorists (e.g., Boszormenyi-Nagy & Spark, 1984) more readily reference variations of myth in their family therapy work. Laird (1989) notes that family therapists have tended toward utilization of the destructiveness of myth in rigid or dysfunctional families, but have shown less appreciation for the central role of myth in all families, as a vehicle for richness and creativity in family folklore. Certainly the expansion of the concept of myth to a wider view of family identity allows for the inclusion of the adaptive narratives described by these families in response to critical events or other circumstances. Clinical practitioners should seek to evaluate shifts in narrative content and construction throughout the course of the therapeutic relationship. Social work research journals today are sprinkled with various articles explaining the value of narrative in therapy as an intervention tool (Borden, 1992) and particularly as a useful tool in multicultural practice (Holland & Kirkpatrick, 1993; Saleeby, 1994).

The Connections to Others category in this investigation is characterized most clearly by its inseparability from both Individual and Family Identity. Identity is formed in conjunction with relationships. An examination of identity development within the context of extended family relationships, kinship groups, intergenerational themes, and cultural ties and traditions yields support for what is already known. Families cannot be understood in a vacuum, because their form is contingent upon what creates and maintains them.

Policy Implications

Policies that support the family structure are abundant in the social service domain. Programs that advocate for keeping families together—with supportive interventions in the home and residential programs for children and adolescents that seek to duplicate a family type environment—are further acknowledgment of the importance of the role of the family in society, and of the need to understand how families define themselves.

In addition, understanding the importance of culture and connections in conducting family therapy as well as family research brings us closer to the inclusion of intergenerational issues as a key variable in policy planning. This focus can be seen in the institution of new programs endorsed by foster care and adoption agencies that support a family's conception of its identity. Families are being considered in their larger context when making a decision regarding who is best able to take care of a child in need, with increasing numbers of children being placed in an intergenerational family home.

Likewise, a number of programs have been developed that include intergenerational care for both children and the elderly at the same site, recognizing the importance of these connections. There are also many new programs implemented in schools, utilizing foster grandparents, which illustrate the same value. As evidence accumulates concerning the importance and the success of these programs for all involved, administrators and policymakers will more readily include provisions for such programs in the future.

Research Implications

Moon, Dillon, and Sprenkle (1990) posit that qualitative research has the potential to reunite clinicians and researchers, as qualitative methods are close to the world of the clinical practitioner. Qualitative researchers ask questions similar to those of clinicians, for example, "What is going on here and why?"; and they utilize adaptations of clinical skills to locate the answers to those questions.

As evidenced by the complexity of these family stories, and the inability to isolate any particular theme without considering its relationship to the previous information and the larger context, qualitative methods may be more effective than quantitative ones in grappling with the full complexity of systems theory, as discussed in chapters 1 and 2. "Like systems theory, qualitative research emphasizes social context, multiple perspective, complexity, individual differences, circular causality, recursiveness, and holism" (Moon, Dillon, & Sprenkle, 1990, p. 354).

A methodological underpinning of qualitative family research is diversity. Qualitative researchers are part of a growing movement of people who understand that families appear in diverse forms in diverse settings, have diverse experiences, and appear differently at different times in history. Even though the families under study in this book lack diversity in its usual meaning, it is possible to note the complexity and diversity of family experience present in this group. The interesting results of this study with a demographically homogenous group point directly toward the need for qualitative research as a method with more a typically defined diverse group of families. This work could be replicated with families of divergent forms: divorced and remarried families; parents and their adoptive, foster, biological, or adult children; extended families in which many forms of families are embedded; families with committed homosexual relationships; elders and the generations born before them; and heterosexual unmarried couples. Comparative results would yield interesting direction for those interested in the continued advancement of family development and particularly family identity.

The results of this chapter are clear. Qualitative analyses of family stories provide a valuable method for understanding family identity. Family narratives offer rich information that clinicians, policymakers, and researchers can utilize in their separate and joint endeavors. Well beyond family myths or beliefs, the parents in this sample detailed structure, struggles, and strengths they discovered in themselves as they worked to raise their children. Finally, we must continue to acknowledge the meaning of events and the impact of experience as perceived by the participants (Borden, 1992). Given the vast array of changes in the world of families, as well as the necessary changes needed in the worlds of practice, policy, and research, understanding family identity issues through the "voice" of family members has the potential to yield promising new answers for those interested in family theory.

REFERENCES

Ammaniti, M. (1991). Maternal representations during pregnancy and early infant–mother interactions. *Infant Mental Health Journal, 12*(3), 246–255.

Ammaniti, M., Baumgartner, E., Candelori, C., Perucchini, P., Pola, M., Tambelli, R., & Zampino, F. (1992). Representations and narratives during pregnancy. *Infant Mental Health Journal, 13*(2), 167–182.

Antonucci, T. C., & Mikus, K. (1988). The power of parenthood: Personality and attitudinal changes during the transition to parenthood. In G. Michaels & W. Goldberg (Eds.), *The transition to parenthood: Current theory and research* (pp. 62–84). Cambridge, England: Cambridge University Press.

Belsky, J. (1984). The determinants of parenting: A process model. *Child Development, 55,* 83–96.

Belsky, J., & Isabella, R. (1985). Marital and parent–child relationships in family of origin and marital change following the birth of a baby: A retrospective analysis. *Child Development, 56,* 342–349.

Belsky, J., & Kelly, J. (1994). *The transition to parenthood: How a first child changes a marriage.* New York: Delacourt Press.

Belsky, J., & Pensky, E. (1988). Marital change across the transition to parenthood. *Marriage and Family Review, 12,* 133–156.

Belsky, J., & Rovine, M. (1984, May). Social network contact, family support, and the transition to parenthood. *Journal of Marriage and the Family,* 455–462.

Belsky, J., & Rovine, M. (1990). Patterns of marital change across the transition to parenthood: Pregnancy to 3 years postpartum. *Journal of Marriage and the Family, 52,* 5–19.

Belsky, J., Youngblade, L., & Pensky, E. (1989). Childrearing history, marital quality, and maternal affect: Intergenerational transmission in a low–risk sample. *Development and Psychopathology, 1,* 291–304.

Borden, W. (1992). Narrative perspectives in psychosocial intervention following adverse life events. *Social Work, 37*(2), 135–141.

Boszormenyi-Nagy, I., & Spark, G. M. (1984). *Invisible loyalties: Reciprocity in intergenerational family therapy.* New York: Brunner/Mazel.

Bowlby, J. (1969). *Attachment and loss: Vol. 1, Attachment.* New York: Basic Books.

Bowlby, J. (1988). Developmental psychiatry comes of age. *American Journal of Psychiatry, 145*(1), 1–10.

Bronfenbrenner, U. (1979). *The ecology of human development.* Cambridge, MA: Harvard University Press.

Byng-Hall, J. (1973). Family myths used as defense in conjoint family therapy. *British Journal of Medical Psychology, 46,* 239–250.

Byng-Hall, J. (1979). Re-editing family mythology during family therapy. *Journal of Family Therapy, 1,* 103–116.

Byng-Hall, J. (1988). Scripts and legends in families and family therapy. *Family Process, 27,* 167–179.

Carter, E. A. (1978). The transgenerational scripts and nuclear family stress: Theory and clinical implications. In R. R. Sager (Ed.), *Georgetown Family Symposium, 3,* Washington, DC: Georgetown University Press.

Carter, B., & McGoldrick, M. (1988). Overview: The changing family life cycle: A framework for family therapy. In B. Carter & M. McGoldrick (Eds.), *The changing family life cycle* (2nd ed., pp. 3–28). New York: Gardner.

Clulow, C. (1991). Partners become parents: A question of difference. *Infant Mental Health Journal, 12*(3), 256–266.

Colman, A., & Colman, L. (1971). *Pregnancy: The psychological experience.* New York: Bantam Books.

Cowan, C. P., & Cowan, P. A. (1992). *When partners become parents: The big life change for couples.* New York: Basic Books.

Cowan, C. P., Cowan, P. A., Heming, G., & Miller, N. B. (1991). Becoming a family: Marriage, parenting, and child development. In P. A. Cowan & M. Hetherington (Eds.), *Family Transitions.* Hillsdale, NJ: Lawrence Erlbaum Associates.

Cowan, P. (1991). Individual and family life transitions: A Proposal for a new definition. In P. A. Cowan & M. Hetherington (Eds.), *Family transitions* (pp. 3–30). Hillsdale, NJ: Lawrence Erlbaum Associates.

Cowan, P. A., & Cowan, C. P. (1988). Changes in marriage during the transition to parenthood: Must we blame the baby? In G. Y. Michaels & W. A. Goldberg (Eds.), *The transition to parenthood: Current theory and research* (pp. 114–154). Cambridge, England: Cambridge University Press.

Ferreira, A. J. (1963). Family myth and homeostasis. *General Psychiatry, 9,* 457–463.

Fischer, L. (1981). Transitions in the mother–daughter relationship. *Journal of Marriage and the Family, 43*(3), 613–622.

Fischer, L. (1983a). Married men and their mothers. *Journal of Comparative Family Studies, 14*(3), 393–402.

Fischer, L. (1983b). Mothers and mothers-in-law. *Journal of Marriage and the Family, 45*(1), 187–192.

Fischer, L. (1983c). Transition to grandmotherhood. *International Journal of Aging and Human Development, 16*(1), 67–78.

Fischer, L. (1988). The influence of kin on the transition to parenthood. *Marriage and Family Review, 12*(3–4), 201–219.

Fischer, L. (1991). Between mothers and daughters. *Marriage and Family Review, 18*(3–4), 237–248.

Fonagy, P. (1994). Mental representations from an intergenerational cognitive science perspective. *Infant Mental Health Journal, 15*(1), 57–68.

Fraiberg, S., Adelson, E., & Shapiro, V. (1975). Ghosts in the nursery: A psychoanalytic approach to the problems of impaired infant–mother relationships. *Journal of the American Academy of Child Psychiatry, 14,* 387–422.

Goldberg, W. A. (1988). Introduction: Perspectives on the transition to parenthood. In G. Y. Michaels & W. A. Goldberg (Eds.), *The transition to parenthood: Current theory and research* (pp. 19–20). Cambridge, England: Cambridge University Press.

Hadley, T., Jacob, T., Milliones, J., Caplan, J., & Spitz, D. (1974). The relationship between family developmental crisis and the appearance of symptoms in a family member. *Family Process, 13,* 207–214.

Haley, A. (1976). *Roots.* Garden City, NY: Doubleday.

Hanson, M. J., & Lynch, E. W. (1992). Family diversity: Implications for policy and practice. *Topics in Early Childhood Special Education, 12*(3), 283–306.

Heinicke, C. M., & Guthrie, D. (1992). Stability and change in husband–wife adaptation and the development of the positive parent–child relationship. *Infant Behavior and Development, 15,* 109–127.

Heinicke, C. M. (1984). Impact of prebirth parent personality and marital functioning on family development: A framework and suggestions for further study. *Developmental Psychology, 20,* 144–53.

Heinicke, C. M. (1984). The role of pre-birth parent characteristics in early family development. *Child Abuse & Neglect, 8,* 169–181.

Hill, R. (1970). *Family development in 3 generations.* Cambridge, MA: Schenckman.

Hoffman, L. (1990). Constructing realities: An art of lenses. *Family Process, 29,* 1–12.

Holland, R. P., & Kirkpatrick A. C. (1993). Using narrative techniques to enhance multicultural practice. *Journal of Social Work Education, 29*(3), 302–308.

Laird, J. (1989). Women and stories: Restorying women's self-constructions. In M. McGoldrick, C. Anderson, & F. Walsh (Eds.), *Women in families* (pp. 427–450>). New York: Norton & Co.

Lane, A., Wilcoxon, S., & Cecil, J. (1988). Family-of-origin experiences and the transition to parenthood: Considerations for marital and family therapists. *Family Therapy, 15,* 23–29.

Lebovici, S. (1983). *Le Nourrisson, la mere et le psychanalyste: Les Interactions précoces.* Paris: Éditions de Centurion.

LeMasters, E. E. (1978). Parenthood as crisis. *Marriage and Family Living, 19,* 352–355.

Main, M., Kaplan, N., & Cassidy, J. (1985). Security in infancy, childhood, and adulthood: A move to the level of representation. In I. Bretherton & E. Waters (Eds.), *Growing points of attachment theory and research. Monographs of the Society for Research in Child Development, 50,* Vol. 1–2, 66–104.

Markus, H., & Nurius, P. (1986). Possible selves. *American Psychologist, 41*(9), 954–69.

Markus, H., & Nurius, P. (1987). Possible selves: The interface between motivation and the self-concept. In K. M. Yardley & T. M. Honess (Eds.), *Self and identity: Psychosocial perspectives* (pp. 157–172). Chichester: Wiley.

Mattessich, P., & Hill, R. (1987) Life cycle and family development. In M. B. Sussman and S. K. Steinmetz (Eds.), *Handbook of marriage and family therapy* (pp. 437–469). New York: Plenum.

Moon, S. M., Dillon, D. R. & Sprenkle, D. H. (1990). Family therapy and qualitative research. *Journal of Marital and Family Therapy, 16*(4), 357–373.

Parke, R. D. (1995). Fathers and families. In M. Bornstein (Ed.). *Handbook of Parenting.* Hillsdale, NJ: Lawrence Erlbaum Associates.

Saleeby, D. (1994). Culture, theory, and narrative: The intersection of meanings in practice. *Social Work, 39*(4), 351–359.

Stern, D. N. (1989). Representation of relationship experience. In A. J. Sameroff & R. N. Emde (Eds.), *Relationship disturbance in early childhood: A developmental approach* (pp. 52–69). New York: Basic Books.

Stern, D. N. (1991). Maternal representations: A clinical and subjective phenomenological view. *Infant Mental Health Journal, 12*(3), 174–186.

Troll, L. E. (1973). The onus of "developmental tasks" and other reactions to Duvall's *Family Development* in its 4th edition. *International Journal of Aging and Human Development, 4*(1), 67–75.

Van IJzendoorn, M. H., Goldberg, S., Kroonenberg, P. M., & Frenkel, O. J. (1992). The relative effects of maternal and child problems on the quality of attachment: A meta-analysis of attachment in clinical samples. *Child Development, 59*, 147–156.

Wallace, P. M., & Gotlib, I. H. (1990). Marital adjustment during the transition to parenthood: Stability and predictors of change. *Journal of Marriage and the Family, 52*, 21–24.

Walsh, F. (1978). Concurrent grandparent death and the birth of a schizophrenic offspring: An intriguing finding. *Family Process, 17*, 457–463.

Wamboldt, F. S., & Reiss, D. (1989). Defining a family heritage and a new relationship identity: Two central tasks in the making of a marriage. *Family Process, 28*, 317–335.

4

Narratives of Temperament: Same or Different?

Carol R. Freedman-Doan
Eastern Michigan University

"Why are children from the same family so different from each other?" This often-voiced question was one of the many questions that led to this qualitative study and collection of family stories. Children's characteristics preoccupy many parents' thoughts. They struggle with how to "define" their children, and often do this by comparing them with one another, using dichotomous characteristics (e.g., "He was the fussy baby, she was the easy one"). This chapter discusses the factors that shape parents' perceptions of their children and considers the potential consequences of these perceptions.

After asking about the gender and birth weight of a newborn, the next most often asked question is, "Is he/she an easy baby?" But what is meant by this simple question? As any new parent will confirm, one of the most important aspects of this question is, "Does the baby sleep through the night?" Sometimes it also means, "Does the baby cry a lot?" "Is the baby colicky?" or "Does the baby eat regularly and take the bottle or breast feed easily?"

However, the answer to the easy/fussy baby question may have a deeper meaning than simply reporting on the regularity of habits of a newborn. The question may also portend what this infant will be like as a human being. Will this child be the kind of adult who fusses at the least little change in the environment, restless and unhappy? Or will this person be satisfied with his/her life, easily soothed by the presence of loved ones, and able to accept the ups and downs of life? In summary, are characteristics of babyhood stable over time, that is, predictive of characteristics through childhood and into adulthood?

TEMPERAMENT

Developmental researchers have long been interested in temperamental differences among individuals. What accounts for these differences? What is temperament and where does it come from? Is temperament stable over the life span of the individual, or does it change as life circumstances and environments change? Is there a difference between temperament and personality?

In the area of temperament development, researchers have attempted to answer these questions by examining both the genetic and environmental factors that contribute to personality outcomes (e.g., Buss & Plomin, 1975; Plomin & Daniels, 1987; Rowe & Plomin, 1977; Thomas & Chess, 1977). As with all debates involving the nature versus nurture controversy (intelligence, pathology, aggression, etc.), personality and temperament researchers generally align themselves along a continuum stretching from extreme environmentalism at the one end to extreme geneticism at the other. Indeed, many individuals believe temperament is a set of inborn, genetically inherited characteristics that later develop into personality characteristics after the environment has had an impact on the individual's temperament. Personality, then, is an interaction between genetics and the environment. It can be defined as a set of enduring characteristics in which individuals tend to behave in predictable ways across various settings.

Researchers who hold a genetic view of temperament tend to examine characteristics that may be more enduring over time. For example, Buss and Plomin (1975) and Rowe and Plomin (1977) outline four temperamental characteristics that are easily identifiable in infancy as well as adulthood: emotionality, sociability, impulsivity, and activity level. Evidence for the heritability of these characteristics comes from the facts that these characteristics tend to "run" in the family (highly sociable parents tend to have highly sociable children); that there is stability of these characteristics during developmental periods in a child's life; that these characteristics are present in adulthood; that these characteristics are adaptive in an evolutionary sense (i.e., the variable rates of activity level seen in humans may have been adaptive in occupation specialization—one highly active human could go out and hunt and gather, whereas the other, less active one, kept the hearth fires burning); and, finally, that these characteristics are also present in animals to some degree.

Although Buss and Plomin (1975) generally hold a genetic view of temperament, they also recognize the important contribution of environment. Plomin and Daniels (1987) attempt to answer the important question of differences within the family by examining the nonshared environments that siblings experience. These nonshared environments, they contend, create more differences between siblings than would be expected if temperament were solely influenced by genetics.

In contrast, Thomas and Chess (1977) hold a view of temperament that emphasizes the bidirectional relation between organisms and their contexts that either do or do not match (fit) temperamental attributes and the psychosocial environment. These researchers who use a "goodness of fit" model examine how the infant's temperament "fits" with the beliefs, expectations, and demands of the environment. It is the interaction between what the individual brings to the environment (heredity), the impact of the environment on the individual, and the impact of the individual on the environment that shapes the individual's personality. Thomas and Chess (1977) examine nine dimensions of temperament that seem to describe infant behavior: activity level, rhythmicity, approach–withdrawal to environmental stimuli, adaptability to environmental changes, intensity of reaction, threshold of responsiveness to stimuli, quality of mood, distractibility, and attention span/persistence at a task. Although these characteristics are inherited to a great degree, the impact of these characteristics on the infant's social environment needs to be examined in order to understand both the stability and malleability of these characteristics in the development of personality characteristics.

PARENTAL EXPECTATIONS AND PERCEPTIONS

The expectations and perceptions of parents regarding infant temperament also need to be considered when attempting to answer the question how children from the same family can be so different. For instance, imagine an infant who awakens for feeding a couple times a night every three or four hours. One parent, who expected the infant to be up most of the night crying to be fed, may interpret the infant's behavior as the sign of an "easy" temperament. Another parent, however, who expected the infant to sleep through the night, just as her/his sibling had done, may describe this infant as "fussy."

Some researchers assert that parental expectations and perceptions may be more relevant in understanding infant temperament than data from trained observers (Zeanah, Zeanah, & Stewart, 1990). Ratings of infant temperament are usually done by mothers when their infants are several weeks old. Some researchers have found that mothers' expectations of their babies' temperament, measured before the baby is born, correlate with their ratings of the babies at 6 months (Zeanah, Keener, Stewart, & Anders, 1985). These findings suggest that infant temperament may reflect the mother's personal characteristics as much as it does the infant's, or that the mother perceives the infant exactly as she thought she would.

The expectations and perceptions parents have of their infant's temperament may be more relevant than the child's "true" temperament (as observed by researchers) in understanding how temperament impacts on the development of personality. Parents often act as social scientists in evaluating their child's temperament. They make predictions, create hypotheses, gather data, assess the validity of their hypotheses, compare their data with other known data sets (sibling behavior), and draw conclusions. In the end, parents' beliefs about what their child ought to be like or what they desire him or her to be like may influence the way they describe their child, the kinds of interactions they have with their child, and the opportunities they make available to their child.

There is evidence that parents have expectations of what their child is like based on gender alone. In an earlier study by Rubin, Provenzano, and Luria (1974), the researchers interviewed mothers and fathers of newborn infants on the day of the child's birth. Fathers were interviewed almost immediately after the delivery and generally had only viewed the infant through the hospital nursery window. (This was, after all, 1974 when the role of fathers in many deliveries was limited.) Mothers were generally interviewed up to 24 hours after the delivery and had been able to hold and feed their infants. The parents were asked to rate the baby on an 18-item bipolar scale of characteristics, including such adjectives as "noisy" versus "quiet," "active" versus "inactive," and "easygoing" versus "fussy." Both parents described their daughters as softer, more awkward, weaker, and more delicate. Boys were rated as larger, better coordinated, more alert, and stronger. These gender-stereotyped beliefs may carry over into the way parents treat their children, which may promote and sustain temperamental differences between boys and girls.

Birth order may also affect parents' expectations and beliefs. The time after the first child is born and before the second child is a unique period when the attentions, affections, and expectations of the parents are focused exclusively on the firstborn. As one mother told us:

> You know, the first one is that exclusive first-child relationship, you know, you have only him and all your attention is focused on him. They do get that exclu-

sive one-on-one attention and get both the parents' attention and without any competition for a while.

Clearly, this is a unique relationship that cannot be duplicated in the family again. The messages firstborn children receive during this time may have a lasting impact on their drives and motivations, and on their personalities. Additionally, after the birth of the second child, parents begin to make comparisons between their children ("She's so much easier" or "He's a lot more active"). They seem to look for and emphasize these differences as a means of characterizing each child's personality (Plomin, 1989). Researchers have found that when the firstborn child is viewed as easy in his or her temperament, the next child is likely to be perceived as more difficult and vice versa (Schachter & Stone, 1985). The temperamental differences parents perceive between their children evoke responses from parents that are consistent with their perceptions, as well as with each child's actual temperament.

Why are children from the same family so different? The answer may simply be to ask their parents. Although many scales have been created to examine infant temperament, very few researchers have used parents' qualitative descriptions of their infants to find out what characteristics are most salient to parents in describing their children. Parents may identify certain characteristics that are important to them based on a host of factors. For instance, parents' previous experiences with children, their own upbringing, or the gender of the child and/or parent may create expectations about how babies ought to behave. These expectations, in turn, cause parents to provide different experiences for their children that either increase or decrease the likelihood that a characteristic will be displayed (e.g., buying toys or providing opportunities to participate in activities that were not available to the parents when they were children). Parents' own psychological and emotional experiences, as described in the previous chapter, may also influence them to see their children in a particular way. As one parent said:

> Your expectations of them are more or less your expectations of yourself. You can't see the way they're different from yourself.

The way the infant responds to the environment also provokes differential treatment from his or her parents. As infants get older, their behavior becomes more predictable. Parents may learn to respond and structure the environment in ways that eventually form the personality and promote the development of certain characteristics. Consequently, what parents actually say about their babies early on in their development may have long-range consequences for the kinds of opportunities they provide for their children and the personality outcomes of each child.

Researchers have found that parents often start off as staunch environmentalists, believing that the environment influences how children turn out in the end (Sameroff & Feil, 1985). Later, after the birth of the first child, and even more so after the birth of the second child, parents become more committed to a genetic perspective. That is, they tend to believe children's behaviors and their personality may be something "inborn" and that parents have little influence over these characteristics. By examining parents' expectations about their children prior to their birth, we can begin to see how and when these beliefs change over time.

This chapter presents data about parents' beliefs and expectations concerning their children's temperaments and characteristics from prior to the birth of the first child through living with the first two children, that is, across the storyboard. First, parents' expectations about what they would be like as parents and the factors that may have influenced their view of their child even before s/he was born are explored. In order to understand some of the differences that parents bring to their parenting role, mothers' and fathers' expectations are compared. Next, both fathers' and mothers' perceptions of the newborn are presented and compared, including their perceptions of the child depending on the child's gender. The stories for the second born child, again comparing mothers' and fathers' responses and gender differences, along with contrasting responses for the firstborn, are then examined. Finally, data are presented that look at how parents' perceptions of their children early in life relate to their current perceptions of their children.

THE STORIES

To examine all these issues, the stories were coded using three different frames; prior to the birth of the first child, the birth and living with the first child, and the birth and living with both children. In the first part of their stories, parents talked about their expectations of themselves as parents and the kinds of values/beliefs they wanted to pass on to their children. Through these expectations and beliefs, we begin to get a notion of the factors that shape parents' perceptions of what their children will be like.

Adults enter parenthood with many life experiences—relationships with parents and siblings, exposure to children, experiences with other couples with young children, etc. All these experiences can influence parents' expectations of what they want their children to be like. The first class, Prior to the Birth of

Child A, contains material in which parents expressed expectations of what their children would be like or what they thought parenthood would be like, prior to the birth of their children. These comments were then categorized by themes. Only themes that were mentioned by at least 10% or more of the sample are discussed here. Two different themes emerged for mothers and fathers. Consistent with the information presented in chapter 3, mothers mentioned their own family of origin experience as an important factor in determining what they wanted their children to be like and the environment they wanted to provide for their children. Several mothers also mentioned certain expectations they had for themselves in terms of their parenting skills prior to the birth of their children. Although some mothers mentioned that their previous experiences with children made them more or less prepared to handle the rigors of motherhood, this was more clearly a theme for fathers. Also, fathers were more clearly apprehensive about the kinds of changes fatherhood would bring about for them.

In order to understand and identify the characteristics parents used to describe their children, a content coding scheme was developed. We looked at the classes Birth of Child A, Living with Child A, Birth of Child B, and Living with Children A and B (Characteristics of Child B); and highlighted parents' comments about the characteristics of the children when they were infants or preschoolers. These comments were then examined for common themes. Again, only themes that represented at least 10% of the sample were included in these analyses. Table 4.1 presents the themes found in the stories for both mothers and fathers. In the section Birth of Child A/Living with Child A, 43 out of the 56 mothers (78%) described their firstborn as an infant and young child using the characteristics outlined previously, and 32 of the fathers (76%) mentioned these characteristics.

As can be seen from this table, what emerged from these statements were dichotomous pairs of concepts. Early on, parents appeared to be attempting to classify their child into a type of individual: easy going/fussy, early developer/late developer, sociable/withdrawn, etc. Some parents had a gender preference for their child, although as will be shown later, the preferences were stronger for the second child. In terms of easy baby/fussy baby, parents generally talked about the amount of sleeping and crying the infant did. A surprising number of children in this study had medical problems, including cerebral palsy, jaundice, and metabolic disorders. The parents of these children described these problems and their impact on the children's lives. Parents often spoke at length about their children's physical development. Of course, the size of the child is of major interest for most parents. To many, this information indi-

TABLE 4.1

**Issues Related to Child Characteristics as Identified
by Mothers and Fathers by Time Period**

Time Period	*Major Themes Across Parent Stories*

Prior to birth of Child A	Mothers influenced by:
	    Family of origin
	    Parenting skills
	
	Fathers influenced by:
	    Experiences with children
	    Apprehension about changes

Birth of Child A/Living with Child A
Characteristics of Child A
  and
Birth of Child B/Living with A & B
Characteristics of Child B
	Desiring a girl
	Desiring a boy
	
	Easy baby
	Fussy baby
	
	Healthy baby
	Sick baby
	
	Early cognitive development
	Late cognitive development
	
	Early physical development
	Late physical development
	
	Positive reaction to baby
	Negative reaction to baby
	
	Mothers only:
	    Sociable child
	    Child is loner
	
	Fathers only:
	    Independent child
	    Dependent child
	    Child creates change in father's life

Living with A & B *Children A & B compared*	Comparisons of easy/fussy babies then and now

cates the health of the baby and how well the mother has cared for her baby pre-natally, but it is also believed to indicate whether or not the child will be big or small later on in life. Similarly, parents often told long narratives about the cognitive development of their child, especially when that development was early or more advanced than anticipated.

Parents shared both positive and negative reactions to their babies. Parenthood brings about change. Sometimes that change, if anticipated appropriately, produces exuberant responses; other times, the change is faced with anxiety and depression. The long-range consequences of such reactions are unknown. In these qualitative stories, we begin to see how parents understand their reactions and how they begin to cope when their reactions are more negative.

It is interesting to note that mothers and fathers generally identified similar characteristics. However, mothers were more concerned about the social aspects of their child's life, whereas fathers were more concerned about the child's ability to be independent and self-reliant.

In the third coding frame, we take a look at parents' comments in the section Living with Children A & B (Child A & B compared). The stories of parents who rated their children as easy or fussy babies early on were examined in these sections to see if parents perceived their children's temperament as stable over time. Do parents who perceive their infants as fussy early on continue to see their children as difficult and irritable later on? Or do these views change as the children mature? Parents' comments about their children's personalities now were compared with comments made about them when they were infants, to see if parents reported stability or change in their children's temperaments.

Prior to Birth of Child A

Family of origin—mothers

Mothers often mentioned their family of origin in their stories about the period just prior to the birth of their first child. Some women recalled what they felt was missing in their own childhoods, and how this motivated some of their behavior with their children:

> I grew up in a European family, the oldest child of four. There were 18 years between the first child and myself—between myself and my little sister. And I guess I was most disappointed in the experiences that were offered to me. Um, there wasn't very much as far as sports, physical activity. I almost had to beg to do the piano, you know, which has become my career. And because of that, I've always wanted to kind of overdo for my own children.

Another mother spoke about the feelings she had as a child that have lingered into adulthood, making her want to provide a different kind of experience for her own children:

> I kind of feel like that with my parents—they really don't make me feel loved enough, and I really want my kids to feel that self-confidence stuff.

These kinds of statements speak to the importance of parents' early family of origin experiences in shaping the lives of children. Over one fourth of the mothers (12 out of 43 mothers) mentioned that they wanted to raise their children differently than they themselves were raised. One mother summed it up by saying:

> You always want to do more for them than what you actually felt you received.

We can only speculate about the kinds of environments these mothers designed for their children as a result of their own experiences. Might these mothers be more anxious about their own responses to their children's distress and to the kinds of activities they do with their children? Might they also be more sensitive to their children's feelings, and they might perceive their children's temperaments and personalities differently because of their own desire to influence their children in a particular way? Although we do not know for certain the answer to these questions, we can begin to see how families of origin shape mothers' beliefs about how they want to raise their children and the opportunities they wish to provide. The mother from the European family who wanted to provide more experiences for her child, quoted previously, also said:

> ... the experience of having that first child was absolutely overwhelming. I wanted to do so well by that child that I just—I just lived, breathed around having that child.

Expectations of parenting skills—mothers

A common expectation mentioned by mothers was that good parenting skills would assure good results. But one mother observed:

> Being a parent ... is a lot different than what you think it's going to be—at least I found it that way. I always pictured it, if you were there, and you could take care of them, and you gave them the attention they needed, they would be these wonderful responsive children—well, baloney!

Another mother said:

> But on childrearing itself, my opinion did change. I guess I always thought—in a sense you think, "Well, if I tell my child to do something or not to do it, of course

they will do it or not do it." Ha-ha-ha. And if you raise your kids right, they will always be polite and cooperative—well, it doesn't work that way.

Prior to the birth of their first child these mothers believed that parents could influence their children's behaviors to a great extent. Their statements indicate that their experiences with their own children did not substantiate this perception. Again, we can begin to speculate about the kinds of environments these mothers created for their children based on these expectations. When the expectations did not come to fruition, mothers had to reevaluate their ability to influence the development of their children's personalities. A mother whose child is unresponsive to his or her warm, nurturing environment may have difficulty bonding with the child. She may perceive him or her as difficult and temperamental, rather than responding within the range of normal infant responses. Additionally, the mother may have been a firm environmentalist prior to the birth of her first child and may since have taken a more genetic view. She may see her child's irritable temperament as a fait accompli. She cannot influence this genetic temperament, and thus gives up trying. This experience, in turn, may shape the way she perceives the child's personality later on in life, and the way she perceives the child's sibling.

Experience with children—fathers

Fathers also had preconceived notions about what their children would be like prior to their births, although fathers were more vague in their ideas. Most fathers reported that having a child "… was all new stuff to me" and that they had "more cold feet about having children than [their wives] did" and were "a bit leery about it … a bit scared." In part, this was due to lack of experiences around children. Fathers who were the oldest of many children in their own family or who had a much younger sibling, tended to be less anxious about the arrival of their first child:

> It was kinda different when my younger brother came along, 'cause it was almost like having a new baby in the house. That was a little indication of what to expect when I got to be a parent. It was. I was 12 years old when he was born, so I kinda understand what it was like to have little kids around the house.

The environment this father provided for his children and the expectations he had for what his children would be like were probably very different than the ones for this father:

> She [my wife] was very used to kids; I was not. I have not been around—I am the youngest. I've got a twin brother. I didn't raise him too much. But I had not been around kids much at all. So, it was all new stuff for me.

Apprehensive about change—fathers

Over 30% of the fathers expressed apprehension about the birth of their children. They were especially concerned about how children would change their lives, as well as their relationship with their wives. One father said:

> So when she did get pregnant with [Child A], I was—she was kind of thrilled but through the whole thing, a lot of times it was, "Do I really want to do this? How's life going to change?" and things like that.

Another father said:

> It was a pretty drastic experience—going from single and having no responsibilities to married and all of a sudden having a kid.

How do fathers cope with this change, and how does it color their perceptions of their children's temperaments and personalities? This theme of fearing change and adapting to changes at the birth of their children recurs frequently throughout the stories the fathers tell about becoming a family. More is said about this theme later in the chapter. However, in their stories about their families prior to the birth of their first child, fathers seem to have created an expectation that their children would change them in some way. Whether they see this change as good or bad may change their perceptions of their children, as well as alter their view of their role as fathers.

In summary, for mothers in our sample, family of origin and expectations about their parenting skills were two factors that may have shaped their perceptions of their children's personalities even prior to their births. For fathers, their previous experience (or lack thereof) with children, as well as their apprehensiveness about change appear to be important expectations they have about fatherhood. We can only hypothesize whether these expectations about parenthood shape their perceptions of their children's personalities. However, in the next sections of this chapter we begin to see how perceptions grow and develop in response to the child's temperament and the environment.

Characteristics of the Firstborn Child

Mothers

Gender Preference.   Only 7% of the mothers expressed a preference about the gender of their first child, and those who did wanted girls. Two of these mothers had daughters for their firstborns. The one mother who wanted a girl but ended up with a boy, said:

But then after we had him, I was—we were happy, you know. His dad was especially happy, I think, that he had a boy. Now, we wanted a girl to tell you the truth, but then, after I had a boy, I never wanted a girl again. It was real weird because after I had thought I wanted a girl all this time, and then I had a boy, it was like, well, I like having a boy, you know?

It appears that despite having a gender preference, this mother changed her expectations after the birth of her son. This mother changed her expectations to meet the reality of the situation. Additionally, her experience with the gender of this first child may set the expectations (or lack of expectations) she has for the next child.

Easy Baby/Fussy Baby.   The majority (61%) of the mothers mentioned that the baby was fussy or easy. These comments were often about the dispositional nature of the child:

She developed just as a normal happy little girl

He was a very crabby baby

She was a very interesting character ... she screamed from the very beginning

When she wanted something, she wanted it now

or the level of activity of the baby:

He was an overactive baby—he was always awake

She was a calm baby

or the eating habits of the baby:

She was colicky

He wouldn't take the breast

Every four hours she would wake up and want to eat. She was really restless—she was always hungry

Interestingly, the percentage of mothers who mentioned that the baby was easy was fairly equal to the number who mentioned that the baby was fussy. And there were no gender distinctions for either easy or fussy babies. Despite popular "wisdom" that boys are fussy babies and girls are easy babies, the parents in our study did not report this was true of their firstborn children. In fact, mothers of boys were twice more likely to mention having a positive reaction to their babies than mothers of girls; but this may be related less to temperament issues than to a societal valuing of male children.

Big Baby/Small Baby and Healthy Baby/Sick Baby.   Mothers were very interested in telling us about the size and health of their babies. Mothers in particular liked to mention if their child was a big baby: "He was a big baby too—9 pounds. And I only gained 17—all beef!" This may be because the size of the newborn is often a reflection of how well the mothers took care of themselves prenatally. As noted earlier, medical problems were quite common in our sample: "We had a quick education in medicine. She spent about 7 weeks in intensive care"; or, "[The baby] decided he would scare us and came out blue and just kind of lay there. They had to call the intensive care." Some of these medical problems prevented parents from taking their newborn home for several days or even weeks. However, no mother reported negative reactions to their babies because of these problems nor because of the separation.

Early/Late Cognitive and Physical Development.   Mothers, in particular, told stories about their child's cognitive and physical development:

> And he was very bright and learned very quickly. And by the time he was 2, I know this sounds incredible, but by the time he was 2, he had taught himself to read.

Another mother said:

> [Child A] has had school problems since probably first grade. In first grade he had a teacher that was—didn't appreciate his antics at all and he was not real—I wish we would have kept him back a year.

Still another mother said:

> I think he was really advanced for his age, hitting baseballs with a bat when he was 2.

Mothers talked about providing early enrichment experiences, such as reading to their 4-month-old, taking their 6-month-old to swimming lessons, or watching *Sesame Street* and other educational programs with their 1-year-olds. Mothers often indicated that their child's early development was due in part to these early learning experiences.

One of the school districts involved in this study had a program for gifted and talented children, beginning in the first grade. Many of the children in our study were involved in this program. Mothers' perceptions and memories of their child's early abilities may be colored by the fact that their child is now in a program for the gifted and talented. However, the rich content and details of the stories these mothers told of their children's early cognitive and physical development suggest that these stories are at least partially accurate, and they offer a wonderful opportunity to view the early development of intellectually and physically gifted children. One mother told us:

> [My son] started talking at 9 months in sentences. And so it wasn't like I was all by myself 'cause I had a conversation … he absorbed more and more things. I started reading books to him when he was about 4 months old—as soon as you could prop him up on the sofa. … And he really liked to read and I read a lot to him.

Another mother said:

> By the time he was 6 months old, I had him in swimming lessons and [my son] really enjoys swimming lessons. He took to the water like a fish. I used to have people come up to me in grocery stores when he was 18 months old and say, "Aren't you the mother that has that little boy at the Y?" I mean, he would go off diving boards at 18 months old—he swam under the water at 6 months. He never cried when, you know, I tried to put him under. And I really enjoyed that time with him.

It is clear that the giftedness of the child was a joy to these mothers as much as a challenge to provide enriching experiences.

Positive/Negative Reaction to Baby.   Only a small percentage of mothers had a negative reaction to their babies (12%). By and large, these negative reactions were due to the fact that the babies were colicky or extremely fussy. The mothers who reported negative reactions toward their babies generally blamed themselves for their baby's fussiness or felt helpless in the face of the situation:

> 'Cause the next week he had his first or second, I don't know, medical checkup, and I was ordered to start giving him formula and he wound up on the bottle after that. And I think I felt kind of rejected after that. And looking back, I think that was another strike against us. I felt rejected cause it didn't work for him. And I was very disappointed.

One mother, who said her baby cried for the first 9 months, finally figured out that the caffeine in the iced tea she was drinking was affecting her breast milk and, thus, making her son cranky. She said:

> I think after he finally got out of it [nursing], I realized why he was so miserable, but it was like, "How could you be so stupid?"

Another mother blamed her baby's temper on her red hair but also felt the baby was rejecting her.

Yeah, she has a temper because of her red hair. But even when she was about 6 weeks old she had a very nasty little temper. She would get upset with different people holding her and would either want me or at times wouldn't want me. And we stopped—I stopped nursing her because she pushed me away. Didn't really want to nurse after about 8 months.

This mother clearly felt helpless in the face of her child's temperament. The mother reported, as did several of the other mothers who had negative reactions to their babies, that things got easier as her daughter grew out of the baby stage. However, as reported later in this chapter, remnants of this early temperament continue to remain with the child later in life.

Sociable/Loner. As mentioned previously, the sociableness of the child was an important characteristic for the mothers. Mothers often mentioned the sensitivity of their child in conjunction with his/her sociability:

His kindergarten teacher told me at the conference, his first conference, that she had never seen a child that age who was so caring of other children. And you know, she told me this cute story of how he'd go and—there's this little [child] who was afraid, really afraid, to be there—every day he'd talk to her and kind of draw her out. So, he was sort of special in that way.

Sometimes mothers merely commented on the child's social skills:

[My child] did have two friends that were 1 year and 2 years older than him in the old neighborhood—they were kind of really good buddies when they chose to be.... [Child] would rather go in the house and read if he didn't like what was going on, if they were combatant or verbally abusive—he just cocooned—I figured that was what he needed at that point.

Other mothers were more openly concerned about social development:

I would be hard pressed for [Child A] to come up with the name of two girls that she really is friends with.... I think part of it is that when she was growing up—when she was little and had the urinary infections, she went all through preschool having almost no control of her bladder. So, she could easily go to preschool and wet her pants and I think she stayed away from kids for that.

Fathers

Gender Preference. Of the 32 fathers who mentioned characteristics of their firstborn, about 12% mentioned desiring a particular gender of child, with the majority, perhaps surprisingly, desiring girls. The following father clearly articulated his preference for a girl, although he ultimately had two boys:

I had always—I wanted a girl first because I thought as a parent I would have been easier on a girl than a son. I would have probably been more demanding on a son and set up expectations for him to meet certain things that, you know, or live my life through him and things like that. And so, I didn't want to have that happen with the first one. I thought I could probably relate to a girl better as far as not trying to set up expectations, or demand too much of her in different performance areas than if I had a son because just the stereotype father puts all these demands on the firstborn son.

Easy Baby/Fussy Baby.   Over 44% of the fathers mentioned the easy/fussy baby characteristics, with more fathers mentioning fussy babies than easy babies. Fathers were particularly concerned with crying infants. One father said: "He was a very difficult baby. I think he didn't stop crying for the first two years." Another father said, "[Child A] was a very easy baby. She didn't cry. She was a no-hassle kid." Still another father commented on his tactics for getting the child to sleep:

> He was up most of the time. It was hard getting him to sleep. I used to have to drive him around at night in order to get him to fall asleep and then carry him into the house. And most of the time he'd wake right back up once I shut off the car.

It seems that the regularity of the infants, their sleeping, eating, and crying habits, have an impact on fathers similar to that on mothers.

It is interesting to compare mothers' and fathers' perceptions about their children's behaviors when they were very young. Do mothers and fathers experience "fussiness" the same way? Some researchers suggest that mothers and fathers agree very little about the temperament and personality of their children (Huitt & Ashton, 1982); others find substantial similarity in temperament ratings made by mothers and fathers (Lyon & Plomin, 1981). In comparing mothers' and fathers' responses on the easy/fussy construct, mothers and fathers agreed on only one "easy" baby. That is, of the 14 babies identified as easy by their mothers, only one of the fathers also identified his child as being easy; the other 4 easy babies identified by fathers were not so identified by mothers. In contrast, for the 12 babies identified as "fussy" by mothers, fathers also identified 6 of them as fussy; in addition, fathers identified another 3 children as fussy. In examining the stories from the mothers and fathers of those children whom both parents called "fussy," it is clear that these children represent the extreme end of the fussiness spectrum. These were children who had medical problems, colic, or extreme irritability that caused seemingly months of crying and irritability. In these cases, both mothers and fathers can agree on the temperament of their child.

Big Baby/Small Baby and Healthy Baby/Sick Baby.   Fathers mentioned the health and size of their baby somewhat less often than did mothers. However, when fathers did report on the health of their child, they generally reported on the same health-related concerns as did mothers. This suggests that when it comes to the health of the child, parents generally perceive the situation similarly.

Early/Late Cognitive and Physical Development.   Fathers were as likely as mothers to tell us about their child's cognitive and physical development. However, their comments tended to be briefer and less elaborate, for example, "She's real bright," "He talked early, I think." And fathers elaborated less than mothers on the kinds of opportunities they provided because of their child's early or late development:

> And then we find out that she's—her intelligence is off the scale when she was little. We had to deal with that.... What do we want her to get involved in and just, you know, find out what she wants to do and things like that.

Positive/Negative Reaction to Baby.   The number of fathers who expressed positive reactions to their babies was equal to the number who were concerned about the kind of changes the infants were having in their lives. Many fathers felt the changes were generally positive. In fact, some fathers were exuberant in their expression of pleasure at the birth of their child. One father told us:

> I'd be his best buddy and we'd do things together and that kind of stuff. Well, you know, maybe I was rushing the idea, but even when he was born, the first thing I did was brought him in and walked him around the house we had, and showed him his room and where ours was, and "Here we can do this and look at that."

Clearly, fatherhood changes one's daily habits and routines, expectations and priorities, but for many fathers the cost of this change is well worth it.

Independent/Dependent Child.   A few fathers were concerned about their child's ability to be independent. For example, one father said:

> And we always tried to kind of give him the feeling of being independent, even from when we were, you know, like I said when he was a baby ... "We go away, you stay with grandma for a while. Yeah, we still love you and everything.... "

Sometimes this concern mirrored the mother's concern about the sociableness of the child. For example, it was the mother of the child highlighted in a previous quotation, who mentioned that her child "cocooned" because his friends were combatant or verbally abusive, noted that he was a "sensitive" child, and suggested that this sensitivity caused him to have difficulties with peers. This same child's father also mentioned that he was a sensitive, introverted boy, but also went on to say:

> And he had a tough time making the adjustment [to a new school], because he didn't want to leave his friends and be independent from them.

It may be that mothers and fathers identify similar personality characteristics in their child, but may attend to different aspects of that characteristic.

One explanation for this parental difference comes from the early work of Talcott Parsons (1955). Parsons proposed a theory of personal development in which mothers play a more expressive, nurturing role in relation to the child, whereas fathers play a more instrumental (i.e., competence-directed, achievement-focused) function. Hence, mothers may see that their role as a parent is to enhance social abilities, whereas fathers believe their role is to enhance achievement motivation and performance. For mothers, they are successful in their task if their children are sociable and friendly toward the environment; for fathers, they are successful when their children are able to assert their independence and express their opinions.

Child Creates Change in Father's Life. One other difference between mothers and fathers in their comments about the child is that fathers tended to mention how much the child had changed their lives (for better or worse). As noted above, fathers were concerned about this issue even before the birth of their child. For example, one father said, "Well, all of a sudden he's home; and I'm going, "Oh my God, I've got 20 years of this. What the hell is happening to me?"" Another father said, "Really it was a change in that, you know, suddenly there's a new responsibility. I think both of us looked forward to it." Still another said, "It really does change your life a lot."

These comments indicate that some fathers saw the change as positive, some as negative, and some were neutral. It may be that as men have historically been less socialized to plan for and imagine their lives as fathers, they are less well prepared to fathom the changes that occur at the birth of a child. Thus, they are more surprised by those changes. Whether their reactions are positive, negative, or neutral seems to depend, in part, on their perceptions of their child and their ability to meet the needs of that child.

Characteristics of the Second Born Child

And what about second born children? Do parents report similar characteristics, and report them with the same frequency, for second born children as they do with their firstborns? There has been considerable research on personality differences between first and second children (Plomin, 1989; Schachter & Stone, 1985). Researchers have found that firstborn children tend to be more adult oriented, helpful, conforming, anxious, self-controlled, and less aggressive than their siblings. One hypothesis is that parental demands and high standards established for firstborns result in these differences.

However, the picture may be much more complex. As mentioned earlier, not only do parents shape children's environments to meet their expectations, but children also shape the environment by contributing their own unique characteristics. So, when the second born arrives, parents' beliefs about their ability to influence and shape their children's behaviors have been confirmed or disconfirmed by their experiences with the older sibling. Parents also now have a measuring stick, however accurate or inaccurate, with which to judge the second child's arrival. The parent who walked the floor night after night with a fussy firstborn may find welcome relief when the second born awakens every 3 or 4 hours. However, the parent who peacefully slept through the night with the firstborn may find this second born's behavior incredibly unpleasant (a fussy baby).

The next section examines parents' stories from the classes, Birth of Child B/Living with Child A and B (Characteristics of Child B). It is interesting to note that parents mentioned the same characteristics for their second child as they did for their first, but with much less frequency. In fact, only 69% of the mothers and 48% of the fathers mentioned any characteristics at all for their second child. Also, for mothers, early and late physical development and sociability characteristics were less salient for their second born children. Additionally, only one father mentioned that the birth of the second child created great change in their lives. In fact, many parents, both mothers and fathers, mentioned that the birth of the second child was less climactic and exciting, and considerably less stressful, than the birth of the first child. As one mother put it:

> ... and I was calmer because I knew what I was supposed to do with a newborn and my expectations were more realistic and less stressful. I knew what to expect.

Mothers

Gender Preference. For the second born child, mothers more clearly identified a preference about the gender of the child (18% mentioned desiring a particular gender of child compared to 7% for the firstborns). This stronger preference about the gender of the second born is probably due to the fact that most families were planning to have only two children; if the parents did not get a particular gender the first time around, they may have been more desirous of that gender the second time around. In general, mothers who stated a preference desired girls, for example:

> I wanted a girl so bad that I was happier than heck when she was born—and it was wonderful!

Most of the mothers did not tell us why they wanted a particular gender, but one mother did.

> I never wanted any girls because my mother and I never were very close, and I didn't want to have to submit my daughter to the same relationship that I had with my mother.

Similar to the processes described in chapter 3, this mother's family of origin experience was an important factor in determining her expectations for what her relationship with her daughter would be like.

Easy Baby/Fussy Baby. The easiness/fussiness of the second born was still an important issue for these mothers, with over 50% mentioning this characteristic. This time, however, easy babies were mentioned over three times more often than were fussy babies. Additionally, although the temperaments of the boy babies were evenly divided between easy and fussy babies, easy baby girls were mentioned much more often than were fussy girls. These results raise two questions: Why do the memories of easy babies linger longer than memories of fussy babies for second born children; and Why were girls identified by mothers as easier than boys the second time around? The first question is easier to answer than the second.

Easy babies may be more memorable the second time around, because the mother's life is much different than it was when the first child arrived. A second time mother not only has to care for a newborn, but also has the added responsibility of chasing after another child, probably a toddler or preschool sibling. Having a child who is easily soothed and whose regular eating and sleeping patterns fit neatly into the busy life schedule may earn her mother's appreciation for these behaviors. Additionally, an easy baby who follows a fussy sibling may be a welcome relief to a young mother who expected her second child to be just like the first. Over 50% of the mothers who mentioned their second child was an easy baby had a difficult time with their first child. In fact, several mothers mentioned the temperament of their second born children by comparing them to the firstborn:

> I mean [Child B] was the kind that you could nurse and then lay down, or he'd sit and look around. It was a whole different experience. So much easier than his sister!

observed one mother.

We do not know, of course, whether the second borns were actually easier, or whether the mothers themselves were better prepared. As one mother said:

> I found [my second child] to be a much happier baby—but, again, I was more experienced and more relaxed, too.

It is unclear why girl babies were identified as easy more often than boy babies for second borns but not firstborns. It could be that by the second child mothers have begun to embrace the societal stereotype that girl babies are easier (less fussy, more sociable) than boy babies. As noted earlier, researchers have found that parents believe genetics play a greater role than do environmental factors in the development of children after the birth of their first child (Sameroff & Feil, 1985). It may be that these mothers, in keeping with the more "genetic" beliefs, ascribe calmer, more easygoing characteristics to their daughters than to their sons.

Big Baby/Small Baby and Healthy Baby/Sick Baby.   Mothers mentioned the health and size of their second born children with the same frequency (approximately 30% of the mothers mentioned this) they did for their firstborns. This suggests that these characteristics may be important for mothers regardless of birth order.

Early/Late Cognitive and Physical Development.   However, mothers were much less concerned with the cognitive and physical development of their second born children (18 and 10%, compared to 30 and 21%, respectively, for their firstborns). It may be that mothers are more relaxed about these issues the second time around. One mother told us:

> [Child A], being the first one, was, you know, he has to be potty trained by this time or he will never be potty trained, and that type of thing. With [Child B], you know, that child is going to learn—you learn to let go a little bit more. You know he's not going to get killed if he plays with this or that, or that kind of thing. I think the first one is sort of like a prototype. You see what happens with this one, and you learn. And we did learn a lot, I think, with [Child A] as far as what would happen and what won't, and not being so structured.

Another explanation may be that second time mothers now have a measuring stick with which to judge the precociousness of their child. They can measure their second born child's abilities in comparison with those of the firstborn:

> So then I had [Child B] and I already had one. Then you kind of had a base of what you could, you know, compare. And [Child B] did everything faster than

[Child A]. Well, for instance, he was like, when he was 2, well he [Child B] walked when he was 9 months old. He did everything fast, and when he was 2 years old all he wanted for his birthday was ice skates, that's it. Well, he had an older brother that played hockey and all his friends, you know, so our life was kind of centered around hockey ...

Positive/Negative Reaction to Baby. Mothers mentioned having a positive reaction to their second born child less often than they did for their firstborn (28% mentioned a positive reaction to the firstborn versus 5% with respect to the second born). However, the percentage of mothers who had negative reactions to their second born child was similar to that of mothers with respect to their first born. The same issues that caused mothers to have negative reactions to their firstborns were mentioned by mothers for second borns: extreme negative temperament of the infant and poor nursing/eating behaviors on the part of the infant (i.e., the mother felt rejected by the infant).

Sociable/Loner. Interestingly, mothers were not as concerned with the sociability of their second born as they were with their firstborn. It may be that second born children, because they have their sibling and their sibling's friends to play with, are naturally more sociable. Alternatively, mothers may not notice the sociability issue as much with the second child because the child has already had experiences interacting with children (i.e., siblings) prior to attending preschool.

Fathers

Gender Preference. Fathers continued to express little desire for a particular gender of child in their stories, even for the second born child. When they did show a preference, the same number desired a boy as desired a girl. This finding, as well as the finding for gender preference by mothers, is in contrast to quantitative research that shows parents have a preference for male children (Arnold & Kuo, 1984; Stattin & Klackenberg-Larsson, 1991). In the Stattin and Klackenberg-Larsson (1991) study, the researchers found that the relationship between parents and children in families whose children ended up being the preferred gender was less conflicted than in those families in which the children's gender was not initially preferred. We saw no evidence of this finding in our data. In contrast, fathers (and mothers) who ended up with a child whose gender was not initially preferred tended to report that gender no longer mattered once the child came. One father said:

I was crushed with the second child because I just had known that it was going to be a boy, and I had a very hard time at first accepting the fact that it was a girl. So I guess I had the postnatal depression. But that only lasted a day until I got a chance to hang onto [Child B—girl]. It was great.

Easy Baby/Fussy Baby.   Fathers also continue to mention the easiness/fussiness of their second born children with the same frequency as they did with their firstborns, mentioning fussy babies somewhat more frequently than easy babies. Fathers and mothers agree about half of the time on which babies are fussy; they agree most often in extreme cases, when the child's temperament is affected by colic or some other physiological disorder (e.g., attention deficit hyperactivity disorder). As noted earlier, the easiness/fussiness of the second child (especially the easiness) appeared to be a very salient issue for mothers. This was less true for fathers. It may be that the differences between mothers and fathers in caregiving responsibilities account for these differences in importance of temperament.

Early/Late Cognitive and Physical Development.   A number of fathers mentioned the cognitive development of their second born children, especially if the fathers felt they were early or exceptional in their development. This was particularly true for fathers of boys:

> I remember at that time [when he was 2 years old] he was looking at something out of his reach, and he pushed a chair over to where he wanted to go, then moved the trash can—he was like problem solving. He really impressed me in that way. He would always keep trying until he got things done like he wanted to do them.

Fathers were much less concerned about the physical development of their second borns. However, one father was concerned about his son's late development because of a physical problem:

> His right side is partially paralyzed so that he has—I think that has an impact on his ability to perform and to achieve things. He was slow to develop things. But, he's very determined ...

Independent/Dependent Child.   The independence/dependence of the child continued to be an important issue for fathers. This issue was especially salient for fathers of boys. Several fathers talked about their child's need (or lack of need) for approval from them resulting in dependent or independent behavior. Another father talked about his son's fears in going to school and meeting new people. These fathers expressed a need to do more to instill independence in their children if this was a problem, or support the independence if their children needed it. One father told us:

> And there's a continuing problem—there's not a great deal of independence relative to playing alone. He likes to play a lot with us or play a lot with friends, but he doesn't like to go by himself. I think over the past couple of years I've probably gotten a lot more involved with him because of [this].

This father clearly seemed to feel his role was to work on addressing this problem so that his son could become more independent. This issue appears to be equally relevant for fathers regardless of the birth order of their child, but seems to be more important for sons than for daughters.

Comparing First and Second Children

How stable are parents' perceptions of their children's temperament over time? Researchers have attempted to answer this question by measuring infant temperament within the first 6 months of life, and then later on when the child is a toddler and is school age. The results have been mixed. Some researchers have found little convincing evidence that temperamental traits are stable over time (Goldsmith & Campos, 1982). Other researchers have found that predictions of temperament observed toward the end of the first year of life, based on newborn observations, are moderately related (Kagan & Snidman, 1991). In another study (Matheny, Riese, & Wilson, 1985), temperament ratings for 110 newborn infants were compared when the children were 9 months old. The researchers found a correlation between the two ratings, but that the characteristics assessed (irritability, contentment, smiling, crying, etc.) were most stable when they were more extreme. Similarly, Belsky, Fish, and Isabella (1991) also found more stability in forecasting negative emotionality than positive emotionality in 9-month-olds, based on ratings at 3 months.

What about the children from our stories? Did parents who told stories of difficult, irritable babies report that their children were cranky and irritable children later in life? The answer is unclear, but in their family stories some parents discussed their children's personalities and characteristics in the section titled Living with Children A & B (Children A & B compared), and often talked about the continuity of their child's early temperament into childhood. Parents also talked about the continuity of their children's cognitive and physical abilities over time, as well as any consequences from medical problems experienced as an infant. However, the most interesting characteristic to follow through these stories is the easy/fussy baby one. As will be seen, this characteristic, as seen by parents, can lead to both positive and negative consequences at both ends of the spectrum. The next section presents data that examine mothers' and fathers' perceptions of their children's easy and fussy temperaments from infancy through childhood.

Mothers

Easy Baby/Fussy Baby.   In examining mothers' stories for their first and second children, there were 14 mothers who identified their firstborns as "easy" babies and 14 mothers who identified their second borns as "easy." Of these 28 mother reports, 9 never mentioned anything about their child's temperament later on in their stories. Eight mothers indicated that their child's easygoing nature continued into childhood. Several of these mothers described their children as "laid back" and "relaxed."

One mother of an easy baby described him this way as a child:

> And then [Child A's] very sincere. He's sort of a sentimentalist. He's kind of a—you know, he's real—that way. I mean, he'll watch a movie and sit down and cry."

Another mother of an easy baby said her child likes to "figure things out on her own" and that "everything still comes easy to her." Still other mothers said their children were very happy, lovable, friendly, and "a honey." The remaining mothers of easy infants reported a variety of behavioral changes, from shy to easily frustrated to fiercely independent to downright "ornery" and hot tempered. Mothers accounted for these changes in a variety of ways. For example, one mother said:

> He thinks when he was little it all came easy for him and he thinks it should stay that way I guess. And he gets to where it's like you just want to shut him in his room; you won't see him the rest of the day. You know, because he's just ornery from that time on.

This mother seems to indicate that her child's temperament was changed by the child's own experience in the world (having an easy time of it as an infant) and by learning a new style of interacting—in this case, from his father, who had a temper. Other mothers mentioned that having a strong-willed sibling also changed how the child reacted. Another mother who described her child as "a little gem" as an infant told us:

> She can be extremely trying, actually exasperating, sometimes, but it's because she feels things differently than other kids. She takes things to heart, I mean, but a lot of it is just the age that she's at right now. Their, you know, their hormones are running rampant, and she's trying to prove herself. One minute she's a little girl that wants to sit on her mom and dad's lap, and the next minute she's trying to sneak makeup in the bathroom.

For this mother, developmental changes have produced personality changes in her child. Whether she thinks these changes are permanent or just an artifact of puberty is unclear. However, it is clear that when mothers recognize changes in their easygoing children's temperaments, they generally attribute those changes to environmental or developmental changes.

In examining the infants, of the 17 mothers of firstborns and second borns who were identified as fussy, 5 did not mention the personality of their children later in their stories. Four children remained fussy, in their mothers' opinions, as they grew older. The mothers of these children described them as very demanding, having bad tempers, and often worrying a lot. One mother of a fussy infant described him thus:

> So when [Child B] came, he was more, more of a fighter, more, more of a rebel. Even now. He was two years old and the kid used to make me cry, just by defying me. Whatever I said not to do, he was gonna do. And he's still strong willed. Me and my husband discussed that, too. He's got such a strong will and you don't want to always yell at him. You don't want to break the will down to nothing.

This mother has clearly been frustrated by her child's difficult temperament from infancy through childhood.

The remaining eight mothers of these fussy infants described changes that suggested the mothers' perceptions changed as much as the child's actual temperament. For example, one mother who said her baby was so fussy she was sure the child was a mistake, said:

> I guess he was very expressive—just enthusiasm—just always had something going, was real bright, interacted all the time—it was very interesting.

Other mothers told us their active, fussy babies grew up to "like to take chances," to "like challenges," and to be very "determined." Still another mother said her colicky baby grew up to be "a lot more studious, serious. She tries hard, she gets it done, and it's good." What these and other stories from this set suggest is that mothers seem to interpret their children's early irritable temperament in more positive ways as the child matures. It may well be that early fussiness is a sign of a very sensitive and expressive child. Because babies have very few methods of expressing sensitivity, they tend to cry a lot. If this sensitivity is coupled with intelligence and disinhibition, the end result may be a child who enjoys challenges and is very determined.

Alternatively, mothers may experience a kind of "reframing" (Haley, 1987) of their children's characteristics. A psychologically healthy response to a noxious situation is to reinterpret that situation as more positive and meaningful. In response to their young child's wails and temper tantrums, mothers may develop a more positive interpretation of their child's behavior. So, crankiness becomes sensitivity, temper tantrums become individualism, and lack of soothability becomes desire for challenges. Understanding this "meaning making," of course, was one of the primary goals of for this study. Through these stories, we begin to see how parents' interpretations may impact on children's personalities. As stories of the child as an infant and toddler get told and retold, the child comes to understand his/her own temperament through the parents' eyes. The reframing the parents do about their child's temperament may have a powerful impact on how the child perceives, and ultimately exhibits, her/his personality traits.

Fathers

Easy Baby/Fussy Baby. In comparing the stories from fathers about their firstborn and second born children, from infancy to childhood, fathers described their children's characteristics as more stable than did mothers. Of the eight fathers who described their first and second children as "easy" babies, five did not provide a description of their children later on in their stories. Three fathers of these easy babies provided descriptions that indicated their children continued to be easygoing and compliant. One father described his daughter as respectful of adult authority; another described his daughter as studious and as someone who "achieves success no matter what."

For the 14 fussy babies, seven fathers described their children as continuing to be difficult, and only one father noted a positive change in his child's temperament. For the children who continued to be difficult, fathers described them as "obstinate," "stubborn," "very emotional," "hyper," and "deliberately provoking." One father of a fussy baby described her, later on in his story, by saying:

[Child A] is strong willed and she's got to be first if you're playing a game. She's got to be the one who starts. If you're playing school, she's got to be the teacher or she will not play.

The one father who noted a change in his child's temperament for the better said:

… and I think pretty much after the first year, though I still—I think she needed a lot of attention in terms of being played with and stuff like that. It was a lot less fussiness and what have you—She's a really good child.

This father, similarly to mothers, appears to be reframing his daughter's fussiness as a sign that she needs extra attention. He goes on to say that she has formed good attachments to him and her mother, and that this has allowed her to be "very well adjusted." This suggests he views temperament as a characteristic that can be shaped by the environment.

In summary, the stories suggest that some parents (over 30% of the mothers and nearly 50% of the fathers) clearly do perceive their child's temperament to be contiguous with their current personality. This may be because children's temperament is as much a function of the parents' beliefs and perceptions as it is genetically inherited. Parents' perceptions may not change over time, and, thus, neither does the child's personality. Additionally, for mothers, but not fathers, nearly 38% changed their perceptions of their child, oftentimes to create a more positive and hopeful view of their child's temperament. These stories help us understand exactly what characteristics changed and why parents' perceptions changed.

CONCLUSION AND IMPLICATIONS

In attempting to answer the question, "Why are children from the same family so different?, these stories illustrate the complexity of the task. Initially we looked at parents' perceptions of what parenting would be like prior to the birth of the first child. Of course, these recollections are retrospective and may not reflect parents' actual experiences. (For a prospective study of adults prior to and subsequent to the birth of their first child, see Cowan & Cowan, 1992, and Fedele, Golding, Grossman, & Pollack, 1988).

Parents in this study identified several issues in considering their own parenting beliefs prior to the birth of the first child. As described in chapter 3, mothers often mentioned their families of origin in their stories and how their experiences directed the kind of relationship they wanted to have with their children. Mothers also talked about their expectations for themselves as parents, the kind of children they wanted to raise, and how skillful they felt they would be at raising this kind of children. Fathers' experiences with children prior to the birth of their first child seems to be an important factor in determining how prepared they feel they are for fatherhood, and how much they think the child will change their lives. The issue of children bringing about change was very salient for fathers. Even prior to the birth of their first child, fathers were concerned about how their children would impact on their lifestyle and on their relationship with their wives.

These expectations about parenthood influence parents' perceptions of their children in several ways. Mothers whose family of origin experiences were conflicted may express more anxiety in anticipation of their relationship with their child. Additionally, having unrealistically high expectations about how children ought to behave or what parenting will be like may create problems in the initial bonding experience for these women.

Similarly, fathers who have little experience with children or who anticipate that having children will impact negatively on their lives may experience anxiety in anticipation of the birth of their first child and may also distance themselves from the child initially. Previous researchers have found that parents' perceptions of infant temperament are strongly related to parental characteristics prenatally, including attachment to the fetus (Wolk, Zeanah, Garcia-Coll, & Carr, 1992) and anxiety prior to the birth of the child (Zeanah, Keener, Stewart, & Anders, 1985). Higher anxiety in parents and poor attachment to the fetus prior to the birth of the child were associated with parents rating their 3-month-old infants as fussier, more unpredictable, and more active than parents who were less anxious and had better attachment to the fetus prior to the birth. The results of these stories illustrate some of the factors that may trigger and maintain anxiety in response to the birth of the first child, as well as cause poor bonding early on.

The question of whether infant temperament has long-term stability or is malleable is not clearly answered. Researchers have found some evidence for the stability of attention span, activity level, irritability, sociability, and shyness, but only at the extremes—those who are very inhibited or very outgoing (Kagan, Reznick, & Gibbons, 1989). Other researchers have attempted to explain the malleability of infant temperament using a goodness-of-fit model (Thomas & Chess, 1977). This model suggests that parents generally create a childrearing environment that recognizes the child's needs but also helps the child learn more adaptive means of functioning. How can these parent stories explain both the malleability and stability of infant temperament throughout childhood?

Parents' descriptions of their children when they were infants begin a story about the life of the child that continues into their childhood. Parents tell us about the gender of their child and the gender they desired. Parents' adjustment to their child's unanticipated gender unfolds a story of parents adapting to changes in perceptions of mother–daughter or father–son relationships and coping with gender stereotyped beliefs in the face of a son or daughter who defies the stereotype.

The health of the infant, and often the size of the infant, was also a story that continued into the present. Parents often explained how more serious health problems (hip deformity, allergies, urinary tract disorder) molded and shaped their children's personalities. Some of the most vivid stories parents told were of their children's physical and cognitive abilities. Parents were quick to recognize advanced development in their young children. They also told us how their child's particular precociousness continued into childhood, and how both they and the school responded to the special needs of their child. Once again, children are told stories about their early development that shape their identity of themselves as competent, creative, resourceful individuals. These stories, and the stories the children themselves create as they venture out in the world, become a part of their schema for their identity, thus shaping and forming their personalities, their drives and motivations, and their abilities.

Perhaps what these parent stories tell us about the development of children's personalities is that personality development is a kind of narrative itself. Infants come into the world with certain temperamental differences, but it is the story parents construct around this temperament that fashions the child's personality. "You were a fussy infant. I had to drive you around in the car until you fell asleep," tells a parent to his or her child. And the child hears the story and incorporates the story as a part of his or her personal folklore. If the child is also very determined, strong willed, and independent, then the story is given further meaning by providing a motive for the child's style of interacting. In this way, parent and child tell and receive a story that gives coherency and meaning to their life experiences.

Thus, temperament appears to be either stable or malleable to the extent that parents either maintain or change the story of their child's temperament. Most parents want to tell a good story with a positive ending: Their children are successes (and will continue to be successful) because their feisty temperament makes them very determined; their children are caring persons (and will continue to be so) because they are (and have always been) good natured, gentle souls. Most parents find ways to make their stories have a happy ending; they maintain stories about their child's easy temperament and reframe stories about their child's difficult temperament. However, as we will see in the next section, some parents are not able to find such happy endings. They are not able to reframe their child's difficult temperament so that the child can be a hero in his or her story. Hence, the difficult temperament becomes a stable personality characteristic over time.

An interesting finding from these data is how mothers and fathers have somewhat different themes in their stories about their children. Mothers tell stories of their children's sociableness; fathers of their children's independence in the world. These themes give us some insight into how mothers and fathers contribute to the child's story of him/herself differently. We know that mothers and fathers have different styles of interacting and playing with their young children. Mothers tend to provide toys, talk with their infants, and initiate conventional games like peek-a-boo, whereas fathers engage in more physical bouncing and lifting games (Parke & Tinsley, 1981). Perhaps what these stories tell us is why parents interact differently with their children. If mothers are concerned about how well their children get along with others, they may purposely teach them how to socialize and converse with others and the social conventions that will help them be accepted by others. Similarly, if fathers are concerned that their children learn to be independent, they may foster activities that promote separateness and individuality.

Practice Implications

We have discussed how parents' expectations and perceptions, formed into stories, help shape a child's personality. But what happens when the story does not have a happy ending? How do children, whose parents continue to have a negative reaction to them into childhood or who continue to see their temperament as difficult and immutable, create a story about themselves that is adaptive and meaningful? These children are most at risk for developing adjustment problems later in life.

As noted earlier, goodness-of-fit models of parent–child relationships suggest that parents create a childrearing environment that is adaptive to the needs of the child. Some parents, however, are not able to create such environments for a variety of reasons (economic hardship, stress, depression, etc.). Parenting that is attuned to the child's temperament is especially important for children with difficult temperaments, who are at risk for many adjustment problems. Difficult infants are far less likely than easy infants to get sensitive care (Crockenberg, 1986; Simonds & Simonds, 1981). By the time the child is 2 years old, the parents of difficult children often resort to angry, punitive discipline which results in defiance and disobedience on the part of the child (Lee & Bates, 1985).

When these families come for help, the clinician is often faced with the dilemma of helping the family recognize that the problem they are presenting is not just about the child him or herself. Rather, the problem must be viewed from a family systems perspective, as described in chapter 1. From a family systems perspective, the family itself is viewed as the client, not the identified child. The goal of family therapy is to change relationships among family members so that the symptomatic behavior (as seen in the difficult child) disappears (Haley, 1987). One major obstacle family therapists must face is overcoming the pattern of homeostasis found in any system. Homeostasis is a process that attempts to maintain a system's stability. Any effort to change the system can cause an imbalance and is met with resistance. Resistance is the system's attempt to protect itself from instability and possible destruction.

The family stories presented here suggest the usefulness of several family therapy techniques. For example, family systems therapists (Bowen, 1978; Kerr, 1981) advocate the use of family of origin work in their theory. They believe that people are born into complex systems. The relationships parents had with their own parents growing up (as well as the kind of relationship they have with them as adults) determine how they interact with their children, as discussed in chapter 3. Most people come to terms with negative experiences during childhood and recognize that other options are available to them as parents (Main, Kaplan, & Cassidy, 1985). Our family stories confirm that the family of origin is important in shaping the expectations and beliefs of mothers, in particular, about their relationship with their children. Mothers in our stories wanted to create better lives for their children than what had been provided for them.

Some parents are not able to come to terms with their early negative experiences. The result may be that the parent is not able to provide a supportive, nurturing environment in which the child can thrive. One technique used in family systems work in order to understand how the family of origin affects current family life, is to ask the parent to draw a genogram (Hartman, 1978; Kerr, 1981) of his or her family showing the various relationship and kinship patterns (married, separated, conflicted, alcoholic, etc.).

This pictorial representation of the family opens up a discussion in the family therapy session of how patterns of behavior are repeated and reinforced in families. A practitioner who hears stories about how difficult and fussy a child was from birth may note that the mother's relationship with a sibling, for example, was similarly conflicted. We often hear parents say, "He's just like his Uncle Pete," or "She's got her grandmother's stubbornness." Helping a parent recognize that the child does not have to have the same relationship with him or her as he or she had with a relative previously is the work of therapy.

Another method of helping parents change the relationship with their child and break through family resistance to change is to relabel or reframe the child's behavior (Haley, 1987). We saw this phenomenon occur with many parents in our study who had fussy, difficult infants and who began to reinterpret those behaviors as more adaptive. In therapy, relabeling or reframing a behavior changes the meaning of the problem, event, or situation to a more useful perspective. So, fussiness may mean the child needs more structure when presented with change, or that the child is tenacious, self determined, and independent. These are all qualities that can lead to positive outcomes. The environment can be restructured to meet the needs of the child and the behavior is now understood in a new light.

Clinicians may ask family clients to tell the story of the birth of the child. Whenever the parent indicates that the child was difficult to manage even at a very young age, the therapist can reframe the meaning of the behavior by saying, "So what you did not realize then was that the child's fussiness was really a very determined personality, that the child has a very strong sense of what he/she wants in the world and is determined to get those things." Then the therapist can ask the parent how he/she thinks those characteristics might be useful to an individual in the future. The temptation is for the parent to think only of the dire consequences of such behavior (as evidenced by Uncle Pete's life or Cousin Mary's disposition). However, the job of the practitioner is to redirect this thinking toward recognizing the positive aspects of such qualities, and how the parents might channel their child's personality more adaptively.

Our family stories also indicate that parents' beliefs about parenthood and their expectations about themselves as parents are important in understanding the kinds of relationships parents establish with their children. Along with family of origin work to get at these issues, family therapists also need to attend to the beliefs and expectations parents had prior to the birth of their children. We know that expectant mothers who imagine themselves as competent caregivers report greater satisfaction in caring for their infant after birth (Leifer, 1980). From our family stories, we know that some mothers expected parenthood to be very different from the way it turned out and that fathers were anxious about the kinds of changes having children would bring about for them.

Practitioners need to ascertain what parents' expectations were before they became parents in order to understand how these beliefs have changed as a result of becoming parents. Parents who feel incompetent and incapable of helping their child make life adjustments (because they have failed in the past), may feel demoralized and depressed when faced with the tasks of parenthood. These feelings may cause them to withdraw further from interacting with their child. The practitioner will need to help parents reestablish feelings of efficacy by encouraging positive interactions between parent and child.

For example, the therapist may suggest the parent and child set aside special times and activities that they engage in exclusively, without other family members present. Family therapists may also help the family learn how to give and receive compliments in order to establish more positive interactions between parents and children. Additionally, therapists may need to teach parents how and when to give positive reinforcement for child behaviors that more closely approximate the parents' desired behavior. For example, the mother in our study who believed that if you "raised your children right they would always be polite and cooperative," might need help learning how to reinforce polite, cooperative behavior.

Policy Implications

Child and family clinicians, schooled in more traditionally behavioral techniques for dealing with problem behavior of children, may simply focus on the child's symptomatology in therapeutic settings. However, our work in family life stories clearly highlights the importance of recognizing parental perceptions and beliefs about the child's behavior even prior to the birth of the child. Social workers and psychologists who work with emotionally disturbed children need clinical training in understanding how the entire family system, including past generations, contribute to the child's disturbance.

Training for child practitioners needs to include not only course work in child development, but also courses that specifically address family systems therapy. Practitioners should be taught how to construct genograms in family therapy sessions; and, through these genograms, they should begin to see patterns of relationships among family members. Child clinicians should also be taught about intergenerational issues and the life cycle of the family, using Carter and McGoldrick's work (1988), so that they can understand how the child's behavior may be impacting on the entire family and how the family may be impacting on the child.

Additionally, our family stories suggest that health practitioners who work with young families with infants, may need to be better trained in recognizing difficult temperament in infants and helping parents cope with these difficult temperaments. Although our stories suggest that most parents eventually adapt to the child's difficult temperament, some parents may be at risk for developing poor relationships with their child. Health providers, such as doctors and nurses, may be unaware of the complexity of the situation. They may simply reassure parents that their child is "normal," without exploring other family issues. Health practitioners need to be trained to ask parents how they feel about their child's temperament and their interpretations of that temperament.

Doctors and nurses can be the first people who offer parents a more positive view of their child's behavior. Excessive crying can be interpreted as determinism, wakefulness as alertness and intelligence, and irritability at changes in the environment as cautiousness and protectiveness of the environment. Additionally, many health care workers may need training in recognizing when families may be at risk for emotional and physical abuse and when a referral to a mental health practitioner is warranted.

Finally, our family stories highlight how woefully unprepared many adults are for the parenting role. Indeed, people prepare less for the parenting role than for other important roles such as employment and marriage (Rossi, 1982).

Schooling and job training prepare individuals for a future career. Experiences of dating and courtship prepare one for marriage. However, many young adults have no experiences with children prior to parenthood and have not been taught important parenting skills such as empathy, caring for an infant, and positive discipline. Some high school health curricula include parenting information, but generally this information is about caring for an infant and does not include information on how to foster the social and emotional development of children (Marshall, Buckner, Perkins, & Lowry, 1996). High school health classes, as well as birthing classes in hospitals and in the community, need to include information about temperament differences among infants and how to deal with infants with difficult temperaments. Informing future parents about these temperamental differences and providing a reframing tool for difficult temperaments in infants may circumvent many problems parents of fussy babies may encounter.

Research Implications

The focus of this research was to identify what infant characteristics parents find most salient in describing their newborn and to examine how temperament, in particular, plays itself out in later childhood. Childhood, of course, is not the end of the story for personality development. Exploring the development of personality from infancy through young adulthood would help us understand how innate, temperamental characteristics interact with the environment to produce enduring personalities. In longitudinal studies of personality, researchers have found that personality is quite stable after about age 30 (Costa, Metter, & McCrae, 1994). However, there has been little research exploring how parent beliefs and attitudes shape personality from infancy through adulthood. Additional interviews with the parents from our study, when the children are adolescents and then later in early adulthood, could illuminate how some personality characteristics change and develop.

The analyses of these stories focused on temperamental changes over time. However, many other themes could have been followed from early childhood through the elementary years. For example, many parents mentioned how certain physical problems such as cerebral palsy and urinary tract problems affected the social and emotional development of their children. Similarly, parents often continued talking about the development of their children who were early or late in their physical and cognitive development. Because there were so few of these stories, the theme was not followed from infancy through childhood. However, parents of physically impaired or highly gifted and talented (or cognitively and physically limited) children could be asked to tell their family stories to compare the developmental trajectories of these characteristics. Looking at these characteristics across time would give us an understanding of how physical handicaps and cognitive or physical giftedness play out over time. We would begin to understand how environment and the child's own temperament interact with high intelligence, for example, resulting in either successful or failed responses to this ability.

In summary, our parent stories inform us about how parents' beliefs and perceptions of their children's early temperament shape and mold them into enduring, stable personalities. When the story the parents tell is initially a positive one, they generally continue that theme throughout the child's life, embedding it in the child's identity and self schema. If that story is initially a difficult one, most parents reinterpret the story to the child's advantage, making the theme one the child can use as an adaptive tool. Other parents may not fare so well in reinterpreting their child's story. In such cases, the parents may need counsel from health and mental health professionals who can help them work through their own family of origin issues and help them relabel their child's behavior in a more adaptive way. Future research may explore these temperament characteristics through adolescence and young adulthood in order to understand how the environment impacts on personality throughout the formative years.

REFERENCES

Arnold, F., & Kuo, E. C. (1984). The value of daughters and sons: A comparative study of the gender preferences of parents. *Journal of Comparative Family Studies, 15*(2), 299–318.

Belsky, J., Fish, M., & Isabella, R. A. (1991). Continuity and discontinuity in infant negative and positive emotionality: Family antecedents and attachment consequences. *Developmental Psychology, 27*(3), 421–431.

Bowen, M. (1978). *Family therapy in clinical practice.* New York: Aronson.

Buss, A. H., & Plomin, R. (1975). *A temperament theory of personality development.* New York: Wiley.

Carter, B., & McGoldrick, M. (1988). *The Changing Family Life Cycle* (2nd ed.). New York: Gardner.

Costa, P. T., Jr., Metter, E. J., & McCrae, R. R. (1994). Personality stability and its contribution to successful aging. *Journal of Geriatric Psychiatry, 27*(1), 41–59.

Cowan, C. P., & Cowan, P. A. (1992). *When partners become parents: The big life change for couples.* New York: Basic Books.

Crockenberg, S. B. (1986). Are temperamental differences in babies associated with predictable differences in care-giving? In J. V. Lerner and R. M. Lerner (Eds.), *New directions for child development* (No. 30, pp. 75–88). San Francisco: Jossey-Bass.

Fedele, N. M., Golding, E. R., Grossman, F. K., & Pollack, W. S. (1988). Psychological issues in adjustment to first parenthood. In G. Y. Michaels & W. A. Goldbern (Eds.), *The transition to parenthood: Current theory and research* (pp. 85–113). Cambridge, England: Cambridge University Press.

Goldsmith, H. H., & Campos, J. J. (1982). Toward a theory of infant temperament. In R. N. Emde & R. Hamon (Eds.), *The development of attachment and affiliative systems*. New York: Plenum.

Haley, J. (1987). *Problem-solving therapy* (2nd ed.). San Francisco: Jossey-Bass.

Hartman, A. (1978). Diagrammatic assessment of family relationships. *Social Casework, 59,* 465–476.

Huitt, W. G., & Ashton, P. T. (1982). Parents' perception of infant temperament: A psychometric study. *Merrill-Palmer Quarterly, 28,* 95–109.

Kagan, J., Reznick, J. S., & Gibbons, J. (1989). Inhibited and uninhibited types of children. *Child Development, 60,* 838–845.

Kagan, J., & Snidman, N. (1991). Temperamental factors in human development. *American Psychologist, 46,* 856–862.

Kerr, M. (1981). Family systems theory and therapy. In A. Gurman & D. Kniskern (Eds.), Handbook of family therapy (pp. 226–264). New York: Brunner/Mazel.

Lee, C. L., & Bates, J. E. (1985). Mother–child interaction at age two years and perceived difficult temperament. *Child Development, 56,* 1314–1325.

Leifer, M. (1980). *Psychological aspects of motherhood: A study of first pregnancy.* New York: Praeger.

Lyon, M. E., & Plomin, R. (1981). The measurement of temperament using parental ratings. *Journal of Child Psychology and Psychiatry, 22,* 47–53.

Main, M., Kaplan, N., & Cassidy, J. (1985). *Security in infancy, childhood, and adulthood: A move to the level of representation.* Monographs for the Society for Research in Child Development, 50 (1–2, Serial No. 209).

Marshall, E., Buckner, E., Perkins, J., & Lowry, J. (1996). Effects of a child abuse prevention unit in health classes in four schools. *Journal of Community Health Nursing, 13*(2), 107–122.

Matheny, A. P., Riese, M. L., & Wilson, R. S. (1985). Rudiments of infant temperament: Newborn to 9 months. *Developmental Psychology, 21*(3), 486–494.

Parke, R. D., & Tinsley, B. R. (1981). The father's role in infancy: Determinants of involvement in caregiving and play. In M. E. Lamb (Ed.), *The role of the father in child development* (pp. 429–458). New York: Wiley.

Parsons, T. (1955). *Family, socialization and interaction process.* Glencoe, IL: The Free Press.

Plomin, R. (1989). Environment and genes: Determinants of behavior. *American Psychologist, 44,* 105–111.

Plomin, R., & Daniels, D. (1987). Why are children from the same family so different from one another? *Behavioral and Brain Science, 10*(1), 1–16.

Rossi, A. S. (1982). Transition to parenthood. In L. R. Allman & D. T. Jaffe (Eds.), *Readings in adult psychology: Contemporary perspectives* (2nd ed., pp. 263–275). New York: Harper & Row.

Rowe, D. C., & Plomin, R. (1977). Temperament in early childhood. *Journal of Personality Assessment, 41*(2), 150–156.

Rubin, J. Z., Provenzano, F. J., & Luria, Z. (1974). The eye of the beholder: Parents' views on sex of newborns. *American Journal of Orthopsychiatry, 44,* 512–519.

Sameroff, A. J., & Feil, L. (1985). Parental concepts of development. In I. E. Sigel (Ed.), *Parental belief systems: The psychological consequences for children* (pp. 84–104). Hillsdale, NJ: Lawrence Erlbaum Associates.

Schachter, F. F., & Stone, R. K. (1985). Difficult sibling–easy sibling: Temperament and the within-family environment. *Child Development, 56,* 1335–1344.

Simonds, M. P., & Simonds, J. F. (1981). Relationship of maternal parenting behaviors to preschool children's temperament. *Child Psychiatry and Human Development, 12*(1), 19–31.

Stattin, H., & Klackenberg-Larsson, I. (1991). The short- and long-term implications for parent/child relations of parents' prenatal preferences for their child's gender. *Developmental Psychology, 27*(1), 141–147.

Thomas, J. R., & Chess, S. (1977). *Temperament and development.* New York: Brunner/Mazel.

Wolk, S., Zeanah, C. H., Garcia-Coll, C. T., & Carr, S. C. (1992). Factors affecting parents' perceptions of temperament in early infancy. *American Journal of Orthopsychiatry, 62*(1), 71–82.

Zeanah, C. H., Keener, M. A., Stewart, L., & Anders, T. F. (1985). Prenatal perception of infant personality: A preliminary investigation. *Journal of the American Academy of Child Psychiatry, 24*(2), 204–210.

Zeanah, C. H., Zeanah, P. D., & Stewart, L. K. (1990). Parents' constructions of their infants' personalities before and after birth: A descriptive study. *Child Psychiatry and Human Development, 20*(3), 191–206.

5

Tales of Social Support Throughout Family Development

Lisa G. Colarossi
The University of Michigan

Susan A. Lynch
University of Arkansas at Little Rock

Support has different meanings for different people. What one person finds supportive, such as receiving advice or having a listening ear, another person may not. Consequently, there are no specific behaviors that are certain to be supportive for everyone in every situation. Despite this, researchers have found that: (a) people who have supportive others in their lives have less physical and mental health problems than those who do not; (b) there are different ways of providing support; (c) the kind of support people find helpful changes over time with age and social context; and (d) males and females give and receive support differently (see reviews by Cohen & Wills, 1985; Uchino, Cacioppo, & Kiecolt-Glaser, 1996; Umberson et al., 1996; and Wood, Rhodes, & Whelan, 1989).

During the course of the interviews with parents in our study, one recurring issue was the help and support they received from their spouses, family members, and friends and how it changed over time as their lives progressed from being single to getting married to having children. This chapter describes these parents' experiences of social support over time and how it related to the development of their families. We begin with a brief review of research that has been done in the area of social support. The remainder of the chapter describes the changes in social support that parents experienced over time as they went from being single adults to spouses and to parents. It also examines the gender differences in these experiences. Research on how support changes with life context, social roles, and relationship dynamics is reviewed; and information from the families in our study is described and discussed. Finally, the chapter concludes with a discussion of how the information from our study can be used to inform policy and practice related to social support in people's lives.

THE IMPORTANCE OF SOCIAL SUPPORT

Social support is an important and growing area of research because both the quality and quantity of support one receives has been found to be related to better physical and mental functioning. For instance, people who are more socially isolated have higher rates of cardiovascular disorders such as heart disease, immune system difficulties related to a variety of illnesses, and mortality (see review by Uchino, Cacioppo, & Kiecolt-Glaser, 1996). Such effects are particularly marked in older individuals, but are also found in younger adults and children, along with higher rates of emotional difficulties such as depression, low self-esteem, and anxiety (Barrera & Garrison-Jones, 1992; Coates, 1985; House, 1981; Turner, 1981). Fortunately, these studies also show that having people to whom one can turn for material and emotional support is associated with improved health and adjustment.

It is argued that support from others influences physical and mental health in many different ways, such as protecting one from stress, helping one cope with difficult situations, and providing a general sense of social integration or belonging. If support from others can help us avoid negative situations altogether, then it will help prevent the development of stress and coping difficulties. This is sometimes known as a main or direct effect of social support. For example, a parent may protect a child from danger, such as running into the street or getting hurt playing with dangerous toys. For an adult, friends and family members may be able to help a person avoid the stress of unemployment by providing information about job openings or providing financial assistance. In these ways, others are able to help one avoid getting into a negative or stressful situation before it happens.

In other cases, stress is unavoidable, but support providers can help one cope with its effects. This is sometimes referred to as a buffering effect. For instance, after experiencing the death of a loved one, others may provide emotional support to help with the grieving process, provide tangible assistance by making funeral arrangements, or provide information or advice on how to deal with a difficult situation. In such cases, others help to reduce both physiological reactions to stress, such as the output of stress-related hormones in the body (Uchino et al., 1996), and emotional distress. Additionally, support may help people avoid nonproductive forms of coping, such as substance abuse, smoking, or even focusing on negative thoughts, while promoting adaptation by engaging us in activities such as exercise or other forms of self-care.

Finally, theorists postulate that support provides us with a general sense of being loved and feeling important. Indeed, it may be these more general beliefs and perceptions about being cared for and having support available when needed that have the greatest effect on decreasing depression and raising self-esteem (Sarason, Sarason, & Pierce, 1990). Obviously, the issue of how and why social support is helpful is complex. In the next section, we discuss the ways in which social support has been defined and conceptualized, then move on to discussing how social support varies by age and gender.

WHAT IS SOCIAL SUPPORT: DEFINITIONS AND CONCEPTUALIZATIONS

In order to understand more fully how support processes work, researchers have developed specific definitions of different types of support and have gathered descriptive data on age and gender differences in the kind and quality of social support that people receive. Researchers view social support in a variety of ways: as a buffer in models of stress and coping, as an actual coping technique, as a risk factor if it is inadequate, and as an individual difference variable related to perceptions or belief systems.

The conceptualization of social support, often criticized as inadequate in early studies (Thoits, 1982), has undergone a series of redefinitions and modifications in recent years. More fully developed theories of social support, stemming from different disciplines and conceptual domains, have produced clearer research on the variables involved and how they interact with different personal characteristics. Social support is now generally conceived to be a complex construct with at least three distinct dimensions: support function, support structure, and perceived quality (Antonucci, 1994; Cohen, 1992; Gottlieb, 1988; Lynch, 1998; Powell, 1990; Streeter & Franklin, 1992; Thoits, 1982).

Support function refers to the type of support actually exchanged (Antonucci & Akiyama, 1987; Levitt, Weber, & Guacci, 1993; Weiss, 1974). Researchers have developed many different scales for measuring functional aspects of social support, and there is some variation in the types that are measured from study to study. However, several basic types are discussed repeatedly in the literature. These include: (a) *esteem support*, also referred to as emotional or expressive support and ventilation such as listening to one's problems, giving empathy, etcetera; (b) *informational support*, also considered to be guidance or advice; (c) *instrumental support*, which is material or tangible in nature, such as loaning money, providing help with transportation, providing a letter of recommendation for a job, etcetera; and (d) *social companionship* or time spent doing activities with someone. These types are highly intercorrelated and researchers often combine them to form a generalized measure of support function (Barrera, Sandler, & Ramsay, 1981; Procidano & Heller, 1983).

Support structure includes such things as the type of relationship that exists between the support giver and the support receiver (i.e., parent–child, wife–husband, etc.) and the size of one's support network. This dimension is a measure of the potential for help available from people with whom one has supportive relationships (Maguire, 1986; Powell, 1990). This dimension assesses the existence of a relationship, but does not speak to the depth or quality of that relationship. These characteristics are assessed by the final dimension, perceived quality.

Perceived quality is the recipient's subjective assessment of the quality of support exchanges and relationships, distinct from what is done by whom. In recent years, it has become increasingly evident that characteristics of support quality are as important, if not more so, as those relating to support quantity (Smith, Fernengel, Holcroft, Gerald, & Marien, 1994; Ward, 1985). For example, individuals' perceptions of support quality are more strongly related to well-being than are reports of actual support exchanges by respondents and members of their support network (Cohen & Syme, 1985; Cohen & Wills, 1985; Henderson, 1981; Hobfoll, Nadler, & Lieberman, 1986; Ingersoll-Dayton & Antonucci, 1988; Sandler & Barrera, 1984; Wethington & Kessler, 1986). Additionally, perceived quality of support has been found to be only weakly related to actual supportive behaviors performed by others (Barrera, 1986; Dunkel-Schetter & Bennett, 1990; Heller, Swindle & Dusenbury, 1986; Lakey & Heller, 1988; B. R. Sarason et al., 1991; Wetherington & Kessler, 1986).

The data in this chapter represent *perceived support*. It is parents' stories about support, or their individual perceptions of support, rather than an outside measure of actual support exchanges that occurred in these families that are used as data. Also, the chapter primarily describes aspects of *support functions* (e.g., emotional support, instrumental support, companionship support, etc.) in people's lives, rather than an analysis of the support structure or network content. Finally, this chapter also illuminates differences in mothers' and fathers' perceptions of the functional support that they give and receive. Such gender differences are found throughout the research literature on social support.

AGE AND GENDER DIFFERENCES IN SOCIAL SUPPORT

People start out life receiving primary support from their caregivers in infancy and childhood. This support is mostly instrumental in nature, as caretakers provide food, shelter, access to school and other activities, and buy things to help a child progress through life. Caregivers also provide some level of emotional support to comfort an infant's or child's needs of safety, security, and belonging.

As children get older, they develop larger networks of support, which include siblings, extended family members, other nonrelated adults, and peers. This trend becomes a major developmental transition during adolescence, when children move away from family members and begin seeking peers and intimate partners to meet their support needs (Cauce, Reid, Landesman, & Gonzales, 1990; Feiring and Lewis, 1991; Furman & Buhrmester, 1992). Adults have even more varied support networks, including their spouses, extended family members, coworkers, and friends. But even for adults, as will is discussed throughout this chapter, these networks vary over time as roles and social contexts change.

Despite the recognition that age does affect the function, structure, and perceived quality of social support, few studies to date have examined social support from a life-span perspective (Ishii-Kuntz, 1990; Levitt, Weber, & Guacci, 1993). Most studies exploring age differences in support focus on cross-generational transactions, ignoring the normative changes that may occur in social support at different developmental stages. It is evident, however, that such changes do occur (Lynch, 1998) and that variations in the function, structure, and perceived quality of social support are related to these changes (Ishii-Kuntz, 1990; Levitt, Weber, & Guacci, 1993).

For example, Lynch (1998) found that between the ages of 30 and 50, friendships are perceived as offering a high level of positive support and are also viewed as relatively undemanding in comparison to relationships with spouses and children. Additionally, Cowan and Cowan (1992) found that young adults may become socially isolated when they start families. As is discussed later, it appears that the birth of the first child can result in a significant decrease in interactions with friends, which can lead to increased levels of stress.

In addition to age-related differences in the structure, function, and perceived quality of social support relationships, research has consistently reported significant gender differences in friend and family relationships (Antonucci, 1990; Antonucci, 1994; Antonucci & Akiyama, 1987; Barnett, Biener, & Baruch, 1987; Lynch, 1998; Schultz, 1991; Silverman, 1987; Vaux, 1985). Adult women report that they provide and receive more support than do men and have more extensive, satisfying, and varied networks; men tend to maintain close and intimate ties with only one person, usually their spouses (Antonucci, 1983; Belle, 1991; Hobfoll, 1986; Sarason, Levine, Basham, & Sarason, 1983). These gender differences begin to emerge even before adulthood. Berndt (1982) concluded from his research that adolescent girls' friendships are more intimate and more exclusive than those of boys. Specifically, girls mention intimate sharing of thoughts and feelings more often than do boys; girls seem less willing to include a nonfriend in an ongoing conversation than do boys; if girls have a reciprocated friendship, they are less willing to make new friends than are boys; and girls may be less willing to make new friends when they already have several stable friends.

These patterns tend to remain stable across adulthood (Schultz, 1991). Overall, findings indicate that the social and family relationships of women, when compared to those of men, tend to exhibit more closeness and intimacy, and that women appear to place a higher value on reciprocal relationships. Adult women frequently report receiving more support from friends and members of their family than do men. Additionally, while women report having close, intimate relationships with a few friends and family members, men are more likely to report having casual relationships with many people (see Schultz, 1991, for a comprehensive review).

THEORIES OF SOCIAL SUPPORT

What makes it likely that we will receive social support and why does it differ with age and gender and over time? Several theorists have tried to provide explanations, with most describing social support as developmental and interactive in nature. Newcomb (1990a, 1990b) conceptualizes the establishment and maintenance of social support as an element of human connectedness, social exchange, and attachment. He hypothesizes that social support quality, adequacy, and satisfaction should remain moderately stable over time and across relationships due to the relative temporal consistency of individual characteristics and social milieu. However, he does note that some change should occur due to evolving, reciprocal, and causal transactions over time.

Newcomb's (1990a, 1990b) perspective proposed that relationships develop over the life course, but early attachment experiences greatly affect later developmental stages to form general attachments to social network members, that will be moderately stable. These early attachment experiences interact with temperament, behavioral competency, new relationship interactions, and cognitive development to create a dynamic interactive model of social support in interpersonal relationships. Unfortunately, this model has not explicitly taken into account gender role dynamics in this developmental process.

Kahn and Antonucci (1980) incorporated elements similar to Newcomb's (1990a, 1990b) model, and included considerations of social role dynamics in their theory. In their perspective, social support develops over time from person–environment interaction that involves attachment processes, social role requirements, and characteristics of the social network composition and its support provisions. These interactions have aspects of both stability and change over the life course, where social context is an important moderating factor in addition to an individual's personality style, role demands, and emotional and behavioral responses.

Thus, the more people in one's social context who have different expectations for men's and women's roles as spouse, parent, friend, and worker, the more pronounced the gender differences in both the provision and receipt of social support will be. For example, women are often expected, as part of their role in the family as wife and mother, to provide more functional support (e.g.,taking care of a sick family member, shopping, nurturing, etc.) than are men. Researchers have hypothesized that such role demands are socialized over time and affect both behaviors in and beliefs about relationships with others, including social support (Jones, Bloys, & Wood, 1990; Murstein & Azar, 1986).

In addition to social context, other researchers have turned toward individual beliefs and motivations in order to understand supportive relationships. Jones and Costin (1995), as well as others (Clark, Ouellette, Powell, & Milberg, 1987), have theorized that the beliefs people apply to their relationships are based on orientations toward *communality* or *exchange*, and are related to traits such as expressivity and instrumentality. Communal/exchange orientation refers to a belief- and expectancy-related system regarding interpersonal relationship processes. Communally oriented people consider the needs and desires of others as a primary force in determining relationship exchanges. These people have a higher degree of expressivity in their relationships, and they report greater satisfaction with social support. In contrast, exchange-oriented people conceptualize relationships as "tit-for-tat" exchanges where there is a comparability of specific benefits between two people. These people have a higher degree of instrumentality in their relationships and often report less satisfaction with social support than do communally oriented people.

A similar concept used to describe these types of relationship characteristics is *affiliation motivation* (Murray, 1938; Wong & Csikszentmihalyi, 1991), which is considered to be motivationally related thoughts and behaviors in the service of establishing and maintaining friendships. Falling under these motivations are social goals of communion versus agency (Jarvinen & Nicholls, 1996) and instrumentality versus relationality (Burks & Parke, 1996). Research has found that these orientations vary by gender and impact on the quality of relationship processes (Burks & Parke, 1996; Jarvinen & Nicholls, 1996; Jones, 1991; Jones,

Bloys, & Wood, 1990; Jones & Dembo, 1989; Murstein & Azar, 1986; Wong & Csikszentmihalyi, 1991). For example, women tend to score higher on communion scales and men higher on agency and exchange. Relatedly, women usually report higher levels of social support from a variety of sources than do men.

In summary, theories of social support postulate that support will change to varying degrees over time due to: (a) one's expected role within a given context (e.g., a child is expected to receive support and parents are expected to provide it); (b) the closeness or attachment one feels toward the person to whom one is providing support; and (c) one's beliefs about the importance and characteristics of relationships (e.g., orientations toward giving to or receiving from others). Lastly, support will differ over time and by gender based on the above aspects of a person's life as well as on the characteristics of each different individual with whom one has a relationship, and on the social context. The following sections provide information about how parents in our study described changes in social support related to social context, social roles, and dynamics in the spousal relationship.

THE STORIES

Participants in our study were asked to begin telling their story by describing their family prior to the birth their first child. Participants talked about what it was like to be a married couple and what it was like to make the transition from that relationship to becoming parents for the first time. Stories were audiotaped and transcribed verbatim. Transcripts were coded for common themes according to the storyboard coding process described in chapter 2 and elsewhere (Harold, Palmiter, Lynch, & Freedman-Doan, 1995). To review, Level I coding separated the transcript information into time frames (e.g., before the birth of the first child, the birth of the first child, after the birth, etc.). Next, this information was coded at a second level, which consisted of four categories of information: birth, family life, child characteristics, and work life. Social support themes were contained in the category of family life.

Themes related to both structural and functional support were coded. This chapter discusses the social support themes that emerged across three time periods: prior to the birth of children, after the birth of the first child, and after the birth of subsequent children. Also, themes are discussed in relationship to parents' social contexts, their roles, and their spousal relationships. Social context factors that were associated with parents' social support included the length of the relationship with their partner prior to the birth of the first child, changes in social networks related to moving to new geographic locations for their own or their spouse's job, and interactions with extended family members and in-laws.

Support themes that related to social roles focused on adjusting to and learning the role of parent and how that changed their relationships with supportive others. Lastly, two different themes arose that related to the spousal relationship: the amount of support men and women provided to each other as a couple, and changes in the spousal relationship that occurred after the birth of their first child. A list of specific themes that emerged during each time period is represented in Table 5.1.

Being a Couple: Social Support Prior to the Birth of Children

Ninety-two out of 98 parents (55 mothers and 37 fathers) in the sample discussed some aspect of social support prior to the birth of their first child. The social context of the time period prior to the birth of the first child primarily involves leaving one's family of origin and starting a family with a partner. The events that couples in our study used to characterize this time period included beginning careers, geographically relocating for new jobs, adjusting to new extended families/in-laws, and spending time doing activities together as a couple and with friends. During this time, many parents experienced rapid changes in support networks as new people entered the network through marriage and work life, and others left due to geographic relocations. Thus, parents in our study often identified the spousal relationship as being the most constant and primary form of support during this time period, followed by extended family

TABLE 5.1
Social Support Themes by Time Period

Time Period	Major Themes Across Parent Stories
Prior to the birth of the first child	1) Companionship support in the spousal relationship 2) Instrumental and emotional support in the spousal relationship 3) Disruptions in the social network 4) Changes in extended family support
After the birth of the first child	1) Social isolation and decreases in support from friends 2) Recreating a support network 3) Extended family: Mixed blessings 4) Spousal roles of parent and supporter 5) Support between spouses: Renewal and divorce
After subsequent children	1) Providing support to children 2) Support received from others 3) Home alone? Support in the parenting role 4) Support between spouses: Renewal and divorce

support. Support in the spousal relationship was dominated by themes related to companionship support and emotional support.

Companionship support in the spousal relationship

Over half of the parents in our study had romantic relationships longer than two years prior to the birth of their first child and several had been together between 5 and 10 years. Couples who were together longer prior to the birth of their first child often felt this factor was significant to their readiness to have a child. For them, this time together seemed to reflect the importance they placed on spending time together as a couple and with friends before starting a family. Many participants commented on how their social activities would change once they had a baby. For example, one father said:

> We were married over 7 years before [the first child] was born. We knew that when we got married we would have children, but we were both fairly young when we got married, so we wanted to do some things on our own. We knew traveling would be more difficult when we had kids, so we took some nice trips and did some things before we had children.

As this father suggests, taking time to do activities together and have fun was an important consideration for many couples. Another father stated:

> We dated 3 or 4 years before we got married and then we got married and waited five years before we had any kids. People used to refer to us as the married single people. But it was a case of doing what you wanted, when you wanted. We could go away for the weekend, go out at night, make plans at the last minute, it was a simple thing to do.

This mother expressed a similar sentiment:

> We didn't have a child for the first 4 years. It was pretty much of a selfish kind of a relationship. We did a lot of fun things. We went out a lot, we kind of developed our own interests.

Also, another mother states:

> My husband and I got married at 19 years old. He was drafted and went away for 2 years, and when he came back we didn't—we weren't ready to settle down. So, we worked, we traveled, we had fun for 10 years and then we decided to settle down and have kids.

Alternatively, parents who had their first child soon after they were married seemed to have a more difficult transition from couplehood to parenthood and felt that they missed doing activities together:

My husband and I were married a month before I found out I was pregnant, so our expectations of the marriage changed immediately. We both wanted kids and we weren't particularly young when we got married. So, it wasn't a horrible experience and didn't scar our marriage, but we certainly couldn't take that trip to Europe, and we had to buy a house right away.

Another mother commented:

It was kinda hard getting used to each other that first year, with both of us working. The first one coming along right away was like all of a sudden you're an immediate family.

Instrumental and emotional support in the spousal relationship

Couples also discussed providing support to each other, as well as receiving support from each other. Although both men and women talked at similar rates about social companionship with each other and with friends, women mentioned providing emotional and instrumental support to others more often than did men. One noteworthy theme that emerged in this time frame, but not at other times during family development, was women's financial support of their husbands so that their spouses could attend school prior to the birth of their first child. These mothers provide examples of this: "We both had just graduated from college when we got married, and about 2 years after that my husband decided to go back to graduate school and at that point I supported us while he went back to school." And, "I went to work and he went to law school." In later stages of family development, women continued to provide instrumental support to their husbands, but not usually financially.

Parents did not place much importance or value on this form of instrumental support provided by women in the early stages of the marital relationship. In contrast, though, there was a lot of discussion of fathers' financial support of the family after the birth of children. As we can see in the themes throughout this chapter, the type of social support provided by and received from others and the value of that support is often related to expected or valued gender roles in the family.

Disruptions in the social network

In addition to the transition from being single to becoming a couple, some parents were coping with changing geographic locations during the same time period. Seventeen parents mentioned extreme disruptions in their network near the time their first child was born, making the adjustment to parenthood more difficult, with less access to social support. Twice as many women as men mentioned the impact of extreme changes in network. Most of these were related to moving out of town. A few others involved losses due to the death of family members, miscarriages, and stillbirths. One example of multiple social disruptions is contained in this mother's description:

> I had been through a divorce right before I married my current husband, so that was a rough thing. I had gone through a lot of changes. I had moved five times and gotten a divorce from my first husband. I had known my current husband through work, and we started dating and immediately got married within a few months and had our first child a year and a half later. So there were a lot of things that I went through.

As mentioned earlier, mothers seemed to be more affected by these transitions than were fathers. Even within the same family, men and women talked about the same transition differently. For example, one mother commented:

> I had just found out that I was pregnant when my husband transferred jobs to a new state. So, he moved first and I stayed behind to get everything settled. I moved up here in July and that's about 2 months before my first child was born. That was a hard time for me because we lived in a hotel for 6 weeks because we couldn't get into the house we had bought. I didn't know anyone here and I was pregnant and stuck in a hotel and the weather was miserable.

However, this woman's spouse made no mention at all in his story of the pregnancy period or the move to a new state. Similarly, another mother stated:

> I had a rough adjustment moving away from my family to a new state and being pregnant and all the feelings you have when you're pregnant for the first time.

In contrast, her spouse only makes a brief statement about the move:

> … then I got a job in another state, so we moved out here and all things progressed normally.

There could be several explanations for this gender difference. First, it may be that men and women feel similarly about such transitions, but women are more likely to express their feelings to others verbally. Alternatively, men and women may have different perceptions of this kind of social transition. Research findings consistently report that women receive a significant amount of support from their friends and coworkers, whereas men tend to rely heavily on their spouses for support (Antonucci, 1983; Belle, 1991; Hobfoll, 1986; Sarason et al., 1983). Thus, with any geographic relocation, it is probable that the husband is taking his most important source of support with him, whereas the wife is likely to be leaving significant relationships behind (Lynch, 1998). Thus, such a change is likely to create more social isolation and loss for women. For the women in our study, this transition was complicated by the fact that most were pregnant or new mothers at the time of the move. It is not surprising, then, that their recollection of this experience is much different from that of their spouses.

Support from extended family members

Another factor that affected the amount and type of social support received by our families involved relationships with extended family members. When one develops a formal romantic relationship with another person, often increases the size of their his or her social network by the addition of the partner's extended family. Most subjects talked about extended family members as providing welcome and positive emotional and companionship support to them. Also, women in our study discussed support from extended family members much more often than men (21 mothers vs. 4 fathers) and focused a lot on emotional support:

> My husband's family is very close. We see each other all the time, every weekend. We've always enjoyed each other, we do everything together.

And:

> I am the youngest of 4 children, 3 brothers, and I was the first one to have a baby. So, my brothers called me every day. They came with their video cameras when the baby was born. I wasn't the kind of mother who needed rest, I was more than happy to see anybody. When I came home from the hospital, mom had everybody over and we were passing the baby around.

And:

> I was pampered by my brother and my mom and dad, and even my spouse's family. They'd be like, you know, 'be careful outside, there's ice out there,' and "be real careful with your wife, keep her arm." I felt a bit resentful, because I thought I was capable and didn't need a constant escort, but I understood why they were doing it.

Two fathers also described feeling close to their extended families:

> Both of us have very, very close families and the families know each other.

And:

> I think our families are alike. Both [my and my wife's] families are from "the old country." And we are all pretty close knit. We all had some pretty strong values

about families and loving each other. I think that was a real connection between [my wife] and I when we first met.

Another father found the addition of his wife's extended family support more difficult to adjust to:

I'm an immigrant. I'm a first generation.... So, I didn't have a real family here [in this country].... That wasn't very easy, but I managed okay. I met [my wife], got married, and then I became involved in her family. And it was foreign to me because her family is pretty close, and I didn't, you know, it was tough, but I got used to it and I enjoyed it.... I'd been a very private person, I guess you'd say a loner type all my life, and it's hard for me to open up to people. And being around [my wife's] family—they were very open and it enabled me to be more open.... I'm a completely different person than I was 10 years ago.... I can talk with people comfortably now.... The interaction with [my wife's] family helped me a lot.

Summary

At this time in their family development, couples engaged in multiple roles, including spouse, worker, and friend. The time period after marriage was marked by numerous changes in social support. These included adapting to a new extended family network, geographic relocations related to job changes for one or both spouses, and adjusting to the marital relationship. The adjustment to the marital relationship was described as smoother and more positive by those couples who spent time together for several years prior to the birth of their first child. Both men and women described this time together as a couple as an important and enjoyable time in their lives.

A few couples were just beginning to think about what the role of parent might be like and how it would change their relationship. This mother describes the preparation for this next period in her family's development:

And the last day [of being pregnant] walking out to go to the hospital, we both looked at the house and we both knew it was the last moment we would ever be alone together. We knew there was a change that was taking place.

This transition would bring dramatic changes in the social support participants would receive and have to give to each other and to children.

Becoming a Family: Social Support After the Birth of the First Child

Fifty mothers and 36 fathers in the sample discussed some aspect of social support prior to the birth of their first child. As parents transitioned from being a couple to being a family with multiple members, so did their support networks. Their description of parenting their first child included changes in support across all areas of their lives. Parents consistently discussed social context changes related to the addition of a baby into their relationship, geographic relocations, changes in work roles, and increased extended family interaction. Themes that arose consistently in parents' stories during this time period included experiences of isolation and loss. For example, spending time taking care of a new baby, geographic relocations, and quitting work to take care of the baby greatly decreased time with friends and the ability to engage in a variety of social activities.

Another prominent social context theme that arose was the struggle to adjust to extended family members' involvement with the new baby and their parenting. Several themes arose that involved adapting to the social role of parent. These included defining, adjusting to, and learning the role of parent, and creating a renewed social network and social activities that integrated their parenting role. Finally, changes in the spousal relationship also occurred as people adjusted to being coparents; and, for a few, those adjustments resulted in the first divorces of couples in our study.

Social isolation and decreased social support from friends

Other researchers have found that parents' social contexts change with the birth of their first child. Cowan and Cowan (1992) note that young adults often become socially isolated when they marry and begin to start families. Especially for women, the birth of the first child often results in a significant decrease in social interactions with nonparenting friends and coworkers. Women have more people in their support network, but often have unreciprocated support in these relationships because they are providing more support than they receive, which can cause stress (Antonucci, 1994). For example, young adulthood is a time when women often begin employment careers, marry, and start having children. Although work relationships, other friendships, and partner relationships may provide adequate support for women before they become parents, these supportive relationships can be disrupted by the birth of the first child (Cowan & Cowan, 1992). This can result in a significant increase in stress, especially if the woman perceives her husband as nonsupportive. Thus, a new mother may find her emotional and physical energy taxed by the demands of a new infant, who cannot reciprocate, at the same time that she is receiving less support from others in her network.

The large majority of mothers and fathers in our study described decreases in social support as a result of becoming parents, but in different ways. Mothers felt more isolated, which was compounded if they had recently moved to a new geographic location. For example, this mother states:

I think it was still hard for me when he was a real little baby because we didn't have any family and I didn't know anyone; and with it being winter and having a new baby and not knowing anybody, you don't go out of the house. I think it was kind of depressing, you know, but, in a sense it was exciting too. But I remember being like, I couldn't wait to get out of the house, you know, being stuck in the house with a baby and he was a very crabby baby, you know, and so, that didn't help.

Another mother more clearly states the loss of support that results from relocation and increased isolation:

We had no family anywhere in the area, so we didn't have any family to turn to. And I was one of the first of my friends to have kids, so I didn't have friends to turn to—even for advice or for things to do.

Another factor that compounded women's sense of isolation was leaving their job, as this mother describes:

… Everything was different. I had been working and then I'm home with a baby. I found it a big adjustment, I really did. Mostly because we were new in the neighborhood, I didn't know anybody. So you're isolated with a baby, it's wintertime, you're in a house alone with a baby all day. It was a lonely time, really.

Another mother states:

The thing that was hard for me was that I quit work—totally. It was hard for me to adjust to that. I was all of a sudden cleaning diapers and I felt isolated and I felt … sort of unimportant, you know, after working full-time and working with adults and having responsibilities. And all of a sudden there I was at home doing what I think are important things but at the time didn't seem important.

For men, the role of parent did not come with the same stress and isolation, although fathers did feel a significant decrease in companionship support or time spent doing activities with friends, which they seemed to find stressful. One father describes:

Maybe I had rose-colored glasses on about having the kids and they're a lot of work, there's clearly no doubt about that. Your lifestyle changes as soon as you become a—have a kid. You go out and it's not like you stay out as late as you want. I mean, you're not the last ones to leave anymore, you're not the ones who are there 'till the end. Because you've got to go home to get the baby-sitter home, I mean, that was always the excuse, but in the back of your mind, it was always I want to go home to see the kids. Some of the things we, you know … we tried to make sure that they didn't dominate our life.

And another father states:

Well, social life was a lot different. Once I became a father, the social drinking stopped. From when I was partying a lot to now— it's like hardly ever.

Recreating a support network

Most mothers described that first year as a time when they needed more social support, and it took some time before they could make adjustments to renew their social network. Some found other parents to connect with, whereas others returned to work to regain contact with their peers. The following mothers describe this transition:

> Probably when they were almost about 1, we met some people; then we just started meeting some people with kids around the same age and we started trading off. And that was good for me, and I knew that I was the kind of person that just needed space for myself and just [being] away, you know, at times. Again, I look back and remember feeling truly unhappy during that first year. I never felt the unhappiness that I felt at that time with my second child. And it must have just taken me that year to—even though, like I said, it was my choice to quit work and I could've gone back anytime. I mean, we [my husband and I] never discussed it. So, that's why I was unhappy. I think it was just it took me a while to really adapt to a different style of living.

And:

> We moved from out of state right into our apartment here. I didn't know anybody except a couple of friends. My husband had friends from his new workplace that kind of adopted us. So we got involved into their family so we weren't alone for holidays and stuff. Then I met more and more moms, joined a nursing mothers' group, and got my own network of friends.

And:

> I felt really isolated like it was just she [the baby] and I. So, what I did was, just to keep my sanity, I took a part time job working 3 days a week just to see some people because there was no one to talk to [at home with the baby]. So just to be halfway decent as a mother too—to keep mentally okay—I worked.

Fathers, though, were more likely to describe the need to accept the changes in their social activities, rather than make specific adaptations. This father's statement is exemplary:

> When he was born I'd go out with [friends] less and less and be home by 10:30, 11 o'clock in case [my spouse] wanted me to watch the baby. Then a lot of them just drifted off completely. So, I'd stay home with my little baby most of the time. Yeah, my friends drifted off 'cause they were all single and liked to go out and

party a lot. And I'd just become a parent, and I started getting out of that stage for a while. Then I got back into it, but I didn't go out a lot—I stayed home and partied. Then, finally, I just got out of it completely.

After the initial adjustment to defining and learning the role of parent, couples found it much more enjoyable. For example:

In retrospect, living with that child after I made the adjustment to the crying and then he started reacting to me and everything, it was really a lot of fun.

Some parents adjusted to this by seeking out support from professionals, such as doctors:

I didn't know what I was supposed to do, all I know is it came easy for me. I was scared in the beginning like most women, I didn't know what to do. I'd call my doctor every 5 minutes, whether he needed it or not or whether she needed, I mean, she's spitting up, she's not doing this, she should be doing this, she's not, you know, and finally everybody goes through that. That's just being new. Then, after that, it just became a pleasure, and I took great pride and pleasure in it.

With this adjustment also came renewed activities between spouses who were able to integrate the child into their time together by taking the baby on trips and, later, by engaging in children's activities such as sports and playing with other kids. One mother describes:

After the first three months I became more adjusted and summertime came and I saw my friends more, and they all had children and we did a lot of things together with our children. So, that was a real nice part of my life.

Another mother states:

Well, he was born in July, and we took him camping. He loved camping, he loved water. So we did—anywhere we went, he went.

And a father provides this description:

Then it was fun! I think we had a good time. We took her right away on a couple of trips with us ... and we still were able to, you know, go out with her. She tended to sleep in restaurants and things like that. Then I figure after about 6 months, we finally got baby-sitters and, I think, probably later on during that time we had met some other people with children her age and got into that kind of a groove. Then, you know, we did a lot of activities.

Extended family support: mixed blessings

Becoming a parent also changed the amount of time and type of interactions couples had with their extended family members. An equal number of mothers and fathers described extended family support (22 parents in all discussed this area to some extent). Most new parents described receiving helpful support and companionship from their extended family, such as taking care of the baby, visiting and spending time together, and providing advice. For example:

> I guess if we had any questions as far as health concerns, you know, if she got sick or something, we always relied on [my husband's] dad because he's a retired OB/GYN.

And:

> My younger brother would watch the baby at times so we could get out of the house.

Also:

> [My wife] and her mother were relatively close. When she had questions, it was easy to call her mom and ask her about things. That worked out real good.

All 11 fathers who discussed support from extended family made positive statements. However, several mothers described feeling a lack of support from extended family members. This was due to feeling criticized for their parenting, rather than receiving helpful advice. One mother states:

> [It was difficult] having the interference from my mother all the time, because she was, you know, kind of always telling me, "Oh you're not feeding him enough" and all this.

Another mother commented:

> Every time he cried, I picked him up. My mom said, "Don't do that." But I had to, it was my baby.

And another mother struggled with criticism about breast feeding:

> I don't remember calling my mom very much or anything like that. I would actually, if something bothered me, I'd probably call a doctor before I'd call my mother, because she would—she had these old theories about, you know, I mean she never breast-fed her kids, and she thought I was being obnoxious breast-feeding my children. You know, I mean, "Mom, this is what I'm doing, just hush up. I'll go in the bedroom if you don't like it, no problem." And grandma kept saying, "you're not feeding him enough, he's waking up too much, you're not feeding him."

Another mother simply stated:

> I nursed for 14 months and my mother kept saying, 'Isn"t it time to quit? Isn't it time to quit that?" You know, blah, blah, blah.

These experiences may have occurred only for women in our study and not for men (at least to the extent to men were discussed in the interview) due to others' perceptions and expectations of women as the primary care-taker of the baby. This difference in the parenting role was described in detail by the participants, as will now be described.

Spousal roles of parent and supporter

Parents found the adjustment to changing social roles and learning to be a parent a noteworthy change in their lives as one mother describes:

> The only problems we had really were, you know, as far as [my husband] and I, you know, was adjusting, you know. I didn't know really what my role was supposed to be, because I still wanted to be a party-er, but I wanted to be a mother, I wanted it all. And I wanted to work. And I wanted to be a good wife, and I wanted to be thin, and I wanted, I just wanted all of it.

Changes in social roles sometimes decreased the amount of support, particularly in the area of activities and advice available from friends for those who were the first of their friends to have children. It also came with the feeling that they were on display as new parents:

> It was really strange [to be a parent]. I was the first one of my friends to have a baby. So whenever we went back to [my hometown] twice a year, I felt like I was on view. You know, "let's see what it's like to have a baby."

As women adjusted to the role of mother as caretaker, men did not perceive parenting as primary to their role. They described fatherhood as more of a "helper" role. In this way, fathers perceived their role to be supporters of their spouse more than as primary caretakers of the baby. For example, this father describes:

> I was ready for it [being a father]. I helped the wife out as much as I could, which was fun. I used to help her, you know, change diapers and all that stuff, feed them, which was, you know, back then it was pretty neat.

This particular man's spouse also described him as, "Pretty good at helping because he would push the stroller." A different father states:

> Well, yeah uh, I didn't know what it was gonna be like. You know, I didn't know if it was gonna be, you know, crying babies all the time or whatever. And then again, I'm—I'm a father. You know, I mean, I try and help, but [my spouse] took, you know, certainly took the primary responsibility and this, that, and the other thing. However, it was neat. It was really really neat. Um, every age, even now,

you know, [my son is] 12 years old now. They go through their phases—it's enter-
taining. You know, different kinds of problems.

This father provides an even more in-depth description of what it was like to
take a secondary role as a supporter in parenting:

> I didn't really know what to expect. So, yeah, he cried, you know, he needed
> changing, he needed this, but he didn't seem to be an overly bothersome type baby
> to me. There were times when, although, clearly it was a case where I would get
> home from work [my wife] would be at the door and say, "He's yours, I'm out of
> here, I'm coming back when he's in bed, see you at 10, I just can't take him any-
> more." And I'd be like, "What are you talking about?" Here's this sweet young
> thing here, he's not doing anything, how can you do this? But, you're not around
> him full-time for that cost and demand and the pressure that they have. They want
> what they want from you. So, as far as what I expected, yeah, he was, he was not
> overly bothersome. He eventually got to sleep through the nights. [My wife]
> breast-fed him, and so she would wake up in the middle of the night to feed him
> and she'd do it in the room and I, you know, I would try to stay there awake; but,
> you know, after the first week or so I was kind of like—I could roll over and just go
> back to sleep. But we tried to share responsibilities as much as we could. I probably
> did more of that with [my first child] than the other ones [later children] because
> it was the first one. But also, because of the situation I had at work, I had much
> more time in the evenings back then than I have with the job I have now.

Fathers also viewed the parenting role as more focused on financial support
than did mothers. For example, these fathers state:

> We started accumulating the various and sundry items, such as a house. We did
> not spend a lot of time planning financially for the different things. I was work-
> ing, sometimes as much as double shifts, 7 days in a row—8 days, 9 days in a row.
> It was that type of a work schedule. So, I did not spend a lot of time with the fam-
> ily because I was doing about 16, 17, 18 hours at work.

And:

> [It was] a lot of stress. So, all of a sudden, that spontaneous intimacy in a variety
> of areas was gone and we had to bargain with the kid. Then we had to start to
> plan what was going to happen with our life. And we realized that we had to start
> doing a lot more planning to accommodate the new arrival. Plus we picked up
> the instant financial burden. All of a sudden, buying diapers. I remember the big-
> gest budget change was when he got out of diapers. We started moving away from
> the expensive baby foods and feeding him normal things.

Support between spouses: Renewal and divorce

Most parents said that having a baby did not change the quality of their relationship a great deal, but their roles in relation to each other did change regarding parenting responsibilities and mutual support. One father stated that:

We both felt it was better for the mother to stay home with the baby. Not like modern times where both parents are still working. That was the major change in our life. And we thought we might actually have some problems. But as it turned out we didn't have any problems, we just cut a few places here and there as far as expenditures. You know, tightened up on the budget a little bit. Ever since then, [my spouse] has been staying home with the kids. We enjoy it a lot more. We certainly have—like we are together more.

Another father states:

It was all new stuff to me. I enjoyed it. We basically, we shared responsibilities. There was nothing really—I don't think it really changed our lives as far as our own relationship between the two of us.

For other couples, adjusting to parenting as a couple meant deciding to divorce because they could no longer negotiate their time together, support for each other, and/or their role as parents. One mother who divorced during this time described her relationship this way:

He stayed the same after the baby was born, but I had to change. You know, he didn't give up anything. I changed for the baby. You know, I had to give up this or that. You know, more with staying home, more giving up things, you know—more responsibility. I took it on, he didn't.

Another mother also described a lack of support from her spouse, as well as a lack of understanding for her role as a mother:

I mean, I loved [the baby], but it was not a lot of enjoyment for me. I think, just because, it was very time consuming. I think because my husband was working, and he continued his work, it didn't [work out]. He'd just come home in the evening; it didn't affect him like it did me. You know, he could enjoy [the baby] for the times that she was enjoyable, but it didn't change his life as much. I think it was hard for him to see why, you know, it was difficult for me just because he didn't go through the same kind of change that I did.

Summary

For our participants, the birth of their first child created numerous changes in the social support that they needed, received, and provided. Mothers described needing more support from friends and spouses because they felt isolated at home caring for the new baby, which took them away from their normal daily routine with friends and coworkers. Fathers did not experience this loss in support, but they did note the loss in activities with their friends, especially after work and on weekends.

Additionally, a noteworthy event that occurred during this time was that fathers took on the role of helper in parenting the baby. In this way, fathers provided support to the new baby by participating in his/her care, but this is not necessarily support provided directly to their spouses. The decrease in companionship and emotional support passed directly between spouses often placed a strain on the relationship.

Couples were faced with the need to adapt to these changes. It was important for them to take steps to reintegrate their support network by finding play groups, going back to work, and making new friends who also had children. Couples adjusted to decreases in their time spent together by organizing new activities as a family. Integrating the child into spousal time together as well as finding child care from family members and baby-sitters in order to spend time alone helped couples rejuvenate their relationship and provide support directly to each other. For mothers, the importance of seeking out professionals for help and advice and sharing parental responsibilities with their spouses were noted as important sources of support to them.

Being a Family: Social Support After the Birth of Additional Children

The families in our study began having second children sooner rather than later (most within 1 to 3 years). Thirty-eight fathers and 43 mothers discussed social support in their lives after the birth of second and third children. As their families grew larger, parents reported less geographic relocations; but social network disruptions did continue to occur through divorce, deaths of extended family members, and even the death of one of the fathers in the study. Although there were continued losses in parents' social networks, the social context of their stories was dominated by providing support to multiple children, extended family relationships, further integration of friends into the life of the family, and negotiating the development of children's own social networks.

Social roles during this time period shifted somewhat for fathers as they became more integrated into the parenting role with the birth of a second child. However, mothers continued to take primary responsibility for parenting. One additional noteworthy change in roles during this time period came about as some couples found themselves caring for their older parents for the first time.

Lastly, most couples continued to struggle with finding time to spend together as a couple, rather than being dominated by activities with children. Also, several more couples divorced during this time period. These divorced parents discussed the difficulties of single parenthood and the need for support from people outside of the family.

Providing support to children

Although most parents were excited and happy about integrating additional children into their family, they discussed the stress of having to provide care and support to an additional child. This mother describes the fulfillment and emotional closeness of the family:

> That first year strengthened our family. It felt more like a family with more than one child. To me, 100% it was like we really were more of a family somehow, maybe because there was more interaction and more closeness.

But these parents describe the difficulty of providing support to two children:

> Anyway, so we went back to [my home state].... I had [my second child] here in [my home state]. And since that time there has been—there's definitely a change in a relationship when there is one child and then when there becomes two, because then a new baby needs a lot of your time and the baby that you had before isn't a baby anymore so they're still vying for your attention. So all of a sudden you have to try and divide everything as equally as you possibly can—your time and working with them and playing with them and cuddling and hugging and kissing them so it gets a lot more difficult after there's a second one.

And:

> Becoming the parent of [an additional child] was pretty much the same but, it's a lot, I guess it is more, it 's harder the second time only because you have, you know, the first child there and you feel like you're neglecting them, and yet the baby has needs and, you know, it's hard to split up your time. I'm not even sure you do it 50/50 at the time. It just seems like you don't want the, your first child to get jealous or anything so you have to be very careful.

Support received from others

Most parents continued to described their spouses and extended family members as supportive, as this mother states:

> It was kind of a change for me to have two children in the house after having one for quite a while—having to adjust to a second one. But I had a lot of help and support from my husband at that time and from family. So, I wasn't, as far as needing him [the baby], I wasn't kind of a clinging mother where I didn't want anyone else to take care of my children.

In general, parents reported that extended family members helped less with parenting over time, but stepped in when there was a crisis, as these two mothers discuss:

I had to have surgery 4 weeks after the second child was born. My mom had to stay with me for about 6 weeks.

And:

After my first child was a year old, my husband died, and that changed our lives a lot. I was able to get family to watch the kids while I worked. My mother helps me a lot.

Although instrumental and emotional support from extended family was described as important, companionship support was the most important focus of parents' relationships with their extended family. Over time, parents developed special activities to do with their extended family, including ritual visits around holidays and summer vacations. This mother describes the importance of regular contact with extended family, at the same time relying on support from friends when family members were unavailable:

We try to, since our families are so far away in [another state], we try to do the best kind of bonding that we can. When they were smaller it was a hello on the phone and the older they got, the more accustomed they got to their week in a compacted visit with the family—and to know who everyone was. And we had a picture on the wall, "This is your grandma and this is your other grandma." So, it was hard, but a lot of other people—it's nice out here because there's a lot of people who have been transported. We're not the only ones who are isolated from their families and stuff.

However, some couples still found that extended family members could be more stressful than supportive due to continued criticisms. One father described it this way:

I guess, being that both kids are the only grandchildren on my side of the family—[I'm] from a fairly large family of five kids, me being the oldest brother of four boys and a girl, and none of them have kids—there was a lot of pressure from them [about how to] raise our kids, and obviously they all knew how to do it and they had done it before. It was, I never really let it bother me. It's my family and I can slough it off. I think [my spouse] always let it bother her a little bit more. It's the same on her side of the family.

Finally, receiving support from friends increased during this time period due to parents' abilities to renew peer networks. Renewing peer support networks required making new friends who also had children or getting involved in local social systems such as the church. These parents (a mother and a father, respectively) described this renewal:

Most of the time we [my child and I] got together—it had to be, we'd drive to a friend's house or we took him to somebody he met from preschool. And I always have done that. Just because we don't live by somebody doesn't mean we can't have friends.

And:

We became quite involved in the church that we still go to. So, we got some stability there. We've been at that church now for over 9 years, and have got to know those people.

Home alone? Support in the parenting role

Mothers talked about spousal support, and the lack thereof, much more often than did fathers (23 mothers compared to 6 fathers). Fathers continued to take on supporter roles in parenting, rather than as direct caretakers, and many mothers described a lack of adequate support from their spouses for parenting. For example, as these mothers described it:

I think it was hard for me with [the two children], because [my daughter] was only 19 months old when [my son] was born. So, that part I think was hard for me because [my husband] was going to school all the time and I felt like I was alone with two babies, you know? And sometimes I felt like I was expecting more of [my daughter] than I should have at her age, you know, because she was—I had two babies in diapers, you know?… And all this time [my husband's] been going to school. And that was different as [far as] my expectations of a family and as parents.

And:

The worst time I had was summers, because my husband likes to play ball. There were many summers I felt like I was stuck with two kids. There was one summer, I was stuck with two kids and he was playing ball 3 days a week. That's a lot to play ball…. And my husband would have 10 more kids, but—he's the type, he'd help out at times when he has nothing to do, but if we go to a family reunion or something, I don't see my husband. I'm stuck with two kids. I resent that.

Some fathers commented on this strain in the relationship, but they did not relate the magnitude of their spouse's stress:

It was tougher on my wife because I'd go away to work and I'd come home and she'd have two kids. I'd have to say there was a decent amount of strain there, but it was also strain for both of us really. We felt a lot of pressure from being tied down.

And:

She [my wife] did a whale of a job working with the kids. It would have driven me crazy I think to be at home all the time with it. She's got tremendous patience. She's used to kids. We both love them, but she's very patient and very good.

And:

> I was never gone away from home that much, but I probably ought to have taken
> her feelings into consideration a lot more than I had in the past. Because she was
> stuck at home sometimes during the day with two kids, and I was less inclined to
> call her and say I was going somewhere after work, or something like that, with-
> out checking the situation out first. I think, in that sense, it made me a lot more
> aware of some of the pressures she was under during the day. It made it tough for
> her at times, I know. And she'd get upset during the day, more so than she did
> when she had one child. And sometimes I'd come home and she'd be on edge
> and she'd kinda jump on me for something and I'd jump back at her. It made for
> … when the kids were real small, I'd say, situations where one or more were on
> edge 'cause of the responsibilities and stuff.

And another father thought a TV would help the situation:

> When we first got married we did not have or want a television. And then, with
> me being out roughly 3 nights a week until midnight every night and then study-
> ing the rest of the time, my wife needed something to occupy her time at home.
> Plus, we only had one car at the time so she was pretty limited in her mobility and
> ability to get out. And so, we went out and bought a television.

This father describes himself as an involved parent, but only after leaving infant care primarily to his spouse:

> And I think as the children have gotten older I've become more involved. I enjoy
> showing them things and asking them questions and listening to their responses
> and seeing where they—how they think about things and where they're at. And
> the more they can interact with people, the more I enjoy it. Whereas, as babies
> they have no interaction and they make messes and they drool. I didn't like that.
> But um, parenting, I guess for me didn't start until they were able to have a little
> bit of interaction with me. So, then it was basically an inconvenience, if I can put
> it that way, because it changed our lifestyle as we used to know it with just the
> two of us, and I wasn't really getting anything back for that. But now that they're
> older, I get a lot of it back. They're a lot of fun just to take to the store or to help
> me with the lawn or whatever. Because not only do they help me, and they're
> willing to do that, but they always come up with the darndest questions. They
> make me laugh a lot and I enjoy that.

However, not all mothers were dissatisfied with their spouse's parenting and
there was a wide range of behaviors that were considered helpful. These two
mothers express the range of helpful coparenting:

> I noticed with each baby my husband would help more. You know, with the first
> baby I would have to ask him to change a diaper and by the second or third one
> he would know what to do.

And:

> And Dad was equally good giving his attention to everybody. In fact, he's—I'm
> not saying this for the tape recorder but—he's about as ideal as they come as a fa-
> ther. I tease him that if he was as good to me as he was to them, we could write a
> marriage manual. He is just superb. Not overly indulgent, but giving of his time.
> If they want to play catch, "I'm tired, but we'll play catch," and that type of thing.
> He gave up some of his interests when the boys started being real busy so that he
> could be at every ball game that they have or every PTA, concert, whatever. So
> it's not one of those, "Mother's a teacher so she's interested and I'm not."

Support between spouses: Renewal and divorce

This theme appears again in this time period as it did after the birth of the first
child. The change and disruption that additional children bring to the spousal
relationship requires that parents renew their relationship as a couple. Again,
some adaptations meant divorce for several more couples, while other participants found ways to maintain mutual support. This parent describes the challenge of making time for each other:

> But, basically that's it—[my husband] and I have—we figured it out the other
> night, my husband and I don't—the only time that we've ever lived alone to-
> gether is for like 6 months out of our entire marriage, which has been almost 15
> years now. It's been kind of crowded. So, we always had family or friends or some-
> body stay with us.

And this parent describes reengaging in companionship support as a couple after the children get a little older as helpful to their relationship:

> I find that as they get older, more independent, there's more time for us. Uh, it's
> like today, he had the day off, I had the day off, so we spent the day together. We
> went to [a small town], went shopping—furniture, looked at furniture, just you
> know—that's good. We find our time together. It's no problem.

This father expresses some ambivalence about feeling close to his spouse, but
yet describing separate, nonshared, activities:

> With the kids, I think, we definitely have a more hectic lifestyle because we're
> running here with one and here with another. It kind of makes my wife and I
> closer. A lot closer family group like. We're more concerned about it than our-
> selves. Obviously. The kids. That's almost all it is. It's so hard for us to get time to
> ourselves or—in fact, we have even taken short vacations separately. She will go
> away for a week with some friends or I go hunting or something. It's just so hard
> for us to get away together that it just doesn't happen, unfortunately. But it's a
> good trade-off.

Other couples were unable to renew their relationship and decided to divorce. For this participant, divorce did not mean an end to the support that her ex-husband provided to their children:

> My ex-husband and all that? Well, it was a close relationship we had, so the kids did grow up in a very loving home. We had some husband–wife squabbles, things like that, but I think both kids came up in a very loving relationship to begin with, and still is, an excellent parent. I couldn't ask for a better father for the children. They love their father very much and they look forward to seeing him. And considering that he does live a long ways away, he does make every effort to be with the children and often has to take time off from work to do it. I think in their growth and development this was a very important aspect for the kids, because there are so many fathers who just don't make this effort to see their children. And I encourage that their father does love them even though he doesn't live with them.

However, not all parents had this experience:

> When she [my second child] came along, I went through a divorce. So, then I basically raised her and my son by myself until just a couple of years ago and I got remarried.

Some parents adjusted to this by adopting a family system where the children were expected to provide more support than they might have otherwise. For example, this mother states:

> The girls benefitted from it [the divorce], I believe for the future, because I became very self-sufficient. I didn't have any child support coming, I didn't ask him for any because he, at that time he wasn't working. And I always felt what's the sense of my going after money from him when it's only going to make him more mad and he's going to take it out on the kids. That's ridiculous. I make a damn good salary. So I always left him alone. But I was always very self-sufficient. The girls have seen me, as they grew up, paying for sitters, doing everything myself, you know, doing everything. I was the total singular parent.... [But] they help me around the house; they cleaned this room. You know, "I'm gonna be late. Make sure the room is clean." They're 9 and 10, and the room is clean for company. And they do their own laundry, they'll do the dishes, they help me 100%. I told them, and explained to them, that this is a group effort, you know?

Summary

Participants described the time after the birth of additional children as a time of reorganization and restructuring of their whole support system. Support from friends and family members became more consistent, fathers became more integrated into the parenting role as children grew older, activities with extended family members became more systematic, and children learned to provide support to the family in ways that were age appropriate. Mothers again described a difficult transition after the birth of their second child, marked by loneliness, strain, and isolation. Parents adapted to spreading their support between two or more children as well as between each other. Many parents who could not negotiate these roles divorced and found new ways to provide support to the children separately.

CONCLUSION AND IMPLICATIONS

The stories the parents in our study shared regarding the development of their families, from being a couple through the birth of their children, highlight, in a personal way, what previous studies have suggested. The birth of the first child, traditionally viewed as the first developmental step in the process of becoming a family (Germain, 1994), can often create a crisis for a couple due to the enormous changes and adjustments necessary to accommodate this addition to their lives (Worthington & Buston, 1986). These adjustments include changes in role expectations; changes in lifestyle; and, as is the focus in this chapter, changes in the amount, type, and quality of social support the parents provide to and receive from each other and external sources.

These changes in social support can significantly affect the relationship each parent has with the child, as well as their relationship with each other. With the birth of additional children, new adjustments in the provision and receipt of support have to be made. In the next section, we discuss the practice and policy implications of the changes in social support that occur as couples become parents.

Practice Implications

Studies examining marital relationships during the transition to parenthood have consistently found a decrease in marital satisfaction after the birth of the first child (Worthington & Buston, 1986). Although this is attributed to several factors, including physical and financial stressors, changes in social support appear to have a major effect (Cowan and Cowan, 1992). This may be due to the fact that these changes are so widespread, affecting multiple aspects of the new parents' lives, from their relationship with each other to their relationships with extended family and friends. This appears to be particularly true for mothers, who often find themselves isolated and cut off from important sources of support after their first child is born.

A new mother may find her emotional and physical energy taxed by the demands of a new infant at the same time that she is receiving less support from others in her network due to a decrease in contact. As is reflected in the stories told by the mothers in this study, many women quit their jobs to stay home with their first baby. And because they have not previously been parents, many first-time mothers do not know other women with infants or small children. Consequently, the birth of the baby can often result in a significant decrease in social interactions with coworkers and nonparent friends.

Another significant issue discussed by several mothers in this study was the effect of moving to a new town. Women are likely to be more negatively affected by being geographically isolated from family and friends, due to the fact that men focus heavily on one provider of support—their wife—whereas women most often turn to family and women friends for support (Belle, 1982; Schultz, 1991). Thus, when couples move, men are probably taking their most important source of support with them, but women are likely to be leaving significant relationships behind.

All of these factors can result in a decrease in social interactions and an increase in stress for new mothers, especially if a woman feels her husband is not supportive. The fact that marital satisfaction decreases more for women after the birth of their first child than for men (Worthington & Buston, 1986) also may be due to new mothers feeling that becoming a parent has been more disruptive to their life than to their spouse's—like many of the women in our study. Despite some cultural changes in gender role expectations, most studies show that new mothers shoulder a majority of the responsibility for infant care, and often feel overwhelmed by their new responsibilities (Worthington & Buston, 1986). Unfortunately, because men and women sometimes do not perceive support in the same way (Burks & Parke, 1996; Ingersoll-Dayton & Antonucci, 1988; Jarvinen & Nicholls, 1996; Schultz, 1991), husbands may feel they are being very supportive whereas their wives may view the support they receive as being less than adequate.

When working with first-time parents, it is important to recognize the effect changes in social support have on the marital relationship and, thus, on the relationship the new parents have with the baby. Mothers who feel overwhelmed and unsupported are likely to have a harder time coping with the demands of an infant. This can negatively affect their interactions with the child as well as their view of their ability to be a good parent (Kissman, 1989; Koeske, 1990). Similarly, new father may be resentful about the loss of his wife's attention and may be hurt and confused by his wife's marital dissatisfaction.

Zaslow and Pederson (1981) identified three areas related to social support that need to be addressed with first-time parents, preferably before the birth of the baby. First, the couple should be encouraged to identify and clarify their individual and joint needs for support. Expectations regarding parenting roles and responsibilities should be discussed candidly to identify areas of potential conflict. Fathers who are aware of their wives' expectations for involvement with child rearing may be more likely to live up to those expectations (Harriman, 1983). This should be presented as an ongoing process, since support needs are likely to change over time as parenting roles and patterns are established, especially with the birth of additional children.

Furthermore, both parents need to maximize the social support they have. This is especially important immediately following the birth of the baby, and entails identifying what is and, as importantly, what is not supportive. For example, many of the couples in our study described their ambivalence about the advice they received from their parents regarding care for the new baby. This is not surprising, because advice can often feel more critical than supportive (Rook, 1992). Expectant parents should be encouraged to discuss with each other their expectations around the day-to-day involvement of the baby's grandparents, each identifying the level of involvement with which they are comfortable.

It may be especially helpful for expectant and new parents to identify people, besides their spouses, whom they feel comfortable contacting when they need support. Normalizing their need for such support is important. As has been mentioned, new mothers who receive less social support often experience more stress, and tend to be less satisfied with and feel less adequate in their mother role (Cowan & Cowen, 1992; Kissman, 1989; Koeske, 1990.). Emphasizing the fact that the need for support is a normal, expected part of being a new parent may allow both the mother and father to reach for help outside the marital relationship with less feelings of inadequacy.

In addition to exploring ways in which first-time parents can access informal sources of support, it is appropriate to discuss more formal sources that may be available. For example, peer groups can provide new parents with informational and emotional support. Dubow et al. (1991) found that parents who received ongoing support from structured peer support groups acquired better parenting skills, including the expression of supportive behaviors toward their children. These children were found to have better adjustment in a variety of behavioral, mental health, and academic areas.

A final issue to discuss with expectant or new parents is the need to find time for each other. It is important that both partners continually work toward mutual understanding and support. Intimacy-promoting activities should be planned, with the couple spending some amount of time weekly focused on each other and their relationship. Again, normalizing the need for the couple to set aside time just for each other may decrease any feelings of guilt at wanting time away from the baby. Furthermore, intimacy, mutual understanding, and support may require that both parents examine their role in the spousal–parenting relationship, as well as in the larger family system (e.g., with extended family), and the sociocultural expectations and constraints placed on these roles. For example, a feminist perspective on couples/family counseling focuses on power inherent in each member's role. This includes economic control over earning and managing money, expectations of "fee labor" involved in taking care of a household, providing emotional support to others, and day-to-day decision making. Relatedly, clinicians should always assess the presence of domestic violence between couples, which may influence how decisions are made in families, the amount of support that is provided by some members of the family to others, and the amount of formal and informal support needed by the survivor of the violence (see Campbell, 1995 and Jasinski & Williams, 1998 for further information regarding the prevalence and assessment of violence).

Policy Implications

Obviously, the transition to parenthood is easier if both parents have an adequate amount of social support available. In the United States, however, there are few cultural structures in place to ensure, or even make likely, that new parents receive the support needed. Since World War II, American families have become increasingly isolated from both informal and formal sources of support that have traditionally been available, including kinship systems, churches, neighborhoods, and communities (Hartman & Laird, 1983). To make matters worse, social policies that affect families in this country tend to be based on the out-dated definition of the normative family as "a working father, a nonworking mother, and two children under the age of eighteen" (Macarov, 1995).

Even national policies that attempt to address family issues in a forward-thinking manner can be less than effective when implemented. A case in point is the Family and Medical Leave Act of 1993, which states, in part, that " … an employer must grant unpaid leave to an eligible employee … for the care of the employee's child (birth, or placement for adoption or foster care…. " The act intentionally excludes the mention of gender, and, therefore, opens the door for fathers to take a more active role not only in the birth of the baby, but also in the care of the new infant during the first few weeks of life. Unfortunately, fathers may find it difficult to take advantage of the act due to a lack of support by their employers (Macarov, 1995). Even if company policies allow extended childbirth leave for fathers, the company environment may inhibit fathers from taking time off for more than a few days.

Work environments tend to be more supportive of mothers in granting extended leave surrounding the birth of the baby; however, such leave policies are only a small part of the type of support most families need in order to negotiate their dual roles of parent and employee. The availability of informal support in the workplace as well as formal family benefits is correlated with increased satisfaction with both job and parenting roles, especially for mothers (Greenberger, 1989). Both mothers and fathers benefit most from work environments that allow for flexible job schedules and show explicit support for parenting roles and responsibilities (Greenberger, 1989; Shinn, Wong, Simko, & Ortiz-Torres, 1989).

According to Rothman and Marks (1987), during the 1970s, managers of offices and factories became aware that low employee morale was related to high absenteeism, low productivity, and poor work quality. Several Gallup poll surveys conducted at this time indicated that many employees were unhappy with their jobs due to the conflict they felt between work and family responsibilities. Therefore, managers began to experiment with flexible work schedules in response to a growing demand from the workforce.

Unfortunately, despite the success of flextime in increasing worker satisfaction and supporting parents who have small children at home, when financially able to do so, many women choose to leave their jobs after their first child is born. One often-cited reason for this decision is that work environments tend to be neither supportive enough nor flexible enough for mothers to juggle successfully the demands of work and a new baby (Greenberger, 1989; Shinn et al., 1989). This is linked to the fact that many organizations still adhere to a traditional professional ethos that see family responsibilities as secondary to those of work. There is evidence that such traditional views lead to policies that deprive both women and men of opportunities for quality family interaction (Rothman & Marks, 1987).

There are several ways social work practitioners can intervene on macro- and microlevels to support families and enhance opportunities for both mothers and fathers to be more active in childrearing. Obviously, social workers need to advocate for family-oriented personnel policies on both a national and a local level. However, it is as important that traditional views of work and family begin to be challenged. Only when national and organizational policies view family needs as being equivalent to employer needs can men and women receive and give the kind of support needed to negotiate the challenges of parenthood successfully. Additionally, policies that improve the availability (i.e., accessibility and affordability) and quality of formal or professional support systems, such as mental health services, support groups, and childcare, will increase the amount of instrumental and emotional support that parents can access as needed.

Research Implications

The majority of research in the area of social support has used survey reports to gain information about people's experiences of support. These survey answers are then quantified to access statistical relationships. This chapter represents one of the few research studies that has analyzed people's verbal, open-ended, descriptions of their social support and how it varied over an important developmental period—becoming a family. The information our participants provided was consistent with the majority of quantitative research studies about the nature and changes in social support. However, our study was able to provide a more personal view of the importance of support in people's lives. Using interview data allowed us to capture the quality and depth of people's personal experiences, rather than collapsing them into frequencies that have been categorized and defined by the researcher. The information provided in the chapter can now be used to exemplify, highlight, and/or personalize future quantitative studies of social support in families.

Future research should continue to clarify which kinds of support (e.g., advice, ventilation, companionship, concrete assistance, etc.) are most helpful for different life transitions and from whom is it most needed (e.g., spouses, extended family, friends, etc.). As our study found, being a couple before having children involved a high degree of companionship support between spouses as the amount of time spent with one's family of origin decreased. However, after the birth of a child, the adjustment to becoming family required an increase in extended family support as well as an increase in instrumental support between spouses and a need to spend time with friends from whom they felt isolated. These support needs changed again in later family development. Future research could continue to specify and clarify the nature and extent of these needs throughout the life span.

Finally, an emerging area of social support research explores the question: If social support has positive effects on people, what makes some people better at soliciting and maintaining supportive relationships than others? This area of research suggests that behavioral skills, personality style, and belief systems have an effect on people's reports of support from others. One important area to explore in family systems research like ours is how beliefs and practices of couples and families affect the amount of support they receive from others. For example, some families believe that asking for help from, or telling one's problems to, professionals or strangers is not acceptable because such information should be kept within the family. However, this kind of belief might restrict a family member from acquiring an adequate amount or type of support to meet his or her needs. Also, family members can become overburdened if they become the only providers of support to each other and if they do not reach out for help from others who might have special knowledge or skills that would be supportive.

Thus, there are a variety of areas needing future research. Studies should use a variety of methods for collecting information from participants, such as interviews, ethnography, observations, surveys, and experimental methods. Only then can we fully understand people's common, and uncommon, experiences and the nature or quality of those experiences.

REFERENCES

Antonucci, T. C. (1983). Social support: Theoretical advances, recent findings, and pressing issues. In I. G. Sarason & B. R. Sarason (Eds.), *Social support: Theory, research, and applications* (pp. 21–38). Boston: Martinus Nijhoff.

Antonucci, T. C. (1990). Social supports and social relationships. In R. H. Binstock & E. Shanas (Eds.), *Handbook of aging and social sciences* (pp. 205–226). New York: Academic Press.

Antonucci, T. C. (1994). A life-span view of women's social relations. In B. F. Turner (Ed.), *Women growing older: Psychological perspectives* (pp. 239–269) New York: Sage.

Antonucci, T. C., & Akiyama, H. (1987). Social networks in adult life and a preliminary examination of the convoy model. *Journal of Gerontology, 42*(5), 519–527.

Barrera, M. (1986). Distinctions between social support concepts, measures, and models. *American Journal of Community Psychology, 14,* 413–445.

Barrera, M., & Garrison-Jones, C. (1992). Family and peer social support as specific correlates of adolescent depressive symptoms. *Journal of Abnormal Child Psychology, 20,* 1–16.

Barrera, M., Sandler, I. N., & Ramsay, T. B. (1981). Preliminary development of a scale of social support: Studies on college students. *American Journal of Community Psychology, 9*(4), 435–447.

Barnett, R., Biener, L., & Baruch, G. (1987). *Gender and stress.* The Free Press.

Belle, D. (1982). The stress of caring: Women as providers of social support. In L. Goldberger & S. Breznitz (Eds.), *Handbook of stress: Theoretical and clinical aspects* (pp. 496–505). New York: The Free Press.

Belle, D. (1991). Gender differences in the social moderators of stress. In A. Monat & R. S. Lazarus (Eds.), *Stress and coping: An anthology* (3rd ed., pp. 258–274). New York: Columbia University Press.

Berndt, T. J. (1982). The features and effects of friendship in early adolescence. *Child Development, 53*(6), 1447–1460.

Burks, V. S., & Parke, R. D. (1996). Parent and child representations of social relationships: Linkages between families and peers. *Merrill-Palmer Quarterly, 42*(3), 358–378.

Campbell, J. C. (Ed.). (1995). *Assessing dangerousness: Violence by sexual offenders, batterers, and child abusers.* Beverly Hills, CA: Sage.

Cauce, A. M., Reid, M., Landesman, S., & Gonzales, N. (1990). Social support in young children: Measurement, structure, and behavioral impact. In B. R. Sarason, I. G. Saracon, & G. R. Pierce (Eds.), *Social support: An interactional view* (pp. 64–94). New York: Wiley.

Clark, M. S., Ouellette, R., Powell, M. C., & Milberg, S. (1987). Recipient's mood, relationship type, and helping. *Journal of Personality and Social Psychology, 53,* 94–103.

Coates, D. (1985). Relationships between self-concept measures and social network characteristics for Black adolescents. *Journal of Early Adolescence, 5,* 319–338.

Cohen, S. (1992). Stress, social support, and disorder. In H. O. F. Veiel & A. Baumann (Eds.), *The meaning and measurement of social support* (pp. 109–124). New York: Hemisphere.

Cohen, S., & Syme, S. L. (1985). Issues in the study and application of social support. In S. Cohen & S. L. Syme (Eds.), *Social support and health* (pp. 3–22). New York: Academic Press.

Cohen, S., & Wills, T. A. (1985). Stress, social support, and the buffering hypothesis. *Psychological Bulletin, 98*(2), 310–357.

Cowan, C. P., & Cowan, P. A. (1992). *When partners become parents: The big life change for couples.* New York: Basic Books.

Dubow, E. F., & Tisak, J., Causey, D., Hryshko, A., & Reid, G. (1991). A two-year longitudinal study of stressful life-events, social support, and social problem-solving skills: Contributions to children's behavioral and academic adjustment. *Child Development, 62,* 583–599.

Dunkel-Schetter, C., & Bennett, T. L. (1990). Differentiating the cognitive and behavioral aspects of social support. In B. R. Sarason, I. G. Saracon & G. R. Pierce (Eds.), *Social support: An interactional view,* (pp. 267–296). New York: Wiley.

Feiring, C., & Lewis, M. (1991). The development of social networks from early to middle childhood: Gender differences and the relation to school competence. *Sex Roles, 25*(3/4), 237–253.

Furman, W., & Buhrmester, D. (1992). Age and sex differences in perceptions of networks of personal relationships. *Child Development, 63,* 103–115.

Germain, C. B. (1994). Emerging conceptions of family development over the life course. *Families in Society, 75,* 254–268.

Gottlieb, B. H. (1988). Marshaling social support: The state of the art in research and practice. In B. H. Gottlieb (Ed.), *Marshaling social support: Formats, processes, and effects* (pp. 11–51). Newbury Park, CA: Sage.

Greenberger, E. (1989). Contributions of a supportive work environment to parents' well-being and orientation to work. *American Journal of Community Psychology, 17*(6), 755–783.

Harold, R. D., Palmiter, M. L., Lynch, S. A., & Freedman-Doan, C. R. (1995). Life stories: A practice-based research technique. *Journal of Sociology and Social Welfare, 22*(2), 23–44.

Harriman, L. C. (1983). Personal and marital changes accompanying parenthood. *Family Relations, 32*(2), 387–394.

Hartman, A., & Laird, J. (1983). *Family-center social work practice.* New York: The Free Press.

Heller, K., Swindle, R. W., & Dusenbury, L. (1986). Component social support processes: Comments and integration. *Journal of Consulting and Clinical Psychology, 54,* 466–470.

Henderson, S. (1981). Social relationships, adversity and neurosis: An analysis of prospective observations. *British Journal of Psychiatry, 138,* 391–398.

Hobfoll, S. E. (1986). *Stress, social support, and women.* New York: Hemisphere.

Hobfoll, S. E., Nadler, A., & Lieberman, J. (1986). Satisfaction with social support during crisis: Intimacy and self-esteem as critical determinants. *Journal of Personality & Social Psychology, 51*(2), 296–304.

House, J. S. (1981). *Work stress and social support.* Reading, MA: Addison-Wesley.

Ingersoll-Dayton, B., & Antonucci, T. C. (1988). Reciprocal and nonreciprocal social support: Contrasting sides of intimate relationships. *Journals of Gerontology, 43*(3), S65–S73.

Ishii-Kuntz, M. (1990). Social interaction and psychological well-being: Comparison across stages of adulthood. *International Journal of Aging and Human Development, 30*(1), 15–36.

Jarvinen, D. W., & Nicholls, J. G. (1996). Adolescents' social goals, beliefs about the causes of social success, and satisfaction in peer relations. *Developmental Psychology, 32*(3), 435–441.

Jasinski, J. L., & Williams, L. M (Eds.) (1998). *Partner violence: A comprehensive review of 20 years of research.* Beverly Hills, CA: Sage.

Jones, D. C. (1991). Friendships satisfaction and gender: An examination of sex differences in contributions to friendship satisfaction. *Journal of Social and Personal Relationships, 8,* 167–185.

Jones, D. C., Bloys, N., & Wood, M. (1990). Sex roles and friendship patterns. *Sex Roles, 23,* (3/3), 133–145.

Jones, D. C., & Costin, S. E. (1995). Friendship quality during preadolescence and adolescence: The contributions of relationship orientations, instrumentality, and expressivity. *Merrill-Plamer Quarterly, 41*(4), 517–535.

Jones, G. P., & Dembo, M. H. (1989). Age and sex role differences in intimate friendships during childhood and adolescence. *Merrill-Palmer Quarterly, 35*(4), 445–462.

Kahn, R. L., & Antonucci, T. C. (1980). Convoys over the life course: Attachment, roles and social support. In P. Baltes & O. Brim (Eds.), *Life span development and behavior* (Vol. 3, pp. 253–286). New York: Academic Press.

Kissman, K. (1989). Social support, parental beliefs, and well-being. *Youth and Society, 21*(1), 120–130.

Koeske, G. F. (1990). The buffering effect of social support on parental stress, *American Journal of Orthopsychiatry, 60*(3), 440–451.

Lakey, B., & Heller, K. (1988). Social support from a friend, perceived support, and social problem solving. *American Journal of Community Psychology, 16*(6), 811–824.

Levitt, M. J., Weber, R. A., & Guacci, N. (1993). Convoys of social support: An intergenerational analysis. *Psychology and aging, 8*(3), 323–326.

Lynch, S. A. (1998). Who supports whom? How age and gender affect the perceived quality of support from family and friends. *The Gerontologist, 28*(2), 231–238.

Macarov, D. (1995). *Social welfare: Structure and practice.* Sage.

Maguire, L. (1986). *Understanding social networks.* Thousand Oaks, CA: Sage.

Murray, H. A. (1938). *Explorations in personality.* New York: Oxford University Press.

Murstein, B. I., & Azar, J. A. (1986). The relationship of exchange-orientation to friendship intensity, roommate compatibility, anxiety, and friendship. *Small Group Behavior, 17*(1), 3–17.

Newcomb, M. D. (1990a). Social support by many other names: Towards a unified conceptualization. *Journal of Social and Personal Relationships, 7,* 479–494.

Newcomb, M. D. (1990b). Social support and personal characteristics: A developmental and interactional perspective. *Journal of Social and Clinical Psychology, 9*(1), 54–68.

Powell, T. J. (1990). Social networks and self-help organizations. In T. J. Powell (Ed.), *Working with self-help* (pp. 71–90). Silver Springs, MD: NASW.

Procidano, M. E., & Heller, K. (1983). Measures of perceived social support from friends and from family: Three validation studies. *American Journal of Community Psychology, 11*(1), 1–24.

Rook, K. S. (1992). Detrimental aspects of social relationships: Taking stock of an emerging literature. In H. O. F. Veiel & A. Baumann (Eds.), *The meaning and measurement of social support* (pp. 157–169). New York: Hemisphere.

Rothman, S. M., & Marks, E. M. (1987). Adjusting work and family life: Flexible work schedules and family policy. In N. Gerstel & H. E. Gross (Eds.), *Families and work,* (pp. 469–477). Philadelphia: Temple University Press.

Sandler, I. N., & Barrera, M. (1984). Toward a multimethod approach to assessing the effects of social support. *American Journal of Community Psychology, 12*(1), 37–52.

Sarason, B. R., Pierce, G. R., Shearin, E. N., Sarason, I. G., Waltz, J. A., & Poppe (1991). Perceived social support and working models of self and actual others. *Journal of Personality and Social Psychology*, 60(2), 273–287.

Sarason, I. G., Levine, H. M., Basham, R. B., & Sarason, B. R. (1983). Assessing social support: The social support questionnaire. *Journal of Personality and Social Psychology*, 44, 127–139.

Sarason, I. G., Sarason, B. R., & Pierce, G. R. (1990). Social support: The search for theory. [Special issue: Social support in social and clinical psychology]. *Journal of Social & Clinical Psychology*, 9(1), 133–147.

Shinn, M., Wong, N. W., Simko, P. A., & Ortiz-Torres, B. (1989). Promoting the well-being of working parents: Coping, social support, and flexible job schedules. *American Journal of Community Psychology*, 17(1), 31–55.

Schultz, K. (1991). Women's adult development: The importance of friendship. *Journal of Independent Social Work*, 5(2), 19–30.

Silverman, D. K. (1987). What are little girls made of? *Psychoanalytic Psychology*, 4(4), 315–334.

Smith, C. E., Fernengel, K., Holcroft, C., Gerald, K., & Marien, L. (1994). Meta-analysis of the associations between social support and health outcomes. *Annals of Behavioral Medicine*, 16(4), 352–362.

Streeter, C. L., & Franklin, C. (1992). Defining and measuring social support: Guidelines for social work practitioners. *Research on Social Work Practice*, 2(1), 81–98.

Thoits, P. A. (1982). Conceptual, methodological, and theoretical problems in studying social support as a buffer against life stress. *Journal of Health and Social Behavior*, 23, 145–159.

Turner, R. J. (1981). Social support as a contingency in psychological well-being. *Journal of Health and Social Behavior*, 22, 357–367.

Uchino, B. N., Cacioppo, J. T., & Kiecolt-Glaser, J. K. (1996). The relationship between social support and physiological processes: A review with emphasis on underlying mechanisms and implications for health. *Psychological Bulletin*, 119(3), 488–531.

Umberson, D., Chen, M. D., House, J. S., Hopkins, K., & Slaten, E. (1996). The effect of social relationships on psychological well-being: Are men and women really so different? *American Sociological Review*, 61, 837–857.

Vaux, A. (1985). Variations in social support associations with gender, ethnicity, and age. *Journal of Social Issues*, 41(1), 89–110.

Ward, R. A. (1985). Informal networks and well-being in later life: A research agenda. *The Gerontologist*, 25(1), 55–61.

Weiss, R. S. (1974). The provisions of social relationships. In Z. Rubin (Ed.), *Doing onto others*. Englewood Cliffs, NJ: Prentice-Hall.

Wethington, E., & Kessler, R. C. (1986). Perceived support, received support, and adjustment to stressful life events. *Journal of Health and Social Behavior*, 27, 78–89.

Wong, M. M., & Csikszentmihalyi, M. (1991). Affiliation motivation and daily experience: Some issues on gender differences. *Journal of Personality and Social psychology*, 60(1), 154–164.

Wood, W., Rhodes, N., & Whelan, M. (1989). Sex differences in positive well-being: A consideration of emotional style and marital status. *Psychological Bulletin*, 106(2), 249–264.

Worthington, E. L., & Buston, B. G. (1986). The marriage relationship during the transition to parenthood. *Journal of Family Issues*, 7(4), 443–473.

Wright, P. H. (1982). Men's friendship, women's friendships, and the alleged inferiority of the latter. *Sex Roles*, 8, 1–20.

Zaslow, M. J., & Pederson, F. A. (1981). Sex-role conflicts and the experience of childbearing. *Professional Psychology*, 12, 47–55.

6

Job Talk:
The Role of Work
in Family Life

Lucy R. Mercier
Rena D. Harold
Michigan State University

"What do you *do*?" is probably the single most asked question when making new acquaintances. Indeed, in contemporary America, work behavior and employment history are linked to personal and family identity, access to resources, and prediction of future economic and social success. Most studies of the impact of work on adults confirm that employment has a positive emotional effect for both men and women, and many recent studies emphasize that the majority of adults have little economic choice about working outside of the home (Menaghan & Parcel, 1991). For most families, then, the marketplace holds the keys to both survival and self-respect.

The very idea of work is value laden. That is, work is closely linked with concepts of goodness, moral purpose, and personal worthiness. Traditional ideas of the inherent value of hard work, sometimes called the Puritan work ethic, have been influential in shaping the cultural landscape in America. Consequently, one's occupation signifies both social status and individual identity. For example, a professional job such as attorney, physician, or business executive may be considered desirable based on social perceptions of difficulty, level of responsibility, salary, and opportunity for advancement. In contrast, employment as an agricultural laborer or factory worker carries considerably less prestige.

Ideas about status and perceptions of prestige pervade the work–family intersection as well. For families, of course, the idea of work is often linked with gender roles, and this traditional view contains a profound cultural conundrum. Structural conditions in American society continue to present powerful gender imperatives for type of work (Perry-Jenkins, 1994; Schooler, Miller, Miller, & Richtand, 1984). In most families, men are expected to be breadwinners and women are expected to demonstrate skills in caregiving and homemaking. Whereas men's paid work is rewarded financially and socially, women's roles as workers are often marked by ambivalence (Ferree, 1987; Larson, Richards, & Perry-Jenkins, 1994; Zavella, 1987) and discontinuity (Moen, 1985), as described in chapter 1's discussion of role theory. In fact, men are expected to work for pay outside the home, and families that contain male adults are assumed to have an economic and social advantage over households headed by women. At the same time, more and more families rely on the wages earned by women, with the result that mothers often return to paid work within weeks or months of the birth of a child. Many women work out of financial necessity, but others work because they gain pride, identity, and interpersonal contact in their jobs (Rosen, 1987).

Because social and cultural norms and values have been so slow to change, gender inequities continue to influence (subtly and otherwise) the work aspirations, employment histories, and relative salaries of most Americans. Development of knowledge about families and work also is slow to change, and research questions and conclusions reflect the larger cultural landscape. Study designs often limit the data collected by asking questions that are restricted by conventional ideas about the lives of respondents. For example, what research has been done on the ways in which *fathers* choose between staying at home or returning to work following the birth of a child?

GENDER AND WORK

The world of work is divided along gender lines. Employment opportunities continue to be gender segregated, with the result that there are fewer full-time jobs for women that offer a living wage. In addition, women's work lives are more likely than men's to be interrupted by the demands of family life, such as caring for a child or elderly relative, school vacations, or a husband's job relocation (Berk, 1985; Moen, 1985). Women also are more likely than men to mold their employment histories to the needs and desires of their families (Rosen, 1987). Some theorists believe that this combination of conditions leads to a unique problem for American women—employers are less willing to offer good jobs to women because of the perception that women are not fully invested in their work; and women are less likely to invest themselves in employment outside of the home that does not offer adequate pay, reasonable schedules, and opportunities for advancement (Ferber, 1982; Kessler-Harris, 1987).

Despite much rhetoric about the liberation of women in the United States, women continue to provide the bulk of unpaid household labor, even when they are employed outside the home (e.g., Warner, 1986). When families include children, demand for home labor increases. Rather than leveling the differences between the work loads of men and women, parenting actually increases gender differences in married and cohabiting heterosexual couples (Perkins & DeMeis, 1996). That is, women substantially increase their housework load, even when employed outside the home, after the addition of children to the family; in contrast, fathers' activity in several household tasks actually decreases with parenthood.

Gender roles influence the perceptions and experiences of daily interactions and activities. An interesting recent study of parents from a working-class community concluded that gender has important implications for individual perceptions of work. In this study, fathers reported more positive emotional experiences in the home, which they saw as a place of leisure and increased personal authority. In contrast, mothers reported more positive emotional experience away from home, perhaps because of the contrast between the structure of the job site and the ever-present and never-ending nature of housework. It seems that men often perceive paid work as an obligation over which they have little control. Ironically, though, only by being employed do women achieve an average level of happiness comparable to men's (Larson, Richards, & Perry-Jenkins, 1994) .

Predictably, much research has found that mothers of infants and young children are more likely to spend more time with their children and are more emotionally involved in parenting than are fathers (Thompson & Walker, 1991). The fact that women more often stay home with children while men work may be seen as both cause and artifact of the gender role messages that are constantly sent and received in families. For instance, Wille (1995) asked couples to rate themselves in terms of their ability to parent an infant. Both men and women demonstrated support for prevailing gender stereotypes by rating mothers as better caretakers overall. Interestingly, however, mothers rated fathers as better caretakers than the fathers rated themselves. Such results suggest that gender roles in parenting are influenced by lack of confidence in nontraditional roles, resulting in maintenance of a status quo that can be cumbersome and unrealistic in contemporary families.

The implications of gendered parenting and work roles are sometimes subtle, sometimes profound. For example, mothers report greater conflict in separation from infants than do fathers (Wille, 1995). Mothers' distress about leaving their infants decreases, however, in families where mothers work more hours in satisfying jobs and share child-care arrangements with fathers. Such findings imply that changes in work roles, as is happening in dual-earner families, can result in increasing feelings of responsibility and increasing comfort with child care (and perhaps other housework).

INTERSECTIONS OF WORK, FAMILY, AND POLICY

Given the importance of work for personal and economic success, it is reasonable to suppose that considerations about work have a major impact on the everyday lives of men and women. Social policies and employment practices link the world of employment to the individual and family work of childbearing and parenting.

The traditional separation of work and family, as exemplified by the two-parent/single-earner nuclear family, is no longer a viable reality in the United States (Akabas, 1984; Thompson & Walker, 1991). Far from being separate worlds, work and family are connected at the level of allocation of resources. Resources flow from family to workplace in terms of the number and quality of worker hours provided by families. They also flow from employer to family through wages, provision of child care, family leave for childbirth and care of family members, and distribution of other benefits such as health insurance. The relationship between families and employment practices is increasing in complexity and shows increasing potential for disruption to both family and workplace when contemporary family realities are not considered in employment policies and practices.

Two decades of research have stressed the importance of a workplace that sustains families, but recent studies seem to indicate that employers continue to ignore the needs of working parents. For example, Seyler, Monroe, and Garand (1995) examined the benefits provided for working parents in one southern state. Their most striking finding was that most companies offered few family supportive benefit options beyond the maternity/disability leave required by federal law. Not surprisingly, larger companies and companies that employed more women were more likely to offer additional benefits, such as flexible work schedules and personal leave to care for sick children. Although previous research has shown that corporate outlay for family supportive benefits usually results in positive outcomes for employers (Seyler, Monroe, & Garand, 1995), it appears that employers continue to resist expanding benefit options because they believe that it is not in their (financial) interest to do so.

Employer benefits are only one of the environmental conditions needed for adequate support of working parents. One recent survey of the literature on parental employment and child care (Chilman, 1993) found consensus among social scientists that out-of-home child care is no longer considered a detriment to the health and development of children. Their study did find, however, that the availability of quality child care, especially for low- and middle-income families continues to be a major roadblock to the employment of women.

It is clear that industrial support for family needs strongly influences the level of stress experienced by working parents (Zedeck & Mosier, 1990). Because women are most often designated as primary child-care providers, they often have the most to gain from workplace policies that support family life. Women who work more than 30 hours per week, however, are *not* more likely to be in jobs that provide supports such as flexible scheduling and on-site childcare; nor are occupational categories that are thought to be predominantly female more likely to exhibit these characteristics (Glass & Camarigg, 1992).

THE EFFECTS OF PARENTAL WORK ON FAMILY

Studies of the impact of parents' work on children's development and well-being are particularly skewed by a social norm that places great pressure on fathers to work outside of the home, whereas mothers care for babies and children in the family home. Social norms compel researchers to ask questions about the impact of a mother's absence from the home, for example, but rarely pressure social scientists to examine the effects of a father's absence during work hours. In spite of these epistemological constraints, however, much of the recent research seems to support maternal employment, at the same time pointing out the particular pressures that working mothers experience. In fact, taken as a whole, the research on maternal employment has demonstrated that nonmaternal child care has neither positive nor negative impact on child outcomes (Parcel & Menaghan, 1994).

The relationship between maternal work and child outcomes involves a complex of factors. Mothers' work conditions seem to impact their children's cognitive and social development depending on the timing of mother's return to work, the working conditions of the mothers' partners, and the availability and quality of child care. Not surprisingly, the benefits of maternal employment for mothers and children are greatest for women with better jobs (Parcel & Menaghan, 1994).

In general, child outcomes in working-mother families are neutral or positive when compared to families with stay-at-home mothers. For example, one study that compared children with stay-at-home mothers to those with mothers who worked outside the home found that children of working mothers had higher self-esteem and more positive moods (Richards & Duckett, 1994). Where it has been studied, fathers' work has been found to affect children indirectly through its impact on fathers' affect and parenting behaviors (Stewart & Barling, 1996). In fact, Depression-era research (Elder, Caspi, and van Nguyen, 1985) indicates that it was the father's behavior during the economic crisis that was the link between family deprivation and how the children fared.

One might suggest that increased parent–child contact brought on by job loss would allow parents the opportunity to provide more cognitive stimulation or "quality time" activities for their children. However, in their study of the jobless in Marienthal, Germany, Jahoda, Lazarsfeld, and Zeisel (1971) found that without the structure that work provided, the unemployed showed little desire to make use of their time.

Moen, Kain, and Elder (1983) wrote that "economic adversity and adaptations to that misfortune become a legacy for members of the next generation, restructuring in turn their options and resources for dealing with adversity as well as the very shape of their lives" (p. 2). Plans for the future, as well as learning opportunities, are not encouraged during periods of unemployment as parents often feel they cannot provide the resources necessary to assist their children, now or in the future. The literature also suggests that the ill effects of joblessness may be created not only by the objective fact of being laid off, but also by the degree to which the effects are translated into a subjective sense of economic distress (Harold-Goldsmith, Radin, & Eccles, 1988; Kelly, Sheldon, & Fox, 1985). Thus, these findings may be true of families with a single income or a dual income who do not feel that their resources are adequate to provide for their needs.

Amato and Ochiltree (1986) found that relationships between family resources and the development of children's competence were stronger for young children than for adolescents. Elder (1974) asserted that younger children were at the greatest risk because they are wholly dependent on reliable parental nurturance, which may change as a result of changes in finances, family relationships, and intensified strains; and Hayes and Nutman (1981) found that younger children may also be more vulnerable to the economic changes that can produce dissonance for the family, resulting in a contradiction that might shape the children's values and orientation toward the future. For example, when parents lose their jobs despite adequate educational preparation and investment, they may have difficulty encouraging their children to invest in school to secure good jobs in the future.

By itself, then, the amount of time that a parent spends with her or his child does not seem to have a strong, direct correlation with child outcomes. In addition, investment in work and career does not seem to be detrimental to children, since work-oriented parents are often child oriented as well (Greenberger & Goldberg, 1989). Parcel and Menaghan's study (1994) is a good example of the complexity of the relationships between various factors in the lives of families where two parents work. When work impacted children and families, it seemed to be the result of the hours worked and the type of work being done by the parent, rather than anything intrinsic to work itself.

EXAMINING WORK AND FAMILIES

Traditionally, work for pay has been studied as a social science construct somehow separated from and superior to the ordinary labors of home and family (e.g. Marx). For the past two decades, however, contemporary social scientists, especially feminist researchers, have laid out an agenda that focuses on understanding the whole of work, including its interactions with personal history, social class, and family constellation. Theorizing about working parents has recentered around the idea that the experiences of workers are often shaped by the constraints of society, including contemporary formulations of the role of parents in work and family life. Dominant ideas about the roles of women are especially subject to change, however, and these dynamics exert a powerful secondary force on the thoughts, feelings, and behaviors of working women (Dyck, 1992). Thus, in spite of lingering conservative ideas about women and work, paid work outside of the home infuses the personal and social experiences of both women and men who raise children. At the time of this writing, the overwhelming majority of fathers and approximately 72% of all mothers participate in the labor force in the United States (U.S. Bureau of Labor Statistics, 1998).

What exactly are the implications of work for parents? Does the meaning of work change as couples begin to develop new family constellations? And what are the differences between women's and men's reactions and responses to the pressures that accompany work in the family?

This chapter looks at the links between work and the family for one group of men and women in the midwestern United States. By focusing on the impact of work on the everyday lives of the mothers and fathers in our study, we try to examine the social implications of work, to understand the complexities of decision making and planning about work, and to explore the effects of work on individual lives. Most importantly, by presenting our respondents in their own words, we scrutinize the *personal* meanings that work has for the women and men interviewed. We hope, most of all, to provide a glimpse into the world of work as it is played out in real lives and real families.

It is important to note that the parents interviewed for this study may not be typical of working parents in all areas of the country or in all socioeconomic situations. Respondents in our interviews were typically employed outside the home in some capacity during the periods of time that were discussed in the interviews, although most of the mothers interviewed suspended paid work when their first babies were born. In fact, nearly all the mothers initially quit work or cut back on work hours to assume primary responsibility for child care after the birth of their first baby although, as chapter 2 notes, 60% returned to paid employment—many after the birth of their second child or when their children entered school.

These interviews took place in the Midwest during a period of significant economic expansion in the United States (Deming, 1996). In this period, local employment grew at a rate higher than the national average, although regional industries were in a period of readjustment due to global competition and many of the new jobs were in the service industries rather than the higher-wage manufacturing sector. Despite dire warnings of a weakening industrial base, this area has been marked by a steadily improving employment–population ratio, one of the indicators of economic health.

THE STORIES

Initially, narrative data from interviews with each respondent were coded for relevance to the topic of work–family life. For each respondent, comments made about work and about the intersections between work and family life were organized into the five family development classes discussed in chapter 2: Prior to the Birth of Child A, the Birth of Child A, Living with Child A, the Birth of Child B and, Living with Children A and B. In addition, data related to mothers' work lives were separated from data about fathers' work lives. In cases where comments could fit into more than one family development class, or were relevant to both mothers' and fathers' work lives, they were included in as many categories as possible.

Data were then examined and coded into general themes suggested by the data themselves, as well as by points suggested in the literature on work and family. These themes were then further divided by the context, tone, and underlying meanings of the narratives. The analysis presented here is just one of many possible, but is our best attempt to present the family stories wherever possible in the voices of the respondents themselves.

Fathers in this study had much less to say about most aspects of their lives, including the role of work in family life. Consequently, the narratives presented here are disproportionately female. When men did comment on their work–family stories, they often related facts about where and how long they worked, or about their wives' adjustment to balancing work and family. Women discussed both their own work and their husbands' work lives in great detail and with strong affect. When women talked about their husbands' work lives, they emphasized career moves, education, father's time away from home and family, and men's worry about financial and job stability. As a result, some of the stories about fathers' work are really stories about their *wives' understanding* of their husbands' thoughts and feelings. Nevertheless, wherever possible, comments about men's work lives are given in their own words.

The following sections represent the major work-related themes of the family stories. First, two overarching themes are presented: work as a source of worry, and gender at the intersection of work and family. Next, themes related to the family development process are discussed. Although data were coded and examined for each phase of family-life development, narratives about work and family make most sense when they are seen as stories about the time periods before and after having children. For that reason, the family development themes are divided into two sections: work and family before babies, and work and family life with children. The section on work and family before babies contains three major themes. The first two, having fun and achievement/security, clearly represent the period in these couples' lives before the birth of their first child. The third theme, concerned with the family following the husband's work is also primarily related to the pre-child period, although some family stories imply that the family does continue to follow the husband's work geographically and socially after the birth of a first child.

The section on work and family life with children contains 11 themes covering the impact of parenthood on mother's and father's identities, family relationships, and strategies for coping with the work–family interface.

Table 6.1 summarizes the themes as they are presented in the following sections.

Overarching Themes

Work as a source of worry

Work is most often described in these stories as a source of concern. Not surprisingly, both men and women discussed work in terms of its impact on their

TABLE 6.1

Overarching Themes and Work Themes by Time Period

Time Period	Major Themes Across Parent Stories
Overarching themes	1) Work as a source of worry 2) Gender
Work and family before babies	1) Having fun 2) Achievement and security 3) Following husband's work
Work and family life with children	1) Women pulled between work and family 2) Decisions about mothers working 3) Leaving baby 4) Parenting roles 5) Women's changing identity 6) Fathers adjusting to babies 7) Fathers' separation from family 8) Women's isolation 9) Stress at the intersection of work and family 10) Creativity in managing work and family 11) Mothers returning to work

families' financial security. What is unexpected is the way in which they described historical and potential/future work almost exclusively as an object of worry. One mother, a high school teacher with a Master's degree, described her ongoing concern with job security:

> My husband changes jobs frequently—by [the] nature of the business. He's at an age where he's real desirable and in a couple of years he won't be, unfortunately, and the old age is getting younger all the time. In fact, he's going Monday for another interview. And it makes me a little nervous that any pensions or anything that he could ever be eligible for never materialize, because you gotta be there 10 years and he's not there. I have some worries that, you know, when [the children] need to go to college, are we going to be able.... You know, we're making fine money now, but how will it be?

Family stories contained passages that seemed relatively innocuous as descriptions of the role of work in family development. With more careful reading, however, the magnitude of work's importance in family life becomes more evident. For example, one woman described her worry over her husband's job security as a major factor in the timing of her children:

> I don't think I would have waited so far in between the kids if circumstances weren't the way they were. And, you know, with [my husband], his job being so

insecure and everything else, I kept saying, "Well, I want another child but I want to wait until things get better—I want to wait until things get better."

Similarly, another mother attributes her divorce to her husband's dissatisfaction at work, combined with social norms that situate men as providers:

… it was a bad situation because [my husband] was having trouble at work and that was a real factor. In fact, it was *the* factor in our divorce. I mean he stuck in a job that he hated, just to be a good provider, because I'm sure that's what he heard all his life. "You provide for your kids, no matter what." And I'm like, "Quit the job. I don't care if we go on welfare. Anything's better than you being a bitch every time you come home." But it didn't work that way. He felt it was *me*.

Gender at the intersection of work and family

Although the theme of work as a source of anxiety was a thread throughout the family stories, the primary overarching theme in these stories about work and family is gender. Gender differences permeated these data in ways that were both familiar and surprising. As expected, both men and women in these families worked outside of the home before the birth of their first child, yet the majority reported making family decisions that mothers would not return to work following the addition of a baby. Interestingly, men had relatively little to say about work, although many sources cite work as the center of most adult men's lives (see Thompson & Walker, 1991). It may be that when asked to tell the story of becoming a family, fathers do not think in terms of including their job history or the role it may have played in the family development.

Thus, it is clear that the role of work in family life is different for men and women. Where mothers' stories were filled with evidence of the conflict inherent in being pulled between raising children and working for a paycheck, fathers' stories rarely suggested ambivalence about personal identity or family role. Women seemed to react more strongly than their male partners to the intersections of work and family, especially in the stories of the period following the birth of a first child. In addition, men and women reported different reactions to the same experiences, often choosing to describe family incidents and situations in very different language. In general, men's descriptions of family life were concise overviews, often lacking emotional reactions to the topics described. Women's narratives, on the other hand, were filled with overt and subtle affect. For example, one father summarized his work–family story:

I've always worked, and [my wife] quit working after she had the first child, and I went to night school and just finished.

The mother in this family had a different perspective on the same set of circumstances:

> … [my husband] was going to school all the time and I felt like I was alone with two babies. All this time [my husband's] been going to school. And that was different as [far as] my expectations of a family and as parents. I think I was more independent. Sometimes I felt like a single mom because I felt like [my husband] had—you know, working full time and going to school there wasn't a lot of—I didn't try to put a lot of pressure on him.…

Gender differences, first evident in the narrative styles of the respondents, were amplified in the family stories that described the period following the birth of the couple's first child. This point in the work–family life cycle, discussed in greater detail in the following sections, was the period of greatest change for women. Many women's stories suggested that the ambivalence and conflict experienced in this period was sustained and intense. Men's stories, on the other hand, supported the notion that the first few weeks following the birth of a child were periods of adjustment, but rarely suggested that this shift was unpleasant in terms of men's roles on a long-term basis. Women's descriptions of adjusting to the addition of a child centered around the shift from the role of worker to the role of mother while their husbands assumed more primary roles as providers. When women in this study talked about their work lives, nearly all discussed the crisis point at which they decided whether to return to work after the birth of a baby or stay home with the kids. Most also described their emotional and social adjustment to their decision (regardless of whether they ended up as stay-at-home mothers or full-time/part-time employees), and their ongoing ambivalence about the world of work.

This basic difference in narratives can be seen as the result of experiences that remain fundamentally distinct for men and women in the family. Women in this study were quite similar to their spouses, in terms of their work lives, before they were mothers, but the addition of a child imposed profound new roles on them and shifted the rules of family and social life. Interestingly, the addition of one or more children after the first baby resulted in relatively minor adjustments in the arena of work and family, presumably because the woman's initial shift (from worker to mother) was sustained in the life of the family.

Work and Family Before Babies

Most of the couples interviewed for this study were two-earner families before the birth of their first child. Because work outside of the home is the norm for

Americans, many of them characterized their pre-child years as typical: "We had a normal marriage—you know, he worked and I worked." In any case, couples characterized their work lives as occupying a central part of their time and identities: " … basically, prior to having the kids, we both worked." For the most part, men's and women's stories that dealt with work lives before the couples had children were similar within families and among the group of respondents. In these narratives, husbands and wives emphasized the details of who worked where, and told stories that imply the meaning of work and money, as well as the ways that they used education as a stepping stone to career advancement.

Having fun

Several couples mentioned the pre-child years as a time of recreation and social activity, characterized by a relatively carefree lifestyle. One man, a sales representative whose wife was a teacher, described the pre-child years:

> Both of us were working and doing just about anything we pleased, had anything we wanted.

Even while these couples described their early years as filled with diversion, they often alluded to the desire to prepare for moving into a new phase of family life. Narratives suggested that these couples saw the emphasis on recreation as transitory:

> So we worked, we traveled, we had fun for 10 years and then we decided to settle down.

None of the family stories examined for this study described the hard work, unpleasant work environments, financial stressors, or other negative issues that must have impacted at least some of these families in their early years together. This may be the result of the retrospective nature of the interviews, or it may be that we did not probe about these specific topics. In any case, the absence of comments on these issues is intriguing.

Achievement and security

In spite of the focus on recreation and social activity early in their family lives, these couples' stories reflected little impulsivity or irresponsibility. Rather, their stories imply that couples *planned* to move beyond this period into a new phase of family life. As their comments on having fun indicated, these couples seemed to have enough money to live comfortably. Like most Americans, they indicate that the function of work in their lives is to secure middle class status.

Many couples noted that they wanted to do some of the things that are associated with financial success before they had children:

> Well, my husband and I were married for 6 years before we had [our daughter]. And that time was spent working. We both had jobs and we worked until we got enough money to buy the house....

Both men and women mentioned buying a home as a specific milestone in family development, and an important factor in their decision to begin having children, as was mentioned in chapter 2:

> So we both worked and it was a very conscious decision as to when—and how we—You know, we would have children when we bought our own home. We were both into our respective jobs or careers at the time.

Following husband's work

Many stories contained a subtheme involving the impact of men's career decisions on family life and family development. Especially in the period before the couples had children, stories often contained references to geographic, financial, or social changes precipitated by husband's work lives. One man summarized this aspect of his married life:

> We were married in April of 1975 when I graduated college. At that time, I decided to go to law school. After I graduated we came here because I was in school. And she was working, and I was working part time. I went through school and in between bought a house, and then decided about the time I was ready to finish up school that it was time to start a family.

However, these stories were most often told by women:

> We both just graduated from college when we got married, and about 2 years after that my husband decided to go back to graduate school and at that point I supported us while he went back to graduate school and then we, when he got out of graduate school. He got a job with [an automotive company] and we moved to [another state].

Or:

> We were both at school there for about 2 years and then we came back here for him to go to law school. I went to work and he went to law school until about—he graduated in '80.

Or:

> Shortly after my graduation, we moved to [a neighboring country] where he felt he had better chances at the time, working in a setting where he had some experience like with the plant industry.

Or:

> ... the reason we were moving around is because he was doing clinical rotations at different hospitals in the country.

The occurrence of frequent, disruptive moves in these families is important because of what it implies about the nature of the couples' relationships. In our sample, for example, no one mentioned husbands following their wives' careers. Also, note that women's narratives often mentioned that wives supported the family while their husbands attended college or other career-advancement training. In such cases, the effect of making men's work primary in the family may have profound individual and social impact. This woman's story hints at the consequences of making her work life secondary to her husband's:

> After a year, he took a different job in [another city], and we moved to [there]. We lived in [there] for 9 months. And, it was quite a change for me because he still left on Monday and came back on Friday, but I had no job.

Family stories that referred to the phenomenon of following the husband's work usually emphasized this issue in the period before the couple had children. It is not known if the couples actually moved more during that period of their lives, or if they simply did not mention family moves after the birth of the children. In any case, there is no suggestion in the narratives that the values and attitudes that supported the frequent moves changed for the couples later in family development.

Work and Family Life With Children

Stories about work and family life after the birth of the first child are largely narratives about women's transitions from employees and partners to wives and mothers. These stories are the most affect laden of the narratives about the intersections of work and family, reflecting the most ambivalence and the deepest emotion about the meaning of family in individual development.

Although the issues discussed by the mothers in this study represented a variety of experiences and worldviews, there were some clear generalities. Mothers discussed employment with emotion; for most, the question of whether or not to work was seen as much more than an issue of logic or logistics. This likely reflects the importance of work for personal identity, especially at the time of the first child's birth. For many of the mothers interviewed here, though, the relationship between work and family was dynamic—that is, the meaning of work outside the home changed over time. For example, some mothers who wouldn't have dreamed of paid employment after the birth of the first baby were eager to return to work once the youngest child entered kindergarten. Others had little objection to full-time paid employment, once they found jobs in which the demands of the workplace did not interfere with the important emotional work of mothering.

Although some narratives suggested that women gave up their identities as workers willingly and freely, others supported the idea that women's work was disposable and transitory. In these stories, women seem to say that they stopped working after the birth of their babies because their jobs were not important enough to interfere with the goals of the family. One mother dismissed her career with "Well, I'm only a substitute teacher."

In these interviews, mothers expressed intense ambivalence about the relationship between work and family. At the same time, however, they revealed remarkable creativity and flexibility in balancing their roles, along with strong dedication to the balance of public and private lives. In the following section, women and men discuss the issues that define the daily experience of work and family life: adjustment to change in the work–family interface, roles and responsibilities, stress and creativity.

Women pulled between work and family

In general, the work and family experiences that women described in this study reflected a pervasive sense of being torn between two worlds following the birth of the first child. For many, the sense of being divided or torn apart was quite powerful. Several mothers described the decision to work or to stay home as central to their definition as parents and as individuals:

> But a lot of the story for me with being a parent was whether I should go to work—should or shouldn't—what my feelings were as a parent, what I should be doing. And again when [Child A] came along, I stayed home for a while, but again I just couldn't stay home all the time. So about the time that she was 2 or 3 months old, I started going back part time again to work.

Sometimes the intensity of the ambivalence and the feeling of being divided between two important tasks was particularly poignant;

> Then I was going to quit work and become a wonderful full time mother and stay home—that lasted about 3 months. And then I was getting bored again. I had been working in the office that my husband worked in prior to then—then I went back on a part time basis. I thought I wanted to stay home with my son pretty much—I thought I did until I got home. When they are infants, I got bored. I wanted something else to do. So I went back to work a while but still wanted to be home mostly.

Decisions about mothers working

The decision to return to work after childbirth is important and complex. Decisions about whether to remain at home with a baby or young child or return to the workplace can rest on economic, cultural, interpersonal, and individual factors, and are influenced by personal control as well as the attitudes of significant others (Granrose & Kaplan, 1994). In daily life, adult men are generally expected to be employed, but labor market conditions intersect with cultural norms to determine the standards by family, community, and class for maternal employment. Women who have been married longer and who have worked throughout their pregnancies are likely to continue work after the birth of a baby. Mothers in the United States are more likely to work full-time hours if they are college educated and working in high-prestige or professional occupations (Pascual, Haynes, Galperin, & Bornstein, 1995). In addition, women who work are more likely to approve of working mothers, and thus are more likely to work after giving birth (Henderson, Lee, & Birdsall, 1993).

Nearly all the women interviewed either mentioned the difficulty of the decision to work or not work after the birth of the first child, or discussed the rationales that they and their husbands used to decide this issue. Underlying many of the narratives for women who chose to stay home rather than returning to work was an assumption that mothers and children ought to be together, especially in infancy and toddlerhood. Some couples reported discussing this issue before the first baby arrived. One mother said:

> One of the things we decided early on is that I wouldn't work after we had her because we didn't want somebody else raising her.

Those who returned to work soon after a baby's arrival (a minority) cited financial concerns and isolation as primary motives for returning to work. Their narratives were filled with references to the stress of balancing work and family:

> I took 6 months off of work after she was born. But then my husband was laid off work when she was 6 months old, and we weren't sure what we would do. I kind of decided I wasn't going back to [my former employer], but then it seemed there weren't any jobs. And I got my job back, and he decided to go back to school and get a degree in computer science.

This mother adds that the logistical and financial difficulty of working while caring for an infant was complicated by dissatisfaction with the idea of day care:

> I realized then that I wasn't the primary influence because I was away from her 10 hours every day. I didn't like that feeling. Even though I had good day care, it was-

n't me. She did not come home with things that were bad or wrong, but they
weren't me and they weren't my husband, and I didn't want that. Part of the reason there is a 4-year gap between [Child A and Child B] is that we made a mutual
decision that I would not have another baby until I could take at least a year off
from work.

Conversely, decisions about women staying home to be full-time mothers
were often predicated on the idea that they didn't *have* to work. This was an
area in which men commented on their wives' experiences. A man who works
for a large automobile manufacturer:

It was fortunate that my salary was enough that one salary would cover the family. She never really had to work. And she wanted to spend as much time as she
could with her children.

Another man, this one a physician:

Fortunately we've always been in a position to be able to have [my wife] at home
because that's what she chooses to do, and we feel that it's important that, you
know, that kids have her around to help nurture—and then [I'd] be here for
them in the evenings and so forth.

Mothers, of course, also commented on the economic resources and financial
sacrifices that played in their decisions to stay home after the birth of a baby:

I'm sure that he would have survived emotionally if I went back to work but I did-
n't have to, so I didn't. It cut our salary in half because we were making equal incomes at the time—it was still worth it, though. I mean, we got by.

Although some of the fathers in these families *did* assume primary care for
their children, rather than acting as the primary breadwinner in the family,
these arrangements were never voluntary. Rather, they were the result of fathers being laid off or fired, forcing mothers to go to work while fathers tempo-
rarily took over home responsibilities. A father, who is also a self-employed
businessman, comments:

… [my daughter] was born in September of '91. That was a bad time during my
business. There was a recession at that time. Fortunately, I was able to maintain
some sort of work. What I'm getting at here is that after [my daughter] was born
[my wife] went back to work part time a few days a week.

Mothers discussed their (temporary) movement back into the workforce mat-
ter-of-factly:

… [Child A] was 2 years old and [my husband] was laid off and I had to go back
to work for a while—which was fine. I don't know how long I worked, it was

never more than 3 months or 6 months. I think out of all the times [my husband] ever got laid off or unemployed—I did go back to work.

Encounters with unemployment and other financial disasters were apparently relatively rare for these couples. In fact, these families are fairly atypical because of their relative affluence, but the stories that include discussion of husbands' unemployment reveal two points. First, when their partners were not employed, women moved back into the workforce, even if they had previously decided to stay home with their children. Second, this role switch was considered temporary by the couple—that is, even when chances for the wife's employment were greater, the couples seemed to stick with their conventional gender-driven conceptualizations of the family.

Leaving baby

Mothers who did not quit work after the birth of a baby often mentioned the "trauma when I had to start working, you know, the separation anxiety." Some mothers, who at first thought that they would return to work, made decisions to stop working because of the emotional impact of leaving their babies. This mother, an administrative secretary, remembers trying to return to paid employment:

> I went back to work after she was 3 months old and could not stand it. And worked for 5 months and I thought it would get easier because I really like the people I worked with and loved my job. I quit when she was 8 months old just because it just tore me apart every day to leave her.

Another mother:

> And when we first had [my son], and I hadn't decided before I had him whether I was going to go back to work or not. But as soon as I had him, I just decided I wasn't—there was just no way I could leave him with someone else. And so it was a joint decision between my husband and I that I would stay home with him.

Surprisingly few parents mentioned out-of-home child care as a factor in returning to work. This may be related to the coding process in the study or to the length of time between the initial search for child care and these interviews. In any case, those who did directly mention it uniformly focused on the negative feelings and social stigma associated with placing a child in the care of others. This mother recalls her experience:

> … when we first moved over here and I started back to work, finding care for them was just a trial for me. I mean, that was just when all the stories were break-

ing about the—out in [another state]—and the child abuse and everything and I was just [anguished cry].

Others referred to this issue indirectly by saying they didn't want "a stranger" raising their children. Recall the mother whose unemployed husband returned to college while she worked. She expressed strong discomfort with child care because:

> I was away from her 10 hours every day. I didn't like that feeling. Even though I had a good day care, it wasn't me. She did not come home with things that were bad or wrong, but they weren't me and they weren't my husband, and I didn't want that.

This mother goes on to say that she and her husband waited until he had finished school and had a good job before having another baby. While she is not a full-time stay-at-home mother, her story typifies many women's narratives:

> I had to give it all to my job or my family, and I can't divide it. So I do something that's not too demanding for money, and spend my time being a mother.

It is noteworthy that none of the fathers' narratives contain references to the pain of leaving their young children to return to work.

Parenting roles

In addition to gender differences in the experience of early attachment, some couples mentioned that decisions about employment were based on traditional notions of the proper role of women in the family, or on personal experiences with families of origin in which women were stay-at-home mothers. It is important to note that these narratives often contained a modern twist—that is, the parents arranged "compromises" where the mothers worked part-time. Or concerns about financial security for dependent women were raised by the couple—yet conventional gender roles continued to provide the foundation for decisions about women and work. One woman commented:

> My mother never worked and I thought it was important that I didn't work; and I've found for my case that was the way to do it. I gave up a good job and haven't regretted that other than maybe possibly a pension.

As mentioned earlier, these couples had the financial advantage of maintaining middle class lives on a single salary. This father explains the decision that his wife would not work after giving birth:

We both felt like it was better for the mother to stay home with the baby. Not like modern times where both parents are still working. That was the major change in our life. And we thought we might actually have some problems. But as it turned out we didn't have any problems, we just cut a few places here and there as far as expenditures. You know, we tightened up on the budget a little bit. Ever since then, [my wife] has been staying home with the kids. We enjoy it a lot more. We certainly have—like we are together more.

Interestingly, in this family, the mother does not mention the mutual decision described by her husband, although she says she did see her husband more after she quit working outside the home.

A few of the narratives indicated that the conventional arrangement of provider—father and nurturer—mother was not an easy fit for some families.

At first my husband was even like, "[Wife's name], I don't want you to work." He came from a very traditional family where mother stayed home, father went to work, they have a house full of kids and that was what mom was supposed to do. And I said, "Well, I think we need to compromise." I'm not willing to completely scrap my—not really like a career because I know that going part time did hurt in a respect but—I wanted to still be active with adults, too. We just didn't want an outside person raising our child or children.

In another family, a father describes his idea of the ideal work–family arrangement for his wife:

One of them [expectations] was that [my wife] would not work before the youngest child was 2 years old and that after that she would work because, even if the work did not bring in lots of income it would at least maintain a professional level of skill, which we felt was necessary for her to maintain the respect of the kids.

Women's changing identity

Several mothers alluded to the problem of forfeiting a sense of self in the transition from worker to mother. Others noted that "you lose the sense of being an adult sometimes" when engaged in the work of mothering small children. Several mothers described the way that leaving the world of employment impacted on their ideas of what they wanted from their lives. All of these narratives suggested complicated, but subtle, cognitive maneuvers by which women forged new identities as mothers. One mother explains:

But it took me until I had him for me to realize that this is what I did want. You know, I knew that before when I was pregnant but it was more or less, "Oh no, I don't know if I really want to do this" because I had to give up a lot. I had to give up school and all that. And then, I thought, "No, this is what I want. I want a family, I want kids."

Another woman, who worked and attended school through her first pregnancy:

> I guess I didn't realize that anything different was happening because I had my routine, and kept going to work and nothing really changed [because of] being pregnant or anything else. And then, after [my daughter] was born, my husband wanted me not to continue working. I struggled with that. I guess I am the type of personality if you tell me I can't have something I want it even more. But looking back, I'm really glad I didn't go back to work. It took me a good 3 or 4 months to adjust to being home and not having a career, kind of fighting being a parent, really. But I enjoyed it.

Slightly less positive is this mother, who highlights the impact of such a sudden change in daily occupation:

> The thing that was hard for me was I quit work totally and I—it was hard for me to adjust to that. I was all of a sudden cleaning diapers and—Yeah, I'd always worked and I really felt tied down or I felt—I don't know if "tied down" is the word but I wasn't prepared for how much responsibility I had.

These narratives seem to suggest that some of the women interviewed struggled with conflicting cultural models of adult gratification. The retrospective nature of these portions of the interviews leaves some questions unanswered: Did these women experience pressure, subtle or otherwise, to conform to the gendered image of the satisfied full-time mother? What was the nature of the internal struggle to adjust to a new identity as mother? What resources were most helpful in making the transition from worker to full-time mother?

Fathers adjusting to babies

Like their wives, the men in this study experienced the birth of a first child as a significant adjustment. It is clear from their stories, however, that their reactions to becoming fathers were qualitatively different from their spouses'. Fathers spoke of the adjustment to babies from their positions as workers, often absent from the home and family for significant portions of the day. One mother summarized her husband's experience of becoming a father:

> I think because [my husband] was working, and he continued his work, it didn't—He'd just come home in the evening. It didn't affect him like it did me. You know, he could enjoy her for the times that she was enjoyable but it didn't change his life as much. I think it was hard for him to see why it was difficult for me just because he didn't go through the same kind of change that I did.

Some fathers had an awareness of the ways in which their experiences and perspectives were different from their wives. None questioned the social norm that mandates fathers to continue working full-time, whereas their wives are faced with the decision to quit work or manage both work and family. Rather, fathers seemed to accept the status quo, even while bemoaning their distance from the family. Fathers often blamed their work responsibilities for their absence from home. One father explains:

> We tried to share responsibilities as much as we could. I probably did more of that with [my oldest son] than the other ones because it was the first one, but also because of the situation I had at work. I had much more time in the evening than I have with the job I have now—than some of the other jobs I've had. So I was around a lot more [at] like 5:00, 4:30 to do things.

Fathers' stories reflected a wide variance in their expressed commitment or desire to spend time with their families. Some stories seem to imply that time with the children is an important value. This father, a medical professional, comments:

> … even though I'm heavily involved in terms of work and there's a lot of commitment there, I think my job has allowed me a fair amount of flexibility and time to participate in the home life, so to speak. And I enjoy that. So hopefully, I'll be able to maintain that all the way through.

Other stories suggest that fathers were happy with the status quo:

> Then, living with the child—It was okay. [My wife] didn't return to work, and reared the child. I went to work and so I didn't—I really didn't interact with the child as much as [my wife] did, of course. And, sure, I changed diapers and, you know, I did that kind of stuff, and fed the baby. But, um, I guess I really didn't relate to babies too well. So, that was that.

One family story stood out as a narrative of separation and disconnection in the work–family arena. This man's story is also unusual in that he is quite articulate about these work–family issues whereas his wife is relatively silent about a series of events that interfered with his connection to his wife and two young children. He described his experience when work required him to be away from the family for an extended period:

> So I was gone for 5 months—I was working in [another state]—while she was up here with [my first daughter]. All of a sudden, I've adjusted to having a wife and a kid and then I have to adjust to living with three other men and then I have to come home and readjust to living with a wife and a kid and then a month later we had two kids. It was tough, real tough. It took me a long while to get used to that, just dealing with being in a house. Because the time when I was gone, [my wife] had become more independent, 'cause I wasn't there.

Father's separation from family

Many of the stories describe fathers as absent or separated from the life of the family because of work obligations. As was mentioned before, work commitment was often given as a reason for fathers to defer or even forgo active involvement in the family. One man, a college graduate working in the auto industry, stated:

> … and again with me working 10 and 12 hours, it was tough for me to get involved especially [working] 6 and 7 days a week.

Another father admits:

> I believe there was some neglect with the kids during that period of time. I believe that I was too busy to pay attention because I was working sixty to eighty hours a week lots of times—all evening, all night, or whatever else.

Employment also interfered with family time when work schedules didn't coincide with family schedules. This father describes being "out of synch" with his family:

> We would like to spend more time together, but it is not always possible. It is very difficult sometimes. I work afternoon shift, and during the school year, the girls are at school and I am home, and then when I go to work, they come home. So, we kinda—I do see [my younger daughter] for about ten to fifteen minutes before I leave for work, and I don't see [my older daughter] in the morning, that's it. During the week, I say "Hi" to [my older daughter], and she says, "Bye, I'm leaving."

Men's stories indicated that some fathers valued being available to their families. One father, an engineer whose wife is a stay-at-home mother, discusses his feelings about his time away from the family:

> I travel quite a bit with business and I'm gone sometimes 3, 4 nights in a week, a couple weeks in a row. And so when I'm at home with the family, the family time is important.

Another father describes missing his son's early development, with some regret:

> … and then when he was just a year, I changed jobs and I got into the insurance business. Starting that off from the ground up—I got my own agency—it's an awful lot of work and time and that. I knew it would be so I kind of felt that during some of the years that I, you know, I watched [my oldest son] develop and so

forth—I kind of missed a lot of that with [my younger son], because it was like 6 days a week, 80 plus hours a week every week for about a 2 ½ year period before it started to taper off somewhat. Even now it's still [many] hours, but I gave up the Saturdays, now I'm there [at work] just 1 or 2 nights a week.

Mothers' stories also described their husbands' absences. One mother described her husband being gone on a business trip when their first child was born.

... he was traveling a lot and—and then when my son was born—that time my husband was in Europe. Well he came—it was a real short trip, like a 5-day trip, and right in the middle of his 5-day trip my son was born. Our son was born. Since I had complained so much about his travel the first time, he decided he would postpone all the travel [until after the birth of Child B].

These mothers also describe the persistent absence of their husbands during their children's early years:

My husband went to 7 years of graduate school at night for his master's degree. And he finished 2 years ago so [my oldest son] was a baby—he started when [my oldest son] was a baby, taking one class a semester. So the whole time that [my oldest son] was small he basically went to school at night one1 or 2 nights a week. And having no family near by it's just me and the (kids) a lot—and [my husband] does travel.

Another woman describes the impact of adding school to work and family life:

We both were working full time and [my husband] was going—is still going—to school at night. So, we were very rarely home alone, if ever, and it just could be very stressful on the marriage, I guess, as well as everything else.

Another woman describes her attempts to deal with her husband's separation from the family:

I was looking for things to keep me more occupied in the evenings and stuff because you know my husband does work long hours and things so rather than just sitting around and waiting for him to get home, I'd rather be doing something....

Women's isolation

Because middle-class Western women rarely raise their children in cooperative arrangements with others, the specter of social isolation, as was discussed in chapter 5, is a real concern for stay-at-home mothers, especially White mothers of young children (Benin & Keith, 1995). In addition to the problem of their husband's work- and education-related absences, several of the women's stories mentioned isolation from other potential sources of support as one of the major challenges of leaving the world of work to raise children. References to the problem of isolation were often embedded in stories about strategies to cope with it. This woman, a teacher, comments:

> So what I did was—just to keep my sanity—I took up a part-time job working 3 days a week, like from an afternoon to an evening. I would drive in just to have some people, 'cause literally there was no one to talk to.

It is clear that mothers and fathers had different ideas about isolation. For example, note that this father seems to imply that being home alone all day is bad for a woman *unless* she has children to care for:

> One of the assumptions that we both agreed on was that for a woman to stay home for any extended period of time would eventually turn her into a vegetable. That was sort of my feeling, and I think she agreed with that. That without any more stimulation that you get from staying home, it will drive you nuts, unless you got kids.

A major source of isolation for mothers, aside from the loss of employment-related support, was separation from family. Mothers experienced lack of extended family on two levels—as missing sources of emotional support and as absent child-care providers. This mother, who moved with her husband's work, describes the implications of her loss of extended family:

> Like I said, it was different not having family out there. Because my husband was working full-time and I had to work part-time, so it was difficult for a while there to be separated from him and to have child care when he was so little.

Sometimes the combination of isolation from extended family and the public life of work caused potentially explosive situations. This man works in the computer industry:

> … at that time [my wife] got pregnant with [our second child] and I was working so much, there was a breakdown in our relationship because I wasn't there—all she had was [our first child] who was 1 year old to talk to. There were no friends, acquaintances, relatives or anything else. [We had] $200 a month phone bills calling back to [home state]. And at that point, my year contract was up. [My wife] said she was coming back to [home state] with or without me to be close to family, relatives, for the help of her sisters and her mother and her aunts and the uncles and, whatever else, when she was going to have [the second child]. And so when my 12-month contract was up I requested and received a transfer to [home state].

Stress at the intersection of work and family

Research on the impact of work on family life indicates that a complex interaction exists. Much of the recent research on the topic centers around role conflict and role overload for mothers employed outside of the home. Multiple roles and work demands, for example, are associated with poorer health for working mothers, especially when women report an awareness of their multiple roles (Facione, 1994). Mothers with rewarding jobs may be protected from the negative effects of role overload, however, indicating that women and their children may actually benefit from outside employment when their jobs are satisfying (Barnett & Marshall, 1992). Wille (1992) found that mothers who worked more hours and mothers who liked their jobs were more autonomous and less anxious about separation and reunion with their infants. The impact of work on fathers' perceptions of stress has been studied less frequently, although one recent study indicated that, whereas mothers' work overload may lead to less-accepting behavior toward children, fathers' work overload leads to increased conflict in the family (Galambos, Sears, Almeida, & Kolaric, 1995). A woman's belief that she can enlist the help of her spouse for child care when she is working is the best predictor that she will experience decreased stress and increased well-being while working (Ozer, 1995).

The family stories reported here indicated that balancing work and children was stressful and exhausting even when mothers were home with their children full-time. For the subset of families where both parents worked, however, the descriptions of work–family stress were quite compelling. One mother comments:

> It's difficult handling the stresses that I have, because I'm just a substitute teacher trying to get a full time position and running a home and handling the children and still trying to have a social life besides.

Another mother described how her stress increased when the second child was born.

> … it's hard to split up your time. I'm not even sure you do it 50/50 at the time. Because it seems like you don't want your first child to get jealous or anything so you have to be very careful. I'm not even sure how you can try to do this, because I was working full time throughout, so I think it gave me a little bit more stress. We both were working full time and [my husband] was going to school at night.

In general, the families in this study seemed to agree with this mother, who expressed her admiration for women who can 'do it all':

> If they can handle a career and a family, then I don't think it affects the kids. I have seen women that can do both, and I really admire them. Because I can't. I

am all or nothing. I tried. It was tough. It was tough, because I gave all to that. I would come home, sit down, and the kids were still young and "Mommy, Mommy, Mommy." And I was exhausted. I would kind of yell at them, you know, "Leave me alone," and push them away.

This quote seems to illustrate that parents' perceptions of stress were often centered around the reactions of their children to mothers' absence from the home. This mother discusses realizing that her daughter was feeling rejected. Note that her reaction is to push herself harder to meet the needs of her child:

This year I noticed, in fact, my husband and I sat down and talked about it—that she [child] showed some feelings or she was showing some behavior that indicated that she was being neglected, especially from me, because I am back working. It's real hard for me to deal with working, your own life and the children have to come first—you have no choice. So, I have tried to do a little more with her.

One mother talked about her decision to quit her job after experiencing an unsuccessful attempt to manage a two-career family with small children:

[My husband] was working long hours and our marriage started going down the skids. You know, I mean—luckily we were wise enough to realize that careers aren't everything they're cracked up to be. Not if it takes a toll on family relationships and offspring and all that so—That's why I said, well, I can always go back to work if things get—if money gets real bad or if I get real fruity, which I do staying at home sometimes.

Overall, the stories about stress in the work–family arena deal with both mothers' and fathers' perceptions of the difficulties of balancing work and family obligations. In fact, though, even when fathers discussed stress in the work–family arena, they emphasized the increased pressure experienced by mothers. This man, who was working on a graduate degree at the time of his second child's birth, describes the situation:

… [at] the time [my son] was born and little, I was going to school too. So that made it even tougher sometimes for [my wife], because I was gone a couple of times a week. And she was home with the kids. Sometimes it was difficult, just having the kids around all day and me not being around there. So, I would say it created more tension that we had to work through and I had to be a little more, you know, sensitive to the fact that she had more responsibility than she had with the one child.

Interestingly, none of the family stories mentioned fathers taking on additional home responsibilities to relieve their wives' increased work loads. This contrasts sharply with Ozer's (1995) finding that the single most important factor in predicting maternal well-being and psychological happiness was mothers' belief that they could enlist the help of their spouses in child care and other household tasks.

Creativity in managing work and family

These family stories indicated that the impact of work and career on family life were considerable at every stage of the family life cycle. In particular, women in this group were faced with significant changes in personal identity, marital relationships, family role, and social interactions. How did they manage their lives? What solutions were found to be most useful in coordinating the daily responsibilities of parenting and employment? In 1992, Dyck wrote:

> Specific avenues of coping must be worked out locally. They may be anticipated to be influenced by socioeconomic status, provision of community resources, the demographics of a local area, and whether women have family members to draw on in working out individual solutions. Role demands, expectations and daily routines all will be shaped within the particular social, cultural, and physical context in which women live. (p. 30)

Most of the stories told by both mothers and fathers in these interviews revealed considerable creativity and flexibility on the parts of both parents when it came to mothers' work lives. In the complex and painful period that often follows the birth of the first child—in which women sometimes feel both exhilarated by new motherhood and bored with the isolation and relative inactivity of staying at home—many mothers began to search for solutions to the problems of the new family system. This mother, who worked in the legal field, discusses her initial solution:

> After [my son] was born, the first month was wonderful to be home. It's fun to sit home and be mom and everything, but I wasn't used to it. I like having adult conversation that is stimulating and a law office gives you lots of stimulating conversation. To be home with a 3-month-old—he slept and you fed him—and as far as I was concerned I could have been anybody, he didn't know. I could have given him to my mother or sister, and he would have been equally as happy, so I didn't feel any reason why I shouldn't do both. So then I decided to go back for a couple of days a week, and I did.

Some of the couples referred to complex decision making that went on before and after the birth of a baby regarding child care. One mother commented:

> I continued to work part-time after she was born. I worked in the evening so that [my husband] could watch her and we wouldn't have to have baby-sitters.

Most of the stories revealed that solutions were generally not so easy to find. Many narratives dealt with mothers' ongoing attempts to find a comfortable fit in the intersection of work and family. One mother said:

> And when we had [my son], I quit work and then went back to work for 2 days a week, which was really healthy for me at that point—worked out well. But they wanted me to work every day, so I quit work altogether when [my son] was 18 months old. Then I was totally relaxed and content to be a mom.

Another mother:

> And, how old was [my daughter]? Well, let's see, [she] was 3, 3 when I went back to work. And then I went back to work full time, but 2 years ago I started job sharing so now I only work 3 days a week.

And another:

> … but when [my son] was born, I only stayed home with him for about 3 months and then [my husband] took him. And [my husband] stayed home with the kids and went to the preschools and he did [a] complete reverse role. Then he went back to work, and then I stayed home for a little while longer. And then I quit again to stay home with the other ones when [my daughter] was born. I've been home for a while now, kind of bored.

These stories support the observation that mothers experienced the intersection of work and family as a dynamic force over the course of their family's development. The commitment to stay home or to seek outside employment was never a final decision for these women. The solutions developed seemed to be linked to a large set of variables, including husband's work situation and schedule; mother's background, education, and experience; the family's financial resources; the children's age and development; and the personality of the woman. Some women managed the conflict between work and family by moving into and out of the workforce when family circumstances dictated. Others managed to maintain consistent employment while caring for their families. One mother mentioned that she manages work and several children, but downplays the difficulty. She suggests that this accomplishment is primarily the result of good organizational skills:

> So, I've just—and I've just maintained a busy work life, just out of habit. I guess I'm just used to it. You become accustomed to it after a while. Where some people can't even imagine working with two children, let alone three. It's just something I—you just gradually work into. You gradually organize into it.

As we noted before, many family stories referred to fathers' absence from the family due to work-related responsibilities. In spite of their separation from their partners and children, however, several fathers mentioned flexibility in their work schedules as an important benefit of their jobs. These men particularly wanted to be available for their children's special events and recreational activities. One father mentioned:

> I started my own business in this city just a mile down the road. It's taken quite a bit of time away from the family but it's also allowed for flexible time. If they have an event at school, a special event, I just make it a priority to take off and be there for their show or parent's luncheon or whatever.

A father who worked in the auto industry:

> And right about the time it was really reaching a peak of pressure, I was promoted and it was like night and day. I don't work 12 hours a day. I have flexible time. If I need to be home at 2 o'clock, I can come home at 2 o'clock. We can go on our vacations.

One father's story told of his gradual metamorphosis from a conventional "provider" into a father whose focus on the family grew out of a growing appreciation for his family after experiencing problems at work:

> I was working, sometimes as much as double shifts, 7 days in a row—8 days, 9 days in a row. It was that type of work schedule. So I did not spend a lot of time with the family because I was doing about 16, 17, 18 hours at work. So all during that time [being laid off from his job], I was learning how to be—certainly—a husband, learning how to be a father, and cutting back on the amount of hours that I worked. The job that I found allowed me to work a maximum, really, of 5—rarely a 6-day week. Long hours, those 5 days, but at least the weekends were available.

The stories about flexibility in managing work and family are filled with references to the difficulty of the work–family intersection as well as a high degree of personal and family resilience. One mother's story brings several themes together:

> [My husband] would be gone for weeks at a time and so forth, so [my son] and I bonded incredibly well. We did everything together the first year of his life. We went shopping and everything, and because of that I think [my son] talked early and everything because he was the only one I had to talk to. For the first year of [my son's] life, [my husband] was pretty much gone, and about every other week he would come home. And that worked out pretty good, I mean really. Because we drove back and forth. And [my son] and I got really good. I mean we were not afraid. I'd just throw him in the car and we'd drive to [another state] or whatever. So he traveled. He probably had more miles on him by the time he was a year old than most kids.

Mothers returning to work

In discussing the role of work in family life, both men and women indicated that the future held changes for the family. Many of the couples interviewed had youngest children who were entering grade school. Predictably, mothers who initially left the workforce to stay home with their infants were considering a return to work. Some stories discussed readjustment to a more public life as the demands of infancy and toddlerhood faded. One mother commented:

> I'm working 1 day a week now, just when the kids are in school. I'm hoping to work a little more as they get older. I work for my brother. He is a financial planner, so it's great I can work my hours around the kids' schedules.

Considerable ambivalence was still evident in mothers' stories when their narratives referred to a potential return to paid employment. A mother who works part-time and has an ambitious schedule of volunteer work:

> ... the future. Umm, well possibly, I don't know if I would ever want to go back to work full-time. Maybe when all the kids are in school, maybe, try teaching again. Umm, because I kind of miss teaching. But then again, then you couldn't do all the extracurricular things, which I kind of feel are important to the kids. You know, like with the dance lessons and Girl Scouts and all.

Another mother:

> And I really, I stayed home, you know, and I felt like that's what I wanted to do. I still have a hard time. I'm thinking [my child's] in kindergarten now, that maybe next year, I should go back to work. But I still—I don't want to miss the field trips and the involvement with the kids.

And another:

> I'm debating right now whether to go back to work part time, and it's a real battle with me. Because they both will be in school full-time this year, and I think, well, I'll be home and I would like to—Probably the biggest reason—I mean I really enjoy my work, I really, really like it—but the biggest reason is for money that I want to go back. I'm just thinking, you know, they'll have to go to latch-key like 2 nights a week after school and that worries me, just because I've never really left them that much. I just think after school when they want to come home and tell me what's happening....

CONCLUSION AND IMPLICATIONS

In concluding this chapter, we return to an earlier statement that is now made abundantly clear by the stories of these parents: The relationship between families and employment practices is increasing in complexity and shows increasing potential for disruption to both family and workplace. How complicated the effects of the work–family interface are depends on: the nature of the men's and women's job opportunities; employment history; education; number of children; timing of children, as it relates to the development of a career; assumptions about gender roles; and the proximity and availability of extended family and friends for support and assistance. These are mostly "personal" variables, but the effects are also highly dependent on whether contemporary family realities are considered in employment policies and practices. Our families have also verified that, given the importance of work for personal and economic success, it is reasonable to suppose that considerations about work (i.e., practice, policy, and research) can have a major impact on the everyday lives of men and women and their children.

Practice Implications

As was discussed in chapter 1, each family member functions in multiple roles that may be prescribed, ascribed, or assumed to insure that all the work of a family is completed. Traditionally, men have been in the instrumental role where they are the breadwinners, and women have carried the emotional, caretaking role. In today's society, where many families need the incomes of two adults, and where many woman may choose to work to fulfill their own goals and aspirations, the picture is not so simple for most couples. In addition, many couples are making a conscious choice to equalize gender-typed roles in their marriage, especially as women return to work after a period of childrearing (Hepworth, Rooney, & Larsen, 1997).

As chapter 3 indicates, the division of labor issue is the most commonly cited reason for disagreement among couples (Cowan, Cowan, Heming, & Miller, 1991). Regardless of where couples saw themselves on the continuum of egalitarianism and traditionalism in their relationship prior to the birth of their first child, once the baby was born there was a shift toward a more traditional division of labor with regard to household chores (Cowan et al., 1991). This shift is compounded by the feelings both partners may have about their identity and roles.

Hepworth et al. (1997) suggest a list of questions that a clinician should consider in working with couples where role conflict, role strain, and role overload may be presenting obstacles in their relationship. The clinician should begin by assessing the extent to which roles are assigned based on gender rather than through consideration of other factors such as ability, interest, availability and flexibility of time. She or he should also assess the rigidity versus fluidity of the roles; the level of satisfaction each partner expresses with the roles they perform; to what extent partners experience pressure, subtle or otherwise, to conform to gendered images of roles; and to what extent the stress of role problems causes problems between the couple or between the parents and children.

The father's story that included his prescription of his wife's work role—"One of them [expectations] was that [my wife] would not work before the youngest child was 2 years old and that after that she would work...."—is an example of parents having preconceived ideas about roles and prescribing tasks for each other. When partners' expectations and ideas about work do not mesh, a clinical intervention may help them sort out what is at the root of the problem and how they might negotiate a compromise that is acceptable to both.

If the practitioner should find that this father, for example, was presenting views that he had incorporated from his family of origin, as discussed in chapter 3, there may be a need for work on changing these messages. It may come down to the question: Who has input into the decision to work? Whatever the decision, it seems to work best when it is negotiated and agreed on, a task in which a skilled clinician can be extremely helpful.

Whether the situation involves going from worker to full-time mother, from mother to full-time worker, or combining both roles all along, a clinician could guide families in discovering what resources would be most helpful in making these transitions and/or in combining roles. Information and referral regarding child care may be invaluable. This is also a point at which support groups with other parents in similar situations might be helpful to combat the isolation stay-at-home parents may feel, or to give strategies to others who are balancing tasks on the home and work fronts. Again, individual or couple therapy around loss of roles, handling role overload, and/or juggling demands of home and workplace might also make a difference in the success of the transition.

Intervening at crisis points is another task for a clinician. For example, our stories tell us that many women moved around to follow their husbands' work or schooling. This geographic disruption, which often overlapped with the birth of the first child, created a crisis in several of our couples' lives. In addition, changing/losing identity (worker to mother or mother to worker) sometimes precipitated a crisis, as did leaving the baby in the care of others—particularly for mothers, who report greater conflict in separation from their infants than do fathers (Wille, 1995).

Two additional practice issues that also have implications for policy interventions require mentioning. In this book, we have cited past work and illustrated with stories the issue that many fathers do not feel prepared to assume active parenting roles, and perhaps cling to gender-typed roles for this reason. Wille (1995) showed that even when women had confidence in their husbands' ability to care for the children, the men themselves did not. This finding suggests the need to create parenting classes for men that can function both as educational forums and as support groups for assuming nontraditional roles with more confidence and success.

Finally, what more natural way to address the complex issues of work and family than by having an Employee Assistance Program (EAP), either on site or available by referral from the employer? These programs, often included as a benefit for workers, can go a long way toward creating better working environments. Issues addressed by EAPs may include strategies for handling the pressures of work and home that spill over into the other domain, facilitation of opportunities for job choice—perhaps including employment or vocational counseling or job sharing—and other support services.

Policy Implications

Clearly, as the literature and these stories indicate, there is a need to facilitate the "ungendering of parenting and work roles." This can be done, in part, through media presenting more models of working women and parenting men, e.g., the Berenstain Bears book *Mama's New Job*, or the movie *Mr. Mom*. In addition, education/training programs beginning in high school, which consciously work to decrease the gender classification of jobs and prepare young adults to assume a variety of roles with confidence and competence, will help alleviate this problem. In conjunction with both of these suggestions, we must talk about the hard work inherent in managing home and family, and acknowledge work at home (either for pay or not for pay) as equally important. Many of the stories presented here suggest that such overt recognition is not the case in everyday life. For example, one father in this sample told an interviewer that his wife did not work. Later, in telling his story, he mentioned that she ran a day-care center in her home.

There is also a need to modify views of employers. We must find ways to help women change the double bind of their dual-focused lives. Many employers are less willing to offer good jobs to women because of the perception that women are not fully invested in their work and may leave their jobs whenever family needs arise. In truth, evidence does suggest that women respond to these conditions by being less likely to invest themselves in employment outside of the home that does not offer job satisfaction, for example, adequate pay, reasonable schedules, and opportunities for advancement (Ferber, 1982; Kessler-Harris, 1987).

Creating a "family friendly workplace" is also a necessary and ongoing task. As this chapter and chapter 5 indicate, family-friendly benefits flow from employer to family through wages, provision of child care, family leave for childbirth and care of family members, and payment of other benefits such as health insurance. Results from a recent survey found that 72% of employers endorse the idea that worker absenteeism would be reduced with the addition of on-site day care centers; that helping employees deal with the stress caused by family–work pressures improves efficiency and creativity; and that flexible schedules can improve morale (U. S. Department of Labor, 1998).

Lastly, there is a need for improved legislation around work issues. Chapter 5 discusses the Family and Medical Leave Act of 1993. This act marked an important point in America's willingness to consider the interface of the complex family–work issue. The "Family Friendly Workplace Act" introduced by Republicans is currently being hotly debated, with Democrats saying their alternative offers "real flexibility" for working families (U.S. Senate, 1998). Whatever the outcome, the debate is crucial in that it raises America's collective consciousness about the critical need of dealing with these issues for the health of the family and the country.

Research Implications

The qualitative nature of these stories reinforces the findings of many previous research studies. More importantly, it gives "voice" to mothers and fathers as they tell of their struggles and successes in combining the worlds of family and work. It also points to areas where further research is needed to understand fully the work–family interaction and each partner's role in it. For example, men's voices were not heard as clearly as their wives' in this study. Perhaps they, too, are not happy with the "gendered" arrangements and would appreciate family benefits as much as their wives. In addition, we need research that will document time at home in a way that values it as work.

There is also a need to study the effects of a father's absence from the home, during working hours and work-related travel. As we have seen, studies on the impact of parents' work on children's development are skewed by social norms that compel researchers to ask questions about the impact of a mother's absence from the home when she works, but rarely examine the impact of a father's being gone. As parents go in and out of roles, that is, worker to parent to parent–worker, it is also important that we look at employment status longitudinally, as a fluid variable that may react on family development.

Research is needed that will explore the experiences of families as women return to work. For example, will the time women took off for childrearing prove to be a handicap as they reenter the workforce and/or try to climb a professional ladder? Will fathers experience a sense of relief as the full burden of financial responsibility is shared? Will fathers change their work behavior? Will mothers who return to work have any relief from housework when they are not

full-time homemakers? What will children think about the decisions that their
parents have made in their efforts to provide for their family and combine work
and family roles? Will decisions of parents to be more available to children be
beneficial for the children, for themselves? These questions demand a continuing, in-depth look at the family story as it unfolds over the life span.

Above all, the lessons from this chapter recommend that practice, policy,
and research endeavors must shift from looking at work as separate from family.
The worlds of work and family are mutually dependent, and must be treated as
such in today's world.

REFERENCES

Akabas, S. (1984). Workers are parents, too. *Child Welfare, 63*(5), 387–399.
Amato, P. R., & Ochiltree, G. (1986). Family resources and the development of child compe-
tence. *Journal of Marriage and the Family, 48,* 47–56.
Barnett, R., & Marshall, N. (1992). Worker and mother roles, spillover effects, and psycho-
logical distress. *Women and Health, 18*(2), 9–40.
Benin, M., & Keith, V. (1995). The social support of employed African American and Anglo
mothers. *Journal of Family Issues, 16*(3), 275–297.
Berk, S. (1985). *The gender factory: The apportionment of work in American households.* New
York: Plenum.
Chilman, C. (1993). Parental employment and child care trends: Some critical issues and
suggested policies. *Social Work, 38*(4), 451–460.
Cowan, C. P., Cowan, P. A., Heming, G., & Miller, N. B. (1991). Becoming a family: Marriage,
parenting, and child development. In P. A. Cowan & M. Hetherington (Eds.), *Family
Transitions* (pp. 79–109). Hillsdale, NJ: Lawrence Erlbaum Associates.
Deming, W. (1996). A decade of economic change and population shifts in U. S. regions.
Monthly Labor Review, 119(1), 3–14.
Dyck, I. (1992). The daily routines of mothers with young children: Using a socio-political
model in research. *Occupational Therapy Journal of Research, 12*(1), 16–34.
Elder, G. B., Jr.(1974). *Children of the Great Depression.* Chicago: The University of Chicago
Press.
Elder, G. H., Caspi, A., & Nguyen, T., van (1985). Linking family hardship to children's lives.
Child Development, 56, 361–375.
Facione, N. (1994). Role overload and health: The married mother in the waged labor force.
Health Care for Women International, 15(2), 157–167.
Ferber, M. (1982). Women and work: Issues of the 1980's. *Signs, 8,* 273–295.
Ferree, M. (1987). Family and job for working-class women: Gender and class systems seen
from below. In N. Gerstel & H. Gross, (Eds.), *Families and work* (pp. 289–301). Philadel-
phia: Temple University Press.
Galambos, N., Sears, H., Almeida, D., & Kolaric, G. (1995). Parents' work overload and prob-
lem behavior in young adolescents. *Journal of Research on Adolescence, 5*(2), 201–223.
Glass, J., & Camarigg, V. (1992). Gender, parenthood, and job–family compatibility. *Ameri-
can Journal of Sociology, 98*(1), 131–151.
Granrose, C., & Kaplan, E. (1994). Returning to work following childbirth: The relationship
between intentions and behavior. *Journal of Applied Social Psychology, 24*(10), 873–896.
Greenberger, E., & Goldberg, W. (1989). Work, parenting and the socialization of children.
Developmental Psychology, 25(1), 22–35.

Harold-Goldsmith, R., Radin, N., & Eccles, J. S. (1988). Objective and subjective reality: The effects of job loss and financial stress on fathering behaviors. *Family Perspective, 22*, 309–326.

Hayes, J., & Nutman, P. (1981). *Understanding the unemployed: The psychological effects of unemployment.* London: Tavistock Publications.

Henderson, L., Lee, V., & Birdsall, W. (1993). Attitudes toward the employment of mothers of preschoolers: Implications for childcare. *Child and Youth Care Forum, 22*(1), 23–42.

Hepworth, D. H., Rooney, R. H., & Larsen, J. A. (1997). *Direct social work practice* (5th ed.). Pacific Grove, CA: Brooks/Cole.

Jahoda, M., Lazarsfeld, P., & Zeisel, H. (1971). *Marienthal, the sociography of an unemployed community* (Trans.) Chicago: Aldine-Atherton. (Original work published 1933)

Kelly, R. F., Sheldon, A. W., & Fox, G. L. (1985). The impact of economic dislocation on the health of children. In J. Boulet, A. M. Debritto & S. A. Ray (Eds.), *Proceedings of the Bush Program's National Conference on Understanding the Economic Crisis: The impact of poverty and unemployment on children and families* (pp. 94–108). Ann Arbor: Bush Program in Child Development and Social Policy, The University of Michigan.

Kessler-Harris, A. (1987). The debate over equality for women in the workplace: Recognizing differences. In N. Gerstel and H. Gross (Eds.), *Families and work* (pp. 520–539). Philadelphia: Temple University Press.

Larson, R., Richards, M., & Perry-Jenkins, M. (1994). Divergent worlds: The daily emotional experience of mothers and fathers in the domestic and public spheres. *Journal of Personality and Social Psychology, 67*(7), 1034–1046.

Menaghan, E., & Parcel, T. (1991). Parental employment and family life: Research in the 1980's. In A. Booth (Ed.), *Contemporary families: Looking forward, looking back* (pp. 361–380). Minneapolis, MN: National Council on Family Relations.

Moen, P. (1985). Continuities and discontinuities in women's labor force activity. In G. Elder, (Ed.), *Life course dynamics: Trajectories and transitions* (pp. 113–155). Ithaca, NY: Cornell University Press.

Moen, P., Kain, E. L., & Elder, G. H., Jr. (1983). Economic conditions and family life: Contemporary and historical perspectives. In R. R. Nelson & F. Skidmore (Eds.), *American families and the economy: The high costs of living* (pp. 213–259). Washington, DC: National Academy Press.

Ozer, E. (1995). The impact of childcare responsibility and self-efficacy on the psychological health of professional working mothers. *Psychology of Women Quarterly, 19*(3), 315–335.

Parcel, T., & Menaghan, E. (1994). Early parental work, family social capital, and early child outcomes. *American Journal of Sociology, 99*(4), 972–1009.

Pascual, L., Haynes, O. M., Galperin, C., & Bornstein, M. (1995). Psychosocial determinants of whether and how much new mothers work. *Journal of Cross-Cultural Psychology, 26*(3), 314–330.

Perkins, H., & DeMeis, D. (1996). Gender and family effects on the "second shift" domestic activity of college-educated young adults. *Gender and Society, 10*(1), 78–93.

Perry-Jenkins, M. (1994). The family division of labor: All work is not created equal. In D. Sollie and L. Leslie (Eds.), *Gender, families and close relationships* (pp. 169–188). Thousand Oaks, CA: Sage.

Richards, M., & Duckett, E. (1994). The relationship of maternal employment to early adolescent daily experience with and without parents. *Child Development, 65*(1), 225–236.

Rosen, E. (1987). *Bitter choices: Blue collar women in and out of work.* Chicago: University of Chicago Press.

Schooler, C., Miller, J., Miller, K., & Richtand, C. (1984). Work for the household: Its nature and consequences for husbands and wives. *American Journal of Sociology, 90*, 97–124.

Seyler, D., Monroe, P., & Garand, J. (1995). Balancing work and family: The role of employer-supported child care benefits. *Journal of Family Issues, 16*(2), 170–193.

Stewart, W., & Barling, J. (1996). Fathers' work experiences affect children's behaviors via job-related affect and parenting behaviors. *Journal of Organizational Behavior, 17,* 221–232.

Thompson, L., & Walker, A. (1991). Gender in families: Women and men in marriage, work and parenthood. In A. Booth (Ed.), *Contemporary families: Looking forward, looking back* (pp. 76–102). Minneapolis, MN: National Council on Family Relations.

U.S. Bureau of Labor Statistics. "Labor force statistics from the current population survey: Employment characteristics of families summary." 21 May 1998. <http://stats.bls.gov/newsrels.htm> (11 June, 1998).

U. S. Department of Labor. "Current events and trends in corporate citizenship: Family-friendly workplace." 29 May 1998. <http://www.ttrc.doleta.gov/citizen/ffnews.htm> (17 June, 1998).

U. S. Senate. "The GOP 'Family Friendly Workplace Act' offers fewer choices, less money." <http://www.senate.gov/comm/Dem-Policy/general/sr/sr-11.html> (17 June, 1998).

Warner, R. (1986). Alternative strategies for measuring household division of labor: A comparison. *Journal of Family Issues, 7,* 179–195.

Wille, D. (1992). Maternal employment: Impact on maternal behavior. *Family Relations, 41,* 273–277.

Wille, D. (1995). The 1990's: Gender differences in parenting roles. *Sex Roles, 33*(11/12), 803–817.

Zavella, P. (1987). *Women's work and Chicano families.* Ithaca, NY: Cornell University Press.

Zedeck, S., & Mosier, K. (1990). Work in the family and employing organization. *American Psychologist, 45*(2), 240–251.

7

Telling the Family Story: Subplots and Next Chapters

Lisa G. Colarossi
The University of Michigan

Rena D. Harold
Lucy R. Mercier
Michigan State University

We didn't have any children for a while and so we were free to go out or on vacation or whatever. And then when you have kids it's a different story. You give, a lot—But that's just how it is. But I think having kids is more important than worldly things. You know, the experience of having them—I would never trade it....

The parents in our study expressed the importance of family in their lives. They provided rich descriptions of the first major transitions in family life development—making a long-term commitment to a partner and having children. These transitions affect many other areas of people's lives, including the psychological areas of identity and mental health as well as the social areas of work, friendships, and extended family. This book has described parents' stories of becoming a family across several different contexts. On an individual level, it looked at how becoming a family affects the identity of each individual member as well as the identity of the family as a whole group or system. On a family level, it considered the influences on parents' perceptions of their children and how these shape the development of the family over time. Finally, on a more social level, it reviewed parents' descriptions of how becoming a family influences parents' work lives as well as their need for social support, and the availability of such support as social systems adapted to the needs of parents.

This information was obtained from interviews conducted with the parents of 60 families. Interviews were used, rather than surveying parents, to capture both the variability and depth of information from parents. As evidenced by the complexity of these families' stories and by the difficulty in isolating any particular theme without considering its relationship to the previous information and the larger context, qualitative methods may be more effective than quantitative ones in grappling with the *full* complexity of family systems. By viewing the family in its totality, qualitative research emphasizes its "social context, multiple perspectives, complexity, individual differences, circular causality, recursiveness, and holism" (Moon, Dillon, & Sprenkle, 1990, p. 354).

One of the methodological underpinnings of qualitative family research is diversity. Qualitative researchers are part of a growing movement of people who understand that families appear in diverse forms in diverse settings, have diverse experiences, and appear differently at different times in history. It is true that the sample for this project is not significantly diverse on such demographics as race, socioeconomic status, and religion. However, it *is* possible to note the complexity and diversity of family experiences that are present in this group. The results of this study with a relatively homogenous group point to the need for qualitative research as a method with more diverse groups of families. This project could be replicated with families of various types: single, divorced, and remarried families; adoptive and foster parents; extended families and kinship networks; and same-sex-parent families. Comparative results could advance our knowledge of family development on both psychological and sociological levels.

This chapter summarizes and integrates major findings across chapters and discuss their relevance for the theories discussed in chapter 1. It then consider next chapters in the development of family life, including the transition to adolescence and to children leaving home. Finally, it provides information about variation in family types and considers the impact of race/ethnicity, class, and gender on family development, before summarizing the overall implications for future practice, policy, and research.

SUMMARY OF MAJOR ISSUES AND IMPLICATIONS FOR THEORY

Reviewing the Theories, the Themes, and Their Connection

Chapter 1 briefly described three theoretical perspectives that framed our study of family development and informed our interpretations of the data: developmental life span, family-in-environment (ecological systems theory), and family roles. Table 7.1 highlights four key concepts of each theory as they relate to families. Each of the three perspectives offers a different, but complementary standpoint from which to view and understand the complexity of the family. They differ mostly in the focus that they assume. The developmental life span perspective views the family with a telephoto lens that moves in and out across generations and across time. The family-in-environment perspective adopts a wide-angle lens that allows a view of the family in a broader context. And the family roles perspective uses a collage of pictures placed side by side and sometimes overlapping. Each perspective assumes a dynamic definition of family.

TABLE 7.1

Theoretical Perspectives and Their Key Concepts

Developmental Life Span	Family-in-Environment	Family Roles
• Family as a three-generational system	• Families are located within and interact with several levels of systems	• In occupying a given role, people's behaviors are influenced by expectations, rewards, and sanctions
• Interaction and potential conflict occurs across time (horizontally) and across generation (vertically)	• Interactive influences and connections exist between individual members and between individuals, families, and environment	• Expectations for role behavior are influenced by societal, familial, community, social class, self, and partner role conceptions
• Focus on family's internal processes	• Dynamic view that people are influenced by personal characteristics as well as their external contextual environment	• Expectations may change depending on a particular social system context
• Looks at transitions and milestones across the life span, e.g., couplehood, adding children, etc.	• Change in relationships in one part of the system may affect all other relationships	• Individuals often feel role conflict and role strain in trying to occupy and function in multiple roles

Table 7.2 summarizes the issues or themes that parents discussed, by time period and across the content areas of the chapters. Identity issues, by nature, are relevant at all points of life. These issues, then, cross time periods. Although themes such as dating and marriage relationship might seem more pertinent to the time period Prior to Having Children, one's identity in that relationship continues to evolve and be shaped After the Birth of Children. Similarly, work issues crossed time periods in two broad categories: gender and work as a source of worry. Although both of these issues may become more important as one assumes the role of parent (e.g., maternity leave, gender-typing of roles, supporting a family), they have relevance for people at all points in their adult lives. Other work issues, however, were seen as being more important either before or after having children. Themes relating to child characteristics and social support were more clearly related to one of the two time periods, as seen in Table 7.2.

How do the themes and issues in Table 7.2 fit and provide depth to the theories highlighted in Table 7.1? Although all three theories can be used as a backdrop to explain some of the themes in each chapter, there are some matches that are more readily apparent. The identity issues discussed in chapter 3 are a prime example of the dynamics described in the developmental life span perspective. Regarding the family as a three-generational system was obvious in parents' descriptions of their expectations, hopes, and plans for their own and their children's lives. One mother said:

> I think the other thing that influenced me was that I was one of five children, and I was extremely aware of how busy my mother's life was … and I didn't want to be a mother of that for a long time because I knew how much work it was.

Another parent, however, said:

> I suspect that a lot of what we had grown up with influenced the way we raise our kids now.

Not only experiences but family messages have an influence:

> I mean, he stuck with a job that he hated, just to be a good provider, because I'm sure that's all he heard all his life, "'provide for your kids, no matter what.…'

This last example might also be explained by looking at family roles theory, where expectations for role behavior are influenced by multiple sources, including family role conceptions. In this case, the traditional "man as breadwinner" role had been drilled into this father's identity. Perhaps the following statement sums up the notion of the family continuum, both vertically and horizontally:

> I just talk to other adult friends, and a lot of them have good memories of their families, and I have others who have bad memories of their families. I just hope my kids have good memories, and I hope I can offer them help when they are adults.

The discussion of child characteristics in chapter 4 can also be viewed in the light of the developmental perspective, particularly as one considers the question of whether childhood traits continue on into adulthood:

> He was 2 years old and the kid used to make me cry, just by defying me. Whatever I said not to do, he was gonna do. And he's still strong willed.

This mother has clearly taken a long term view of her son's characteristics, projecting this past behavior into the future and seeing it as one of his "life issues."

Other parents talked about their own growing up experiences impacting on their perceptions of their children and even on their desire to have a child of one gender or another:

> I never wanted any girls because my mother and I never were very close and I didn't want to have to submit my daughter to the same relationship that I had with my mother.

Some parents focused on characteristics that were similar between generations of their family. One mother discussed her daughter's apparent lack of needing friends by comparing it to her own sister's experience:

> It could be heredity. I have a sister that's 13 months older than me and she's exactly the same. My sister has no friends.

The inherited characteristic of red hair was tied to having a temper for one little girl. Interestingly, having a temper was also seen as being learned or modeled or ascribed to particular role behaviors as in the case of the boy whose mother said:

> You know, I think he's watched—of course being a boy he's going to look up to his dad—so his dad has a temper—when things don't go right his way, you know about it.

Finally, some parents perceived their children as replications of themselves and had difficulty in separating their individual identity from that of their children:

> Your expectations of them are more or less your expectation of yourself. You can't see the way they're different from you.

TABLE 7.2

Issues Related to Identity, Child Characteristics, Social Support, and Work by Time Periods

	Prior to Having Children	After the Birth of Children	Across Time Periods
Identity issues			Individual identity • Description of self Family identity • Dating & marriage relationship • Family beliefs • Expectations, hopes, and plans • Critical events Connections to others • Extended family relationships • Kinship groups • Intergenerational themes • Cultural ties and traditions
Issues Related to child characteristics as identified by parents	Mothers influenced by: • Family of origin • Parenting skills Fathers influenced by • Experiences with children • Apprehensive about changes:	• Gender: girl/boy • Temperament: easy/fussy • Health: healthy/sick • Cognitive development: early/late • Physical development: early/late • Reaction to baby: positive/negative • Sociable child/loner • Independent/dependent	

Social support issues	• Companionship support in the spousal relationship • Instrumental & emotional support in the spousal relationship • Disruptions in the social network • Changes in extended family support	• Social isolation decreases in support from friends • Recreating a support network • Extended family: Mixed blessings • Spousal roles of parent and supporter • Support between spouses: Renewal and divorce • Providing support to children • Support received from others • Home alone? Support in the parenting role	
Work Issues	• Having fun • Achievement and security • Following husband's work	• Women pulled between work and family • Decisions about mothers working • Lwaving baby • Parenting roles • Women's changing identity • Fathers adjusting to babies • Fathers' separation from family • Women's isolation • Stress at the intersection of work and family • Creativity in managing work and family • Mothers returning to work	• Work as a source of worry • Gender

Social support issues discussed in chapter 5 can be understood by considering both the developmental life span and the family-in-environment theories. Many parents talked about the need for having a strong support network of both family and friends to help them through the life transitions of becoming a couple, having children, and, sometimes, relocating. One mother said:

> I am the youngest of four children, three brothers, and I was the first one to have a baby. So, my brothers called me every day. They came with their video cameras when the baby was born.

A father related the importance of his wife's family in his own personal development:

> And being around [my wife's] family—they were very open and it enabled me to be more open.... I'm a completely different person than I was ten years ago.... I can talk with people comfortably now.... The interaction with [my wife's] family helped me a lot.

The lack of family and friends in a couple's environment produced the opposite effects:

> We had no family anywhere in the area, so we didn't have any family to turn to. And I was one of the first of my friends to have kids, so I didn't have ... friends to turn to—even for advice or for things to do.

Similarly, removing a potential source of support, that is, a circle, from a parent's ecological map, left a significant void. For example, when women left work for motherhood, many felt a sense of loss:

> Everything was different. I had been working ... and then I'm home with a baby. I found it a big adjustment, I really did.... It was ... a lonely time, really.

As this last quote demonstrates, both the family-in-environment and the family roles theories explicate the experiences related in chapter 6's discussion of work. Many mothers made the transition from full time worker to full time mother, some by choice, some by necessity, some because of pressure they felt from spouses, families, or their community. Like the woman just quoted, another mother talked about the difficulty of adjusting to the change in roles:

> I was all of a sudden cleaning diapers and ... I felt isolated and I felt ... sort of unimportant, you know, after working full-time and working with adults and having responsibilities. And all of a sudden there I was at home doing what I think are important things but at the time didn't seem important.

Many couples discussed making decisions about work based on societal or familial role conceptions:

> We pretty much agree on the upbringing of kids and [our] thoughts were pretty much the same as far as having ... the woman home and man working ...

Intergenerational patterns could also be seen as described in the developmental life span theory:

> At first my husband was even like, "I don't want you to work." He came from a very traditional family where mother stayed home, father went to work, they have a house full of kids and that was what mom was supposed to do.

The world of work held a central position in every family's ecological environment. For some, it was primarily a necessity, a means to an end:

> Well, my husband and I were married for 6 years before we had [our daughter]. And that time was spent working. We both had jobs and we worked until we got enough money to buy the house.

For others, it was a way to maintain another part of their identity:

> Then I was going to quit work and become a wonderful full-time mother and stay home —that lasted about 3 months ... then I went back on a part-time basis.

Others concurred that raising small children on a full-time basis sometimes left them with the feeling that "you lose the sense of being an adult sometimes," a feeling that work outside the home counteracted.

Gender Differences and a Feminist Perspective on the Family

It is noteworthy that the themes/issues listed in Table 7.2 and discussed by the parents are not always consistent across gender. That is, mothers and fathers in our study differed in their perspectives on family development in several important ways. Table 7.3 summarizes some of those differences.

Both men and women described their excitement and fear about becoming parents, but women's adjustment to parenthood seemed smoother in terms of role adaptation. However, many women also found their role as parent to be more isolating and stressful than it was for men, as they were most often the ones who left work, were isolated within the home, experienced a lack of help from their coparent, and had primary responsibility for the child. Thus, many women who were caretakers, supporters, and nurturers as part of their roles as friend, spouse, parent, family member, also became "sacrificers" for husband and children. Perhaps because of this, the women also had different concerns about their children's characteristics, the role of work in their lives, and the need for social support.

TABLE 7.3
Differences Between Mothers' and Fathers' Themes Across Chapters

IDENTITY	CHILD CHARACTERISTICS	SOCIAL SUPPORT	WORK
Both mothers and fathers: Reported fear, anxiety, difficult adjustment, increased feelings of responsibility, and loss of personal freedom in terms of their expectations of parenthood Responded to parenthood with expressions of excitement and happiness Mothers: Described more concern about a lack of preparation for infant care in anticipation of parenthood Reported more sadness, boredom, isolation in response to parenthood Fathers: Commented more on mothers' role as the in-home child-care provider	Mothers: Commented more on their own family of origin experiences as a factor in expectations of what they wanted their children to be like Were more concerned about the social aspects of their children's lives Perceived their children as having changed over time to become more positive Fathers: Commented more on their past experiences with children as a factor in expectations of what they wanted their children to be like Were more concerned about children's ability to be independent and self-reliant—and even more so for sons than daughters	Mothers: Had greater overall social isolation and more disruptions in the social network Felt extended family support more important Were more aware of providing fair and equal support to multiple children Took on primary role of child caretaker Fathers: Described greater loss of companionship support, but for some this also meant perceived loss of wife as support as she became a mother Took on role of supporter of their wives	Mothers: Described more ambivalence regarding the work/family intersection, especially concerning leaving the children for work Had a changing sense of self after having children in relation to work and family roles and to isolation Fathers: Made comments about being separated from their children that most often referred to geographic separation due to work assignments Had a changing sense of self after children that referred most often to an increased sense of responsibility as a fiscal provider

Several researchers have proposed reasons for these gender differences. First of all, theories of psychosocial development (such as life span, ecosystems, and role theories) are themselves affected by a gendered social order. That is, cultural ideals of masculinity and femininity (as well as race and class) shape, and in turn are shaped by, theories of development (see Gilligan, 1993 for an overview of this process). As a result, characterstics of women's lives and personalities have often been minimized, misunderstood, and/or devalued. This description by Carol Gilligan (1993) clearly echoes the gender differences we found in our study:

> Sensitivity to the needs of others and the assumption of responsibility for taking care lead women to attend to voices other than their own and to include in their judgement other points of view.... Women's place in man's life cycle has been that of nurturer, caretaker, and helpmate, the weaver of those networks of relationships on which she in turn relies. While women have thus taken care of men, however, men have in their theories of psychological development tended either to assume or devalue that care (p. 67).

Illuminating gender differences in the family can further an understanding of the social structure of the family and its implications for maintaining the broader social order through parents' expectations of themselves and of their children. To do this we must consider how the theories that guided our study are influenced by gender. General theories of family development describe people's common experiences (i.e., emotional, cognitive, and behavioral changes over time) from birth to death, and the major life transitions that affect these experiences (e.g., adolescence, work, marriage, and childbirth). However, such theories rarely consider the unique experiences of women over the life span related to the way in which women's lives develop within the constraints of social expectations of women's roles—that is, gender discrimination in a wide variety of contexts, including school, work, religion, and health care; and the frequent occurrence of violence against women, including sexual assault, incest, assault and battery, and sexual harassment (for more detailed information about these issues see Golombok & Fivush, 1994; Koss et al., 1994).

As discussed in chapter 1, life span development is set within the larger ecological system of social structures. These systems are guided by a cultural framework that carries prescribed notions about gender on which the above developmental experiences are based. For example, beliefs and ideals about women's and men's personalities guide perceptions of social roles, such as wife–husband, mother–father, friend, family member, and coworker, as well as physical characteristics, intelligence, and capabilities, which, in turn, influence the frequency and acceptance of differential treatment and differential

attributions. One example is the work of Eccles and her colleagues (Eccles &
Harold, 1991; Eccles, Jacobs, & Harold, 1990; Eccles et al., 1993), who discussed the roles that parents and teachers play in socializing children's self-perceptions and the ways in which these are influenced by the gender of both the
adult and the child. Additionally, gender does not operate outside of, or separate from, issues of race and class. Family structures and practices vary by gender, race, and class within and across cultural/ethnic contexts (e.g., see
Goldenberg & Goldenberg, 1998). These important factors are often omitted
from family assessments in research and practice.

Forced Choices and Surprises

One other element was pervasive throughout the stories and crossed the
bounds of time period and topical issue. As researchers, we initially thought of
people describing their family stories in terms of the choices they made, that is,
what they chose to do, when they chose to do it, and how they chose to do it.
For example, we thought that the following comment would typify the kind of
process that most people described:

> So we both worked and it was a very conscious decision as to when—and how ...
> would have children when we bought our own home.

The interactive relationship between data collection and data analysis
(Altheide, 1987; Berg, 1989) referred to in chapter 2, reminded us however, to
examine parents' stories and hear their voices through them. Thus, we discovered that several of the men and women in this study would probably subscribe
to the phrase "Life happens!" Some seemed genuinely surprised by the turn of
events in their lives; others would probably feel that their choices were not
freely made but rather were forced by circumstances, seemingly beyond their
control:

- Yeah, let's have children, and yeah, it's going to change our life and that's
  about as far as you go. And then, as soon as the child comes, then all of a
  sudden all of these other ramifications come into play. Life insurance.
  Deeds and wills. Schooling, oh gosh.... All of these things start hitting you
  all at once and you have to start thinking about them, and they do change
  your life.

- Well, we got married in 1976 in April and we moved out here in Novem-
  ber. And I was pregnant with [Child A]. He was not a planned baby. And I
  had a rough adjustment moving *f* away from the family, being pregnant,
  and all the feeling that you have when you're pregnant for the first time.

- ... the biggest change, I guess, was the realization that these kids were yours and that you—It's not like baby-sitting where you could get rid of them at night and take them away.

- I think what happened if you want our life story in a nutshell: We got together, we fell in love, we screwed a lot, we got married, the kids came, and it was instant adult and time to grow up, and both of us bolted.

- It was a pretty drastic experience—going from single and having no responsibilities to married and all of a sudden having a kid.

- Well, all of a sudden he's home; and I'm going, "Oh my God, I've got 20 years of this. What the hell is happening to me?"

- My husband and I were married a month before I found out I was pregnant, so our expectation of the marriage changed immediately.

- It was kinda hard getting used to each other that first year, with both of us working. The first one coming along right away was like all of a sudden you're an immediate family.

The notions of planning and choice as part of a family life story are interesting to consider. To what extent do couples ask themselves and each other these questions prior to committing to a long term relationship? What makes it easier for some couples to weather the unknown and unplanned? What implications do these issues have for practice, policy, and research?

NEXT CHAPTERS

Developmental Transitions in Family Life

When we asked parents in our study to tell their family story, their children were between the ages of 8 and 10 and they had been through a major developmental phase in the life of their family, namely, becoming a family. In the past few years, these families underwent another major developmental transition: becoming the family of an adolescent. Conflict and stress between teenagers and parents has long been portrayed as a characteristic of this transition from childhood to adolescence. Traditionally, research describing parent–adolescent interactions has focused on linear effects and has compared parents' and teens' views via questionnaires (e.g., Ohannessian, Lerner, Lerner, & von Eye, 1995; Carlson, Cooper, & Spradling, 1991). However, many theorists postulate that parents and teens are part of a larger, more complex and reciprocal family system (e.g., Bronfenbrenner, 1979), and that other investigative methods should be considered in studying parental and adolescent views of their shared environment (Carlton-Ford, Paikoff, & Brooks-Gunn, 1991).

Just as the storyboard was used to capture the initial stories of *Becoming a Family*, other qualitative research tools such as the eco map, which plots the family with a genogram in the center of its ecological environment (Hartman, 1978), might be used to analyze individuals' perceptions of family relationships and compare how parents and their teens view relationships within the family and between the family, and the ecological systems of which it is a part. Such data can provide researchers with the opportunity to explore the congruence between family members' depictions and descriptions of the relationships in the family, by comparing perceptions of dyadic relationships across subjects as well as by looking at how individual members choose to portray family relationships.

Such data also allow researchers to examine congruency both in themes seen as important and in the explanations given by various family members. For example, what changes do parents and teens themselves describe as important experiences during the shift from childhood to adolescence? Beginning interviews with adolescents and their parents (see Harold, Mercier, & Colarossi, 1997) give us the following illustration: Many parents and teens agreed that the amount of time spent together during this developmental transition was an important issue for the family. However, some family members said that because the teens were involved in activities away from the family, it left more time for the parents to be alone together and that this had a positive impact; others said that parental relationships were negatively affected because they were spending more time attending to the adolescent's academic or recreational activities. In summary, one of the "next chapters" should deal with the developmental needs of adolescents and discuss how the family system adjusts to issues of individuation and autonomy/identity development on the part of the teen, as well as understanding the changes that occur in the adolescents' social system as her/his focus shifts from family to peer and school to work.

The next transition that could be captured through qualitative stories or mapping is that of the "empty nest." For some parents, this means back to couplehood with either long-term or new partners. For others, it may mean being single again. It also involves the process of becoming the extended family/family of origin for those whose children become partners and/or parents. Again, the use of the eco map to depict family relationships graphically and to compare perceptions across family members can provide a technique for viewing family dynamics, particularly during the transitional stages of adolescence and postadolescence, that is, children leaving home. It offers the opportunity to examine how changes that occur at these times affect each member of the family, and to look at how different families and different family members adapt to and cope with these changes. Similarly, individual and family stories about this life stage paint a colorful picture and enrich our understanding.

Diverse Family Types: The Importance and Valuing of Difference Within and Across Family Systems

The proportion of nuclear families in the United States is decreasing, and the proportion of what have been considered "nontraditional" families is on the rise. According to figures from the *Current Population Reports* (Saluter, 1994), children under the age of 18 are considerably more likely to be living with only one parent today than two decades ago. The number of single parents went from 3.8 million in 1970 to 9.7 million in 1990 (U.S. Bureau of the Census, 1995). As the proportion of "traditional" families decreases, the number of families with diverse structures increases. These include single-parent, remarried, adoptive, and foster parent as well as grandparent and kinship households, and same-sex partners raising children (Copeland & White, 1991).

For example, the complexion of families with adopted children is changing. Traditionally, these families were made up of infertile two-parent heterosexual couples with their adopted healthy infants, or those two-parent heterosexual couples who wanted additional children. Now adoptive families include rising numbers of couples who adopt children with disabilities, intrafamily adoptions that occur within remarriages, and adoptions by same-sex couples and single individuals who wish to have children (Hanson & Lynch, 1992).

Also, the number of children residing in foster care has grown by approximately 50% since 1985 (Pelton, 1991). This is attributed to rising numbers of children who are born exposed prenatally to drugs and alcohol. These children's special needs require a change in the qualities previously sought in potential foster parents. Children who have suffered abuse and neglect in their biological families are also residing for longer periods of time in foster care, despite recent efforts to intervene and reunite families of origin (Pelton, 1991). In an effort to facilitate adoption of these children, some states have added a cap to the length of time a child can be kept in foster care before the parental rights are terminated and the child is adoptable.

Social and technological change have provided more opportunities for same-sex couples and unmarried heterosexuals, individuals and couples, to raise children. Often counted or identified as single parent households, these families are frequently hidden from view. However, they face the same issues involved in family development as do two-parent heterosexual families, as well as the added burdens of social stigma and discrimination. Lesbian mother families constitute a significant population. The most commonly cited statistics concerning the number of lesbian mothers in the United States range from 1.5 to 4 million (Patterson, 1994; Rodriguez, 1991), but accurate estimates of the actual numbers of lesbian mothers are difficult to find. Most researchers seem to accept estimates of between 6 million and 10 million children with lesbian or gay parents (Harvard Law Review, 1990).

These changes in the make up of "family" require that family practitioners, policy makers, and researchers expand their understanding of contemporary families to be more accurate, inclusive, and effective in their practices. We must recognize that family definition, family identities, and family pressures are in the process of dynamic transition. Hanson and Lynch (1992) proposed the following definition:

> Family is considered to be any unit that defines itself as a family including indi-
> viduals who are related by blood or marriage as well as those who have made a
> commitment to share their lives. The definition includes the "traditional" nu-
> clear family but also embraces lifestyles that range from extended family and kin-
> ship networks to single parents and to same-sex partners living together. The key
> elements are that the members of the unit see themselves as a family, are affili-
> ated with one another, and are committed to caring for one another (p. 285).

This is a somewhat more expansive definition than White & Epston's (1990), which was described in chapter 1. White & Epston's definition of family as intergenerational, and thus involving children, closely fits the struc-ture of the families in our study. It was, therefore, useful for our purposes, but theory and research should continue to adopt flexible, inclusive definitions of families for many reasons. As economic challenges and social pressures ne-cessitate the need for new family structures, and cultural norms evolve to ac-cept a greater diversity of lifestyles, the traditional nuclear family unit will represent a smaller proportion of the overall society. Therefore, researchers must expand their scope of study in their search for knowledge that will guide inclusive, comprehensive, and relevant conceptual and practice frameworks. In order to meet this goal, Figures 7.1 and 7.2 diagram two conceptual frame-works for studying the family systems. We suggest that diversity be seen as a framework linked to a philosophical position in which we strive for inclusive or population-based thinking, as opposed to exclusive or normative-based thinking. The latter, exclusive, thinking is concerned with a search for the ideal, model, or nominally normative. Inclusive thinking is concerned with variation among members of a group.

Figure 7.1 illustrates an exclusive model of the family: the first marriage, two parent heterosexual family as the norm, from which any other form is a divergent type—with connotations of being "less than," negative, or problem oriented. It follows that discriminatory actions are based on perceived deviations from the norm. Take the model a step further and visualize the norm as the "Ozzie and Harriet" family—first marriage, heterosexual, White, Anglo Saxon, Protestant,

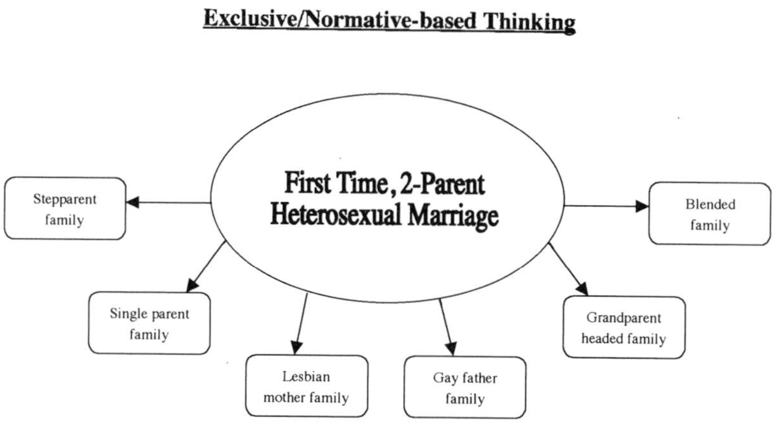

Exclusive/Normative-based Thinking

FIG. 7.1.   A family example of a representation of exclusive/normative-based thinking.

working father and stay-at-home mother, birth children; each characteristic used to define the family creates possibilities for defining other families as deviant. Membership in the normative group provides one with the highest status offered by the model. There is an "in-group/out-group" phenomenon operating. Variation occurs outside the norm, as is indicated by the unidirectional arrows and placement outside of the center.

Contrast this with Fig. 7.2, inclusive thinking, in which variations in family membership, structure, and roles are valued as adding depth to our understanding of the particular family we are studying. When *family* is used to denote a generic category rather than a normative ideal, each subset or type of family can be seen as having particular strengths and weaknesses, being of equal value and worthy of study and advocacy on its behalf. This model encompasses and embraces variation. Recent census data indicate that while a majority of adults are in heterosexual marriages, that majority is quite small, at 56%, and has been slipping since 1970 when it was 68%. Thus, the normative model does not account for 44% of adults. The inclusive model attempts to include several types of grouping, all under the heading of family. Other characteristics that may occur in any of the family types are depicted as circles with bidirectional arrows indicating within-group variation. Another "next chapter" should include stories of those families who represent these variations.

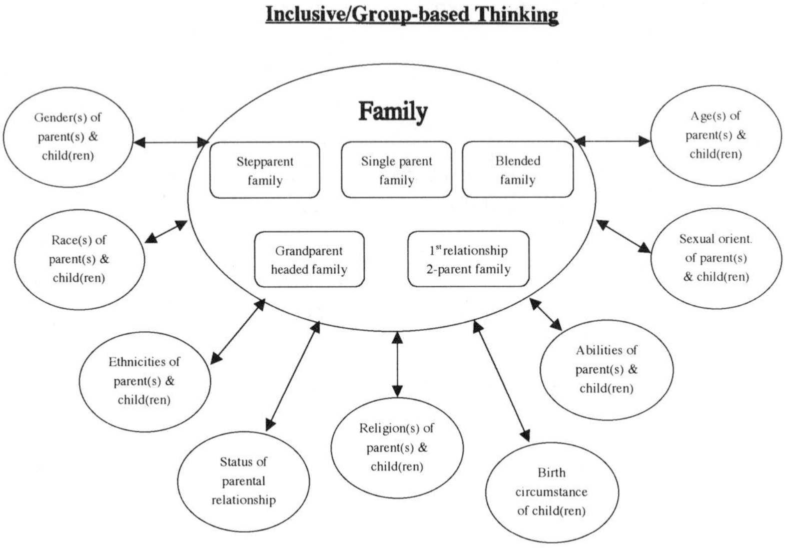

Inclusive/Group-based Thinking

FIG. 7.2.   A family example of a representation of inclusive/group-based thinking.

FINAL REFLECTIONS ON THE RESEARCH

Clearly, the underpinning of this book is the perspective of *person-in-context*. Thus, individuals are considered not only in the context of the family but also in the larger social context in which they live. All of these contexts or systems reciprocally affect each other. Therefore, the implications for practice, policy, and research on a broader social level can have an important impact on family development. Each chapter in this book reviews these implications as they relate to the specific topic discussed in that chapter. Table 7.4 offers an overall summary.

We found that there were several advantages and disadvantages of using the methodology described in this paper. One advantage of our interviews was the versatility of the data gathered. The transcripts allow for multifaceted analyses to be conducted, from context analyses to development of thematic coding schemes for descriptions and comparisons across the sample, to in-depth analyses or case histories of one participant or one family system. One difficulty with our data, though, is the limited sample diversity across a variety of social experiences, including race, ethnicity, class, and sexual orientation. However, the data do provide information that is representative of a large segment of the broader, "majority group," population that can be used to compare and contrast with other studies using different samples from other segments of society.

Another advantage of our study is the possibility of consciousness raising for the participants and the researchers alike. We felt that our storyboard tool provided both a verbal and visual picture of the individual and the family set within time and social context, and allowed for reflection on life choices (or forced choices) and the effects of the social system on those choices. We heard especially from women that some of their choices to marry, have children, and start or stop a career were influenced by social expectations of them as women, and they were able to reflect on how these expectations facilitated or hindered their own personal autonomy and goal fulfillment.

What does this information tell us about the standpoints of the researchers in relation to the participants? We felt that the similarities between the researchers and informants in family constellation, age, education, race, and class led to the ability of researchers and participants to relate to each other on many levels, build rapport, and create a more open dialogue. However, it is important to reflect on the power differentials that did exist between researchers and participants, and how this affected the development of the interviews, the process of conducting them, and, ultimately, the information that participants provided and its future interpretation. To this end, we were in the role of developers and conductors of interviews, and that in and of itself changes the agency of the researchers in relation to the participants.

We also had a higher social status related to education and job characteristics. This differential was true to a greater extent between the female researchers and participants, whereas the male participants were more similar to the researchers in social power referentials by virtue of their higher educational level, job status, and male sex. And, indeed, interviewers did have very different personal experiences of the interview process with male and female participants. A typical male-participant/female-interviewer scenario involved men's greater likelihood to ask questions about the interviewers themselves, the study, and the interview process. We have also reflected on our own experiences during these interviews as sometimes being engaged in a debate over the questions or issues presented, and of feeling that the men often engaged in symbolic power struggles during the interview. Perhaps men felt more watched or judged by female academics, but discussions of the fathers' experience of the interview was extremely difficult to elicit from these participants. Alternatively, perhaps due to social power differentials or to gender similarity that encouraged rapport, interviews with female par-

TABLE 7.4
Summary of Practice, Policy, and Research Implications Across Chapters

	PRACTICE	POLICY	RESEARCH
Identity	• Incorporate family myths and narrative techniques into intervention • View individual development as embedded within family development • Understand identity development within the context of extended family, kinships, intergenerational issues, and cultural ties • Be aware of transitional issues that include parenting skills, division of labor, role adaptation, and stress	• Consider individual and cultural identity in family policies affecting foster care and adoption • Promote programs that integrate child and elderly care at the same site to foster intergenerational connections	• Keep the definition of family diverse and flexible • Use multimethod designs and comparative studies • Use family narrative techniques
Child characteristics	• Help parents create good "fit" by shaping an environment that is adaptable to the needs of the child • Help parents resolve their own family/childhood experiences and define how they would like to be similar and different with their own child • Use a genogram as an assessment tool • Reframe children's characteristics in a positive light and look for their strengths • Clarify parental beliefs and expectations of their child to assist with positive socialization processes • Help parents feel (as well as become) competent and capable as parents	• Focus behavior modification programs on the family systems as a whole rather than just symptoms for long-term change • Include course work on child development, parenting, life transitions, and the use of genogram techniques in the training of clinicians • Incorporate parenting training programs into social services agencies, workplaces, high schools, and childbirth classes	• Explore how parenting beliefs and practices affect long-term personality characteristics and identity • Study the interaction of environment and temperament • Use narrative research techniques to understand cognitive schemas about individual and family identity

Social support	• Help couples define needs and expectations for support and negotiate help from each other and outsiders • Decrease isolation for mothers by helping them develop a network of similar others and increasing men's time taking care of children • Normalize the stress of this transition on the couple's relationship and the need for external sources of support • Use eco-map techniques to identify and evaluate social networks	• Develop work policies that increase both men's and women's child-care leave without penalties or effects on evaluation and advancement • Increasing training for clinicians regarding the social network assessment and intervention • Increase community programming for couples, parents, and families • Increase the availability, accessibility, and quality of professional support services, such as individual counseling, support groups, community mental health programs and chid care	• Conduct multimethod research using participants from diverse backgrounds • Clarify which kinds of social support are most helpful for what kinds of problems and from whom • Explore how personality characteristics affect the way in which people seek out and utilize support from others
Work	• Assess to what extent decisions about work and family roles are based on gender, ability, interest, availability, and flexibility• Assess the rigidity and fluidity of roles as well as individual satisfaction • Help families discover resources available for making easier transitions from one role to another or in combining roles • Intervene at crisis points in the couple's work/family life	• Create parenting classes for men, to educate and support the assumption of their role as fathers • Establish Employee Assistance Programs as a benefit for workers experiencing problems including or impinging on their work/family life • Work to "ungender" parenting roles • Create a "family-friendly workplace" including improving legislation around family leave	• Give "voice" to study participants through qualitative work and by combining methods • Document parents' time at home as work • Study the effects of absence from home due to work • Explore the experiences of moving in and out of the world of work • Look at the worlds of work and family as mutually dependent

ticipants ranged from passive responses to a full, open engagement in dialogue about their views and experiences.

Not only did these experiences allow us to reflect on a variety of levels of social power and social roles, but they provided us qualitative data from male and female perspectives on the family. As such, feminist research need focus not only on women's experiences to understand the social structure, but also on the comparison of men's experiences to women's in the same social context, the same family, and across social contexts. This creates a deeper and broader understanding of the interplay of gender and power.

On a different level, the similarities between the researchers and participants allowed us to relate to their experiences and to work together to meet each other's needs, if not common goals. For example, the participants were financially compensated for their time and effort, but this was not seen as a critical need to them. Participants were more interested in gaining information and assistance from us in regard to the college application process (for the children in the future), the college environment, parenting skills, resources like articles and community referrals, and sometimes mental health resources. We were able to provide this information in an efficient and helpful way because the participants' life knowledge and experiences were similar to our own.

Finally, it is important to reflect on those whom we did not study and whose voices and experiences are missing from our process and the resulting data. We did not interview people from less dominant social contexts, including those of race, ethnicity, sexual orientation, physical disability, and socioeconomic status. As a result, we have data that we can analyze from a predominantly insider perspective, rather than issues of outsider standpoints. We hope to accomplish our stated goals with this group of people, but we acknowledge that this is only one piece of social reality that can only be fully understood in the full context of diverse voices and experiences within and across cultures.

This chapter concludes this segment of the story for these families. They have enriched our knowledge by sharing their experiences. Their lives and challenges continue as does their story as the children grow to adolescents, mature, and leave home to establish their own lives and, perhaps, become families. This final sentiment is one shared by many of the families that we interviewed as they reflected on what the future would bring:

> ... but I hope they have good memories and that they always feel like they were loved. That is the most important thing to me, that they know they were wanted and loved, and that they are very special to me, and they're not a burden, and I'm really glad that they were born.

REFERENCES

Altheide, D. (1987). Reflections: Ethnographic content analysis. *Qualitative Sociology, 10,* 65–77.

Berg, B. (1989). *Qualitative research methods for the social sciences.* Boston: Allyn and Bacon.

Bronfenbrenner, U. (1979). *The ecology of human development: Experiments by nature and design.* Cambridge, MA: Harvard University Press.

Carlson, C. L., Cooper, C. R., & Spradling, V. Y. (1991). Developmental implications of shared versus distinct perceptions of the family in early adolescence. *New Directions for Child Development, 51,* 13–32.

Carlton-Ford, S. L., Paikoff, R. L., & Brooks-Gunn, J. (1991). Methodological issues in the study of divergent views of the family. *New Directions for Child Development, 51,* 87–102.

Copeland, A. P., & White, K. M. (1991). *Studying families.* Newbury Park, CA: Sage.

Eccles, J. S., & Harold, R. D. (1991). Gender differences in sport involvement: Applying the Eccles' expectancy-value model. *Journal of Applied Sport Psychology, 3,* 7–35.

Eccles, J. S., Jacobs, J. E., & Harold, R. D. (1990). Gender-role stereotypes, expectancy effects, and parents' role in the socialization of gender differences in self-perceptions and skill acquisition. *Journal of Social Issues, 46,* 183–201.

Eccles, J. S., Jacobs, J., Harold, R., Yoon, K. S., Arbreton, A., & Freedman-Doan, C. (1993). Parents and gender-role socialization during the middle childhood and adolescent years. In S. Oskamp & M. Costanzo (Eds.), *Gender issues in contemporary society* (pp. 59–83). Newbury Park, CA: Sage.

Gilligan, C. (1993). Women's place in man's life cycle. In A. Dobrin (Ed.) *Being good and doing right: Readings in moral development* (pp. 37–54). Lanham, MD: University Press of America.

Goldenberg, H., & Goldenberg, I. (1998). *Counseling today's families* (3rd ed.). Pacific Grove, CA: Brooks/Cole.

Golombok, S., & Fivush, R. (1994). *Gender development.* New York: Cambridge University Press.

Hanson, M. J., & Lynch, E. W. (1992). Family diversity: Implications for policy and practice. *Topics in Early Childhood Special Education, 12*(3), 283–306.

Harold, R. D., Mercier, L. R., & Colarossi, L. G. (1997). Using the eco-map to bridge the practice-research gap. *Journal of Sociology and Social Welfare, 24,* 29–44.

Hartman, A. (1978). Diagrammatic assessment of family relationships. *Social Casework, 59,* 465–476.

Harvard Law Review. (1990). *Sexual orientation and the law.* Cambridge, MA: Harvard University Press.

Koss, M. P., Goodman, L. A., Browne, A., Fitzgerald, L. F., Keita G. P., & Russo, N. F. (1994). No safe haven: Male violence against women at home, at work, and in the community. Washington, DC: American Psychological Association.

Moon, S. M., Dillon, D. R., & Sprenkle, D. H. (1990). Family therapy and qualitative research. *Journal of Marital and Family Therapy, 16*(4), 357–373.

Ohannessian, C. M., Lerner, R. M., Lerner, J. V., & von Eye, A. (1995). Discrepancies in adolescents' and parents' perceptions of family functioning and adolescent emotional adjustment. *Journal of Early Adolescence, 15,* 490–516.

Patterson, C. J. (1994). Lesbian and gay families. *Current Directions in Psychological Science, 3*(3), 62–64.

Pelton, L. (1991). Beyond permanency planning: Restructuring the public child welfare system. *Social Work, 36*(4), 337–343.

Rodriguez, P. (1991). *The status of lesbian families in the 1990s: An exploratory study of current trends.* Unpublished master's thesis, California State University, Long Beach.

Saluter, A. F. (1994). Marital status and living arrangements. *U.S. Bureau of the Census, Current Population Reports*, Series P20–478. Washington, DC: U.S. Government Printing Office.

U.S. Bureau of the Census (1995). *Current Population Reports*, Series P23–180. Marriage, divorce, and remarriage in the 1990's. Washington, DC: U.S. Government Printing Office.

White, M., & Epston, D. (1990). *Narrative means to therapeutic ends*. New York: Norton.

Author Index

Subject Index